RIGHT
HERE
RIGHT
NOW

RIGHT HERE

STEPHEN J. HARPER

POLITICS AND LEADERSHIP
IN THE AGE OF DISRUPTION

RIGHT
NOW

SIGNAL
McCLELLAND
& STEWART

Signal and colophon are registered trademarks of Penguin Random House Canada Limited.

Library and Archives Canada Cataloguing in Publication
Harper, Stephen, 1959-, author
        Right here, right now : politics and leadership in the age of disruption / Stephen Harper.

Issued in print and electronic formats.

ISBN 978-0-7710-3862-4 (hardcover).--ISBN 978-0-7710-3863-1 (EPUB)
        1. Conservatism. 2. Political leadership. 3. Populism. 4. Globalization.
5. Economics. 6. Social history--21st century. I. Title.

JC573.H37 2018   320.52   C2018-902517-4
                                                     C2018-902518-2

Jacket and book design by Rachel Cooper
Typeset in Dante by M&S, Toronto
Printed and bound in the United States of America

Published by Signal,
an imprint of McClelland & Stewart,
a division of Penguin Random House Canada Limited,
a Penguin Random House Company
www.penguinrandomhouse.ca

1   2   3   4   5   22   21   20   19   18

To the people of Canada, for ten great years.

CONTENTS

PROLOGUE

I f you are interested in politics, you will remember where you were on November 8, 2016.

I was watching the U.S. presidential vote in my basement living room. My (interim) successor as leader of the Conservative Party of Canada, the Hon. Rona Ambrose, was with me. So was the leader of the United Conservative Party of Alberta, the Hon. Jason Kenney. I did not expect Donald J. Trump to be elected president that evening. But unlike most observers, I did think it was at least possible. It had taken me a long time to even get there.

In the year and a half of the Republican presidential primaries, Trump had not impressed me. He seemed to me less conservative, less convincing, and less politically capable than virtually all of the other candidates. He had a presence and a forcefulness, but not much else.

Let us be frank. It was obvious that Trump was not really a conservative and not even a Republican. After all, he had not been either of these for most of his life. As a GOP supporter in the previous few years, he had been noteworthy only as the embarrassing proponent of the Obama "birther" theory. Such outrageous statements and outlandish conduct have continued to mark his public persona.

But Trump won the Republican nomination, and now he was winning the presidential election. So, I asked myself: What happened?

I could have concluded what most commentators concluded. They had predicted Trump could not win—that he could *never* win—because he is a fool and a bigot. Therefore, they surmised, the voters must be fools and bigots as well.

For many liberals, wedded to the belief that those who disagree with them are fools and bigots by definition, that answer may be good enough. For us conservatives, who fancy ourselves students of human nature and human experience, it should not. The ones with the foolish and preconceived notions were those who got it so wrong. It is time to re-examine our assumptions.

So here is my re-examination in a nutshell. A large proportion of Americans, including many American conservatives, voted for Trump because they are really not doing very well. They are not doing well in the world that we conservatives created after the Cold War. And they are not doing well, in part, because of some of the policies we conservatives have advocated.

In short, the world of globalization is not working for many of our own people. We can pretend that this is a false perception, but it is not. We now have a choice. We can keep trying to convince people that they misunderstand their own lives, or we can try to understand what they are saying. Then we can decide what to do about it.

===

Conservatives won the Cold War. Ronald Reagan, Margaret Thatcher, and their generation stood against communism abroad and socialism at home. And they were largely successful. Our values—free societies, free markets, free trade, free movement—have spread around the world.

The problem is this: globalization has been very successful for many of the world's people, but not so much for many of our own. A billion people worldwide—mostly in the emerging economies of Asia—have moved out of poverty. Yet, in many Western countries, the incomes of working people have stagnated or even declined over the past quarter-century. This is especially true in the United States.

Trump clearly understood this. The other Republican candidates stood on the stage telling conservative voters that the solution to the failures of globalization in their lives was more free trade, more open borders, and an American government focused on the rest of the world. Many were not buying it.

Of course, some conservatives were buying that story. A few of them even voted for Hillary Clinton. Yet, ironically, many Democratic voters were not buying what she was selling—conservative orthodoxy on globalization supplemented with the liberal social agenda. They voted for Trump in much larger numbers. That is why he is president.

The 2016 presidential election may have been a choice between two unpopular candidates, but it was at least an interesting choice. It was not between a traditional conservative and an old-fashioned liberal. It was shaped by a political spectrum that is shifting entirely. The uneven impacts of globalization are altering the political dynamics of the United States and other Western nations in some specific ways. Many traditionally conservative voters, particularly those not doing well economically, are starting to question old market dogmas. At the same time, many liberals, especially those faring exceedingly well, are embracing aspects of the global marketplace.

I put it like this: there is a widening chasm between the perspectives of establishment institutions of all kinds—corporations, banks, bureaucracies, academia, media, entertainment—and those who do not identify with such institutions. It is a split between those whose economic interests are global and those whose interests are local. It is between those whose lives cross borders and those who live within them. It is between those whose identities are international and multicultural and those whose identities are national and traditional. Most importantly, it is increasingly between those who believe they are getting ahead and those who can see that they are not.

This is, of course, not limited to America. The same dynamics—"elites" versus "populists"—were behind the surprise outcome of the Brexit referendum. Something similar is happening in Europe as well, as the space occupied by traditional political parties of both the centre right and centre left is gradually shrinking in the face of insurgent political movements.

I do not know whether Donald Trump's presidency will succeed or not. Given the erratic behaviour, the simmering scandals, and the opposition from within, I think probably not. But what I do know is that the issues that gave rise to his candidacy are not going away. They are only going to get bigger. And, if they are not faced honestly and addressed correctly, they are going to get worse.

To fellow conservatives I say it is time to stop obsessing about the flaws of Trump and the Brexiteers. It is more critical to figure out where they have got it right and what got them to victory. Conservatism is successful over time because conservatism works. We have to make it work for the mass of our citizens once again.

We also have to remember that voters have a lot worse options available to them. For every Trump, there is a Sanders. For every Farage, there is a Corbyn. The Trumps and the Brexiteers at least want to fix what is not working with democratic, market-based economies. The Sanderses and the Corbyns of this world, permanently stuck in their adolescent rage, would burn the system to the ground.

Present-day populism is not an all-or-nothing proposition. There are parts of it that reflect legitimate grievances with the elite consensus. There are others that should be opposed. But, in all these things, it is critical that conservatives be the champions for working men, women, and families in the twenty-first century.

I believe I know something about this. I started my elected political career in a "populist" conservative party. During my time as prime minister, Canada embraced free trade and robust immigration, and saw the wages of working- and middle-class people grow despite the global financial crisis.[1] The deepening cleavages of other Western democracies have not appeared in my country—yet.

I also know that what is happening requires understanding and adaptation, not dogma and condescension. Populists are not ignorant and misguided "deplorables." They are our family, friends, and neighbours. The populists are, by definition, the people. In a democratic system, the people are our customers. And, according to our conservative market values, the customer is always right.

=

Which brings me to the purpose of this book.

I will begin by asking, to borrow a quote from Donald Trump—my favourite Trump quote—"What the hell is going on?" I will tell the story of populism, especially in its modern manifestation as the backlash to globalization, and will review its history and its key themes.[2]

I will then explore those populist themes—reactions to market outcomes, trade deals, ideological globalism, and increasing migration. I will look at their emergence in the past generation and the widening gap in views between elites and regular working citizens.

Then I want to talk about the solutions. Obviously, I will look at how political leaders should respond, particularly conservative political leaders. But I will also comment on how business should navigate this political disruption and contribute positively to addressing it.

All of these chapters will reflect my own background. I have not just lived through this era. I have had some unique experiences as both a populist political outsider and a G7 head of government.

My ultimate goal is to put forward a positive vision for reformed democratic capitalism, with renewed working-class opportunity and greater community cohesion. I want to bridge the divide between perception and reality, fact and fiction, and populism and establishment. It is partly about understanding what was behind the political surprises of 2016. But it is mostly about where we go from here.

I am going to have a lot to say about conservatism in this book. Most of it is positive. But some of it is critical. In particular I will decry the way that U.S. conservatism has at times become abstract and disconnected from the interests of regular working families. The subsequent prescriptions are a blueprint for putting these families back at the centre of conservatism. The book is, in this sense, a manual for conservative statecraft in a populist age.

Why is this important? Because I believe conservatives are uniquely positioned to advance an agenda that makes markets and globalization work better for everyone. Our respect for social institutions—including the nation-state, community, faith, and family—is a big reason why this is so. But it is also because of conservatism's focus on practical matters rooted in real-world experience. It is about seeing the world as it is rather than how we wish it to be.

Of course, seeing the world as it is means recognizing that conservatives are hardly responsible for all the problems of globalization. Many of those are the consequences of the ideological tangents down which the liberal left have taken it. Left to their own devices, liberals will take us further down dangerous paths, like corporatism, elitism, alienism, and the extremes of "open borders." When populism fails, as pure populism invariably will, conservatives will need to be there with an alternative to left-liberal options.

Part of developing these alternatives involves challenging some preconceived ideas about populism. Populism is not entirely incompatible with markets, trade, globalization, and immigration. My own political career is proof. Besides this, the problems that have given rise to present-day populism demand solutions. This will require applying conservative experience to new problems. As Ronald Reagan himself once said, "I do not want to go back to the past; I want to go back to the past way of facing the future."[3]

I begin by looking at market economics. The market is a powerful institution for resource allocation and wealth creation. However, conservatives must resist market dogmatism. Policy-making does not occur within a textbook version of reality. It happens in the real world, with trade-offs, imperfect options, and non-economic considerations. Markets are a tool of good economic policy, but they are not an objective in and of themselves.

Growing public concerns about economic dislocation and trade are far from being without merit. However, they require a careful response that resorts neither to protectionism nor state dependency. People want meaningful work, as well as the financial security and personal dignity that come with it. Conservatives must be champions for paid work and must set out an agenda that creates the conditions for it.

It is the principal responsibility of national governments to protect and advance the interests of their citizens. The notion that we live in a "post-national" world is theoretically unsound and factually incorrect. A healthy nationalism is a normal part of a healthy society, as are basic elements of civil society, like family, faith, and community. Conservatives must advance a vision that sustains and strengthens these institutions as the foundation of democratic capitalism.

Finally, immigration policy should be designed to first and foremost advance the needs of host countries. That does not mean that it cannot address humanitarian considerations or the aspirations of immigrants themselves. On the contrary. But it must align with national imperatives, including employment conditions and community cohesion. Immigration is a privilege to be granted, not a right to be claimed.

These are foundational conservative ideas. They are tried and tested, and they remain relevant and useful in the globalist–populist age. The challenge is to translate them into concrete actions to improve working-class opportunity and strengthen social bonds. That is what I aim to do in the chapters that follow.

At the same time, this book is not limited to a readership of conservatives or even politicians. It is for anyone trying to understand the current trends of global politics. For instance, businesspeople grappling with rising political volatility should find it useful. These forces are not just about public governance, after all. The global financial crisis showed us that all institutions must take a hard look at themselves and figure out how to strengthen public trust and contribute to the common good.

=

Let me conclude with this. There are a lot of obituaries being written, citing the decline of the West in general and of America in particular.

These contain some elements of truth. For many of their authors, however, such a decline would clearly be a welcome development.

I do not share this perspective. There is no question that the Western world—most notably the United States—is going through a period of tumult and disruption. Nonetheless, democratic capitalist societies have historically shown unparalleled dynamism, resiliency, and adaptability. I am confident that, with the right ideas, right choices, and right leadership, we will come out of this era better and stronger.

1

IN PLAIN SIGHT

I do not want this book to focus too much on Donald Trump. For one thing, we are all tiring of the endless focus on him. For another, he just seems to enjoy it way too much.

Nevertheless, of all the instances of disruption in leadership and politics today, none can compare with Donald Trump's heading up the most powerful nation on earth. Brexit was a shock to the system, and other populist political movements in Europe are providing more. But nothing is as consequential as what has happened in the U.S. election and since.

There has been an avalanche of commentary purporting to explain how the Queens developer, turned billionaire, turned reality TV star, turned anti-establishment politician, became the president of the United States. The same pundits, press, and pollsters who deemed Trump utterly unelectable are now telling us why he won. They have become instant experts on what happened and what to do about it. If you are not skeptical, you should be.

The good thing is that we do not have to look under rocks or rely on talking heads for an answer. Trump's triumph is really not that much of a mystery. The president has been frank about the economic and social forces that motivated his voters and ultimately put him in the White House. In truth, he saw these trends earlier and more clearly than anyone else.

We need look no further than Trump's inaugural speech. It was a clear distillation of what was behind the populist uprising of 2016. It was an unorthodox yet powerful address, and it was right there in plain sight.

The media largely overlooked the speech. They were too busy focusing on the crowd size and fawning over the celebrities who refused to perform. Everything got attention except what should have. The address was a revealing look into Trump's populism and the voters who supported it.

Do not get me wrong; there was much to disagree with. The tone lacked Ronald Reagan's soaring rhetoric or George W. Bush's sunny optimism. There were no odes to America's freedom and liberty, and no homage paid to its conservative values and beliefs. There was a veneer of anger, even a tinge of darkness.

That does not mean, however, that we have nothing to learn from it. This was something different and worthy of attention. It was a break not just from old conservative mantras, but from the typical left–right model altogether. Trump was articulating a vision that challenged much of what had come before him.

=

We should try to understand Trump's victory by, first and foremost, understanding who voted for him. Who were these people? Were they all angry and deluded bigots? Were they all members of some vast alt-right conspiracy that no one had previously uncovered? Were they all dupes, living under the influence of Russian hackers?

These explanations are laughable at best, and insulting at worse.

Some sixty-three million Americans voted for Donald Trump. Most of them were traditional Republican voters supporting "their" candidate.[1] In the end, however, the real key to Trump's win was voters who do not normally support a GOP candidate but who cast their ballots specifically for Donald Trump.

These voters came overwhelmingly from regions and social groups whose economic lives have been stagnant or declining for a considerable number of years. They face high levels of economic insecurity for the foreseeable future. Some have already lost their jobs. Others are worried they soon will.[2] All know people who have. Virtually none of them are hopeful for their children.[3]

These voters do not tend to have college degrees.[4] They disproportionately work in industries, such as manufacturing, that are facing ongoing disruption from low-cost competition and new technology.[5] In short, they are in the parts of the Western economy that have fared poorly in the post–Cold War era, the age of globalization.

And they were feeling voiceless. This is a common finding in different studies of both the Trump election and the Brexit referendum.[6] The concerns of these people have been either largely ignored or, if acknowledged at all, vigorously denounced. There can be no doubt about the extent to which these voters believe that the political establishment does not care about them. They have come to mistrust both the traditional liberal/centre-left and conservative/centre-right options.

Can you blame them? The typical story about Washington centres on its political division. But the real story is how much the Democratic and Republican establishments actually agree, especially on matters that affect working-class people. In practice, both sides have embraced trade deals, deficit financing, high levels of low-skilled immigration (legal and illegal), weak financial regulation, and corporate bailouts. No wonder these voters felt like they had no real choice.

There is no greater example of this political convergence than the banking bailouts (which, thankfully, Canada did not have to engage in). Washington's political gridlock had stood in the way of progress on various fronts for several years. But, in a mere matter of days, Congress was able to pass a three-page bailout package. Hundreds of billions of dollars. Few questions. Minimal accountability. No consequences for Wall Street. Right in the middle of a recession that was ravaging the lives of ordinary people, this is what got Washington moving.

I do not say this to denounce the policy. It was a severe crisis and the options were limited. I am merely pointing out that there could not have been a greater disconnect between the elite consensus and the perspectives of ordinary people. And this is not strictly an American phenomenon. In a slew of Western nations, the financial bailouts have poisoned the political culture ever since.

Voters were understandably dissatisfied with the status quo. And they were even unhappier with the options the two parties planned to put before them. They simply did not want a Hillary Clinton or a Jeb Bush. I know both. They are very smart and accomplished individuals, and I suspect most voters would agree. But it did not matter. As members of prominent political families, they personified the status quo at a time when voters wanted change.

Thus, we had the twin phenomena of Bernie Sanders and Donald Trump. Their agendas may have been diametrically different, but there was something common in their appeal. How else do you explain the Sanders–Trump "switcher?" About 12 per cent of Sanders supporters in the Democratic primary crossed over to Trump in the general election. In several key states—Pennsylvania, Wisconsin, and Michigan—the number of Sanders-to-Trump defectors was greater than Trump's margin of victory.[7]

Ironically, both Sanders and Trump were deeply flawed candidates. Under normal circumstances, it would be hard to imagine how they could be successful. Two seventy-somethings. Both politically unpolished. One a socialist, the other a neophyte. One sabotaged by his party and the other barely tolerated. Parties, by the way, that neither candidate had belonged to for most of his adult life.

But that was the key. Both were truly outsiders. Both challenged the consensus in Washington. Neither looked like a politician or sounded like a politician. And so, the polls, the pundits, and the professionals told us that they had no chance. But what the "experts" missed was that Trump and Sanders were paying attention to regular people. They were giving voice to the voiceless. And people responded.

The voters, it turns out, were prepared to put up with a lot in order to vote for someone who spoke for them.

=

I mention Trump and Sanders in the same breath because they have been accused of the same political sin—"populism." This, we are told, is the common explanation for the appeal of both candidates and, most importantly, is the guiding force of the Trump presidency. But what exactly is populism?

At least since Trump's damp and dreary inauguration day, "populism" has become a loaded term. It has been made the default explanation for any political view or event that diverges from establishment opinion. Opposition to trade deals? Populism. Protest against immigration? It must be the populists. An unexpected election result? What else but populism? And so it goes.

One academic has the gist of it: Most uses of the term "populism" are motivated by an establishment desire to denigrate any opposition to the "liberal consensus."[8] Put differently: there is a tendency, particularly among contemporary liberals, to call political outcomes that they support "democracy," and ones that they do not "populism." In other words, they seek to equate populism with demagoguery.

That effort is itself demagoguery, for populism can have a positive interpretation. Put simply, it is any political movement that places the wider interests of the common people ahead of the special interests of the privileged few. If you think about it, in most every democracy, every political party tends to frame its core appeal in such terms, at least to some degree.

Is this such a nonsensical concept? In fact, there are times when the consensus of the political establishment diverges from the weight of public opinion. For instance, the desirability of trade deals and of unskilled immigration are areas where the leadership of both the U.S. Republican and Democratic parties has often parted company with the bulk of their own supporters. When such divergence occurs, it is the tendency of elites to try to take such political debate off the table. Populism is a force that can put these issues back on the agenda.

There have been many instances of elite consensus being challenged by the wider public. Economic orthodoxy in one period has become economic heresy in the next. Wars have been undertaken when they should not have, and pacifism has been practised in the face of inevitable conflict. Elites often have interests and perspectives that are distinct from those of the general public. And they are sometimes wrong.

Think of it this way. Populism is a framework for identifying political priorities and making political decisions. But it does not tell us much about the underlying policies per se. So-called populist politicians have stood for ideas that could be classed as left-wing, right-wing, or even centrist.

I am familiar with this because my electoral career began in a self-described "populist" party. In 1987, I worked under Preston Manning to help form the Reform Party of Canada. Reform shared the populist roots of a number of historical parties that have been founded in Western Canada. These parties have been of the right, left, and centre.

Reform's economic agenda included support for balanced budgets, free trade, and market-oriented economic reforms—the antithesis of what is labelled populist today. But Reform was genuinely populist in that it was founded largely by regular working- and middle-class people, it emphasized "grassroots" policy-making, and it had virtually no support from the corporate establishment. Its successor party, the Canadian Reform Conservative Alliance, later merged with Peter MacKay's much older Progressive Conservative Party. I led the resulting new Conservative Party of Canada into government in 2006.

If the Reform Party's complexion appears eclectic, that is actually a characteristic of populist movements. Populists almost invariably borrow their natures and their agendas from different sides of traditional political debate. Donald Trump himself is a case in point, which is why his support broke through some traditional party divisions.

Is this, as many claim, evidence of unprincipled inconsistency, of naked opportunism, and even of demagoguery? It well could be. But it could also be evidence of political innovation, of new ways of thinking about issues, and of new answers to problems that traditional politicians are failing to address.

There is one thing I know for sure: in this age of widespread disruption in the United States and other Western societies, we do require some new approaches.

═

Populism is not new. The term was originally associated with the People's Party—better known as the "Populist Party." It was a farmer-led movement that arose in the U.S. late in the nineteenth century. That was a tumultuous period of change, in many ways not unlike now.

Today, we remember the period for the enormous progress it witnessed. However, there was also massive economic dislocation and social disruption. Living standards rose, but so did wealth concentration. Concerns about inequality and the so-called plutocracy spread in what Mark Twain called the "gilded age."

Technological disruption back then was not from the Internet but the telegraph. There was the coming of railroads and steamships. Agricultural equipment in particular produced considerable labour displacement. Occupational churn peaked at an astounding 50 per cent from 1850 to 1870 and remained elevated into the pre-war period.[9] Workers were forced from the farm to the factory and from the country to the city. In 1880, workers in agriculture outnumbered industrial workers by a ratio of three to one. By 1920, the numbers were approximately equal. Employment in the manufacturing sector had expanded four-fold.[10]

The wage picture from the era is complicated, but big inequalities emerged. High-skilled workers realized significant growth in earnings while the lot of the average worker improved only modestly. The incomes of traditional, artisanal workers stagnated badly. And some, like the "robber barons," amassed previously unimaginable wealth.[11] Sound familiar?

By the eve of World War I, the globalized trading system was nearly as connected as it is now. Back then, U.S. manufacturing was leading the way. Manufactured goods jumped from one-fifth of U.S. exports in 1890 to one-half by 1913.[12]

U.S. immigration flows were also without precedent. America accepted more than twenty million immigrants between 1880 and 1920. The immigrant share of the population was three times greater in 1914 than at any time since.[13]

These were the conditions in which populism came to dominate much of the political culture of the era. There have been countless scholarly analyses of how *The Wizard of Oz* was really a parable about populism.[14] The ruby red slippers, tin woodman, cowardly lion, and even the yellow brick road were references to the era's politics—including monetary policy, trade, and labour turmoil.

The Populist Party ultimately failed, but many of its themes were taken up by voices in the mainstream parties. Democrat William Jennings Bryan and, especially, Republican Teddy Roosevelt became its most notable proponents. Progressive taxation, protectionism, financial regulation, and the breakup of big corporate "trusts" were among the eventual consequences. That was just in the United States. Europe descended into war.

=

We are now living through another period of disruption and dislocation, one that is arguably even more dramatic. Gains from new technology and globalization may be even less broad-based than in the past. Much of the upside is found in the developing world, where poverty has fallen and living standards have jumped. In advanced countries, the costs have been born disproportionately by working-class people. Millions are beginning to question whether it is all worth it.

This is not just a case of nostalgia or ignorance. There is ample evidence that globalizing trade and productivity-enhancing innovation are producing a large number of so-called losers. Those people are not imagining it. For example, the U.S. labour force participation rate is at a thirty-year low.[15] The share of adult men without paid work is now nearly one in three.[16] The most dramatic effects have been in manufacturing, where total employment has fallen by one-third since 1980.[17]

Non-college-educated workers have been disproportionately impacted by these developments. One estimate is that globalization has depressed their wages by as much as $1,800 per year.[18] In fact, working-class incomes are basically stagnant, particularly for men, and have not really risen since sometime in the 1970s.[19]

Policy has contributed to this problem. As we shall see, trade choices really have been a factor. They have led to the loss of employment for literally millions of workers, and in a large proportion of cases, these individuals' income and employment prospects have not recovered.

These are the facts. They have been imposing real costs on people, their families, and their communities for decades. Yet no one seemed to be paying attention. The elites were too busy focusing on historic gains in the stock market or other economic metrics disconnected from the lives of regular working people.

This is where Trump came in, which brings us back to his land-mark inauguration speech. The new president was giving voice to the issues and anxieties that had gone unnoticed or unchallenged in previous years. He was telling us what he had seen and heard that others had missed.

There were four major themes that came out of the speech. They were unique. They distinguished Trump's approach from those long taken by establishment politicians in both major parties.

The first was, for lack of a better term, a certain economic real-ism. Particularly atypical for a Republican, there was no talk about the morality of markets or praise of economic liberty. This was not a speech for think-tank scholars or philosophical conservatives. Instead, Trump articulated a hard-headed focus on bringing industry back to America and restoring jobs for American workers.

The second was trade. Trump challenged the assumption that free trade is inherently and always good for the United States. He called out trade deals that create an uneven playing field between American-based firms and international competitors, particularly trade agreements with China and Mexico. In their place, he offered a focus on domestic growth and "protection" of the industrial heartland.

The third was nationalism, which includes the "America First" philosophy. Trump criticized representatives from both parties for putting global priorities ahead of national imperatives. He pledged to govern in the national interest without nuance or apology.

The final theme was immigration. Trump broke with the bipartisan consensus in its favour. He notably rejected policy that effectively allows large numbers of low-skilled workers into the country. Instead, he spoke about "protecting our borders" and committing to an immigration policy rooted in the interests of American workers and families.

While each of these subjects deserves further discussion, Trump did not have much to say about practical solutions. There were few policy proposals or commitments that went beyond slogans like "winning again." Eighteen months into his presidency, this is still proving to be a weakness.

This does not, however, diminish Donald Trump's insight into the electorate. It does not change the fact that he saw things that much more experienced observers had not. Indeed, in his inaugural speech, he was telling us what he had tapped into and why he won. He was revealing the blueprint that got him to that podium and into the Oval Office.

2

SEEDS OF DISCORD

I arrived at the White House on November 14, 2008. It was not my first visit there, but by any measure, it was the most consequential. The occasion was the inaugural meeting of the newly christened Group of 20, or "G20." George W. Bush had invited the leaders of the world's largest economies and international organizations for dinner. The hall was glittering, the food exquisite, and fine wine would be served. The atmosphere, however, was sobering.

The world was lunging from an economic slowdown to an economic meltdown to total panic. Financial markets were frozen. Stock markets were plunging. Shipping volumes were in freefall. The global economic situation was visibly worsening by the day. In short order, the U.S. economy alone would lose nearly nine million jobs, see ten million foreclosures, and shed nearly three and a half trillion dollars in retirement savings.[1]

As leaders, we were not under any illusion about finding perfect solutions. The options before us were all bad, and the only objective was to avoid imminent calamity. The meeting's final communiqué committed to "whatever further actions are necessary to stabilize the financial system."[2] And we meant it. The stage was set for massive worldwide deficit spending, unprecedented and coordinated monetary interventions, and huge corporate bailouts.

In the weeks and months that followed, a measure of stability returned. The panic subsided and financial institutions stopped collapsing. The stock market bottomed out. In fact, it returned to pre-recession levels faster than most of us had imagined. Corporate profits, too, recovered comparatively quickly.

For many people, however, things would never be the same. As the Great Recession faded for some, employment and wages lagged behind for most. It took nearly a decade for U.S. household incomes to come back. Labour force participation is still down. In many countries, the effects on regular folks have been lasting.

This experience has taken its toll on the public's enthusiasm for markets, capitalism, and globalization. I know there are conservatives who can recite with ease the missteps of governments before and during the crisis, and there can be no doubt that governments did many things wrong. But that exercise cannot succeed in fully shifting the blame. The fact is that markets had failed on a massive scale.

To add insult to injury, when the crisis hit, the result was unremitting capitalism for the working class and socialist protection for the Wall Street financiers who caused the meltdown in the first place. Still, in many elite circles, the old narratives quickly returned. Even bank executives were soon back to paying themselves bonuses—not that they had ever really stopped—and decrying any attempt to re-regulate their sector.

I am not saying these things to denounce or disparage the market system. I still believe in the general efficacy of markets—more precisely, of well-governed markets. History shows unambiguously that capitalism usually produces far better outcomes than the alternatives. The market has a unique ability to connect capital and ideas with customers, and to drive sustained economic growth. The tendency of government, by contrast, is to politicize the allocation of wealth and opportunity at every turn.

These are, however, empirical observations, not expressions of faith. Yet, somewhere along the way, long before the sub-prime-mortgage bubble and the collapse of Lehman Brothers, this distinction was lost. There arose a market dogmatism among conservatives and a comfortable corporatism among liberals. With it came a growing gap between how the political, bureaucratic, and business establishments think and talk about markets and capitalism, and how the rest of the population does.

The crisis and the bailouts turned that gap into a chasm. The result would be the great populist shocks of 2016 and since. But the harvest should not have surprised us. The seeds had long been planted and nourished. We should only wonder why it took so long for the voters to get fed up.

=

As I have thought back to that Washington dinner, it has struck me how much my life and its circumstances have changed over the previous thirty years. Three decades earlier, I had left home and headed to the oil boom in Alberta. That is where the jobs were. In Canada back then, there were not many jobs anywhere else.

Our country, like so many other Western nations, was descending into a sustained period of slowing growth and rising prices. This had begun in earnest with the first OPEC oil embargo of 1973. The economic policy of the day, so-called Keynesianism, was clearly not working.

The term honoured the Depression-era British economist John Maynard Keynes. He had theorized that business cycles in a capitalist economy could be effectively tempered by government "macroeconomic management." This meant using the money supply and, more importantly, the government's budget to control speculative booms and eliminate spectacular busts. Closely related was the idea of robust social safety nets to lessen the economic insecurity of working people.

Keynes was not a socialist. He advocated open markets and international trade, and he did not counsel widespread government economic ownership. Nevertheless, his support for significant government intervention often aided the cause of those who did.

Keynesianism thus generated a growing range of government bureaucracies and a technocratic class of public officials. These visible hands of government strove to engineer economic outcomes in various sectors and to solve social ills of various kinds. There seemed to be nothing that government "experts" felt they could not fix.

For nearly three decades following World War II, the ideas of Keynes and his followers held sway. And, for a long time, they appeared to be right. The depressions and inflations that followed World War I did not re-occur. The Western world went into a sustained period of stable economic growth and social improvement. Indeed, it was one of the most successful periods in history, with steadily growing middle-class wealth and opportunity. U.S. wages, for example, nearly doubled between 1948 and 1975.[3]

This "golden age" was in stark contrast to the struggles and strife of the previous decades. It made converts of many who had initially been skeptical of government planning and economic management. In 1971, even Richard Nixon proclaimed, "we are all Keynesians now." Nixon was supposed to be a conservative. His election had been endorsed by William F. Buckley Jr. and *National Review*, no less. And so the talk of "the end of the ideology" became commonplace.

The Keynesians became ever more confident in their ability to steer the economy down a path of steady growth. At their height, they saw the economy as a giant machine whose buttons could be pushed and levers pulled to produce particular economic outcomes. This is not just a metaphor. A New Zealander at the London School of Economics, William Phillips, actually built something called MONIAC. It was a hydraulic machine that purported to show how an economy functioned and could be managed.

Phillips was the fellow immortalized by the economic theory of the "Phillips curve." Its premise was that Keynesian managers could "fine-tune" the economy through carefully managed trade-offs between unemployment and inflation. If unemployment rose and inflation fell, the budget could go into deficit and the money supply could be expanded to produce growth. If unemployment was low and inflation began to rise, the budget could go into surplus and the money supply could be contracted to cool things down.

By 1978, however, most Western economies were experiencing what came to be called "stagflation." Unemployment and inflation were rising at the same time. In fact, they were often into double digits, as were interest rates. Rising deficits were not creating growth, just higher debt levels.

The Keynesians produced new theories to explain away these apparent contradictions. Their penchant for intervention to fix the economic mess became even broader and deeper. The experience of the United States, the United Kingdom, and Canada with government-imposed comprehensive wage and price controls was just one example.

Another was something in Canada called the National Energy Program. In 1981–1982, the government of Pierre Trudeau capped a decade of socialist experimentation by deciding to use the power of the federal government to re-engineer the oil and gas industry. It was the height of bureaucratic hubris. A booming sector rapidly slumped, and the economy as a whole entered a deep recession.

It was under circumstances like these that a new generation of conservatives came to office throughout the West. These reformers were proposing to solve problems not through more government intervention but through less. It was not long before the ideas of markets and entrepreneurship, of personal incentives and business innovation, would begin to shape a new era of public policy. Ronald Reagan and Margaret Thatcher were their most famous advocates, but the period pulled a whole generation along with it. That included me, then a twenty-two-year-old economics student.

═══

I recount this history so that its lessons are not lost. It had proved impossible to reduce the complexity of a modern economy to the predictability of a simple machine. The notion of fine-tuning became an object of derision. In retrospect, it is apparent that economic and social forces well beyond the control of macroeconomic managers were largely responsible for the growth during the post-war period.[4]

It is also clear that only the arrogance of technocratic experts had allowed Keynesianism to go as far as it did. The Keynesians had developed a detailed and sometimes accurate assessment of the limitations of markets. They had, however, failed to ask probing questions about the limitations of government itself to address economic challenges. For instance, Keynesianism took for granted the notion that government policy-makers could be all-knowing. Going even further, it made the extraordinary assumption that those who shape policy will always act in the broader public interest.

Do politicians and bureaucrats not have their own unique self-interests and imperfections? Will a politician really put the best economic outcome ahead of an electoral objective? Will a bureaucrat always prioritize the management of economic cycles ahead of padding his or her own budget? These were plainly obvious questions that Keynesians failed to ask and refused to address.

I actually did my own graduate research in economics in this very area.[5] I examined federal fiscal policy in Canada over the period of 1953 to 1990. Specifically, I wanted to see if government policy really adhered to Keynes's theory of counter-cyclical budgeting. And I found that, in important ways, it did not. In fact, there was a tendency toward higher deficits most of the time, irrespective of economic circumstances. The timing of elections also mattered. In short, real-life implementation was far messier and more complicated than the theorists had assumed.

And these kinds of failings really mattered. The post-war consensus had buckled under them. Large-scale budgetary deficits had pushed up interest rates and crowded out productive investment. High taxation and big handouts had discouraged entrepreneurship and work. Public ownership, heavy-handed regulation, and trade protectionism had limited competition, undermined productivity, and stymied new industries and innovative competitors. Things had to change.

==

The 1980s would prove to be as exciting as the 1970s were dismal. Reagan and Thatcher and their cohorts would relentlessly pursue ambitious agendas of tax reduction, deregulation, and other market reforms. Reagan's lowering of the top personal income tax rate from 70 per cent to 50 per cent to eventually 28 per cent was a stellar example.[6] Thatcher's privatization legacy—including British Petroleum, Telecom, and Airways—was another.[7]

Both leaders were philosophical conservatives, but it is simply wrong to caricature them as ideologues. Their programs were practical responses to the real economic problems of the day. Reagan in particular was flexible in his choice of policy approaches and always kept a careful eye on public opinion. If Thatcher was more rigidly principled, she was also faced with a more existential challenge. The United States had to be pulled out of a decade-long slump. The United Kingdom had to be rescued from over a half-century of what seemed to be terminal decline.

It is also important to note the "populist" elements of these leaders' electoral support. Contrary to modern mythology, both Reagan and Thatcher were opposed not only by the left but by elements of the traditional right as well. The corporate establishment may not have fought them the way union bosses and government officials did, but it was hardly supportive. Small businesses ("shopkeepers"), private-sector workers ("Reagan Democrats"), and taxpayers were their bastions of support among voters.

But while the economic programs of Reagan and Thatcher were practical, their adherence to values was inspirational. And these two things came together in their shared opposition to communism and its denial of human freedom. Indeed, this agenda would become the foundation of an international transformation.

Where Keynesianism had led to stagnation, communism had reached the depths of human despair. Thus, when Soviet leader Mikhail Gorbachev attempted to reform communism, he unwittingly unleashed a tsunami of hopeful enthusiasm. In it, his system and its world would drown.

I remember watching the fall of the Berlin Wall. People who had for decades lived in a giant, decaying prison were suddenly free. It was as uplifting as it was stunning. The Soviet Empire, the second-largest on earth and one of the most systematically oppressive in human history, would disappear in two short years. And hardly a shot would be fired.

=

By the 1990s, Reagan and Thatcher were gone, but the democratic capitalist revolution they had unleashed was only beginning. One by one, countries everywhere moved in the direction of markets. In the two-decade span following Reagan and Thatcher's arrival in office, the number of states with communist, socialist, or fundamentally non-market economies shrank to a handful of rogue regimes. Capitalism had gone global.

In the former Soviet bloc, the transformation was most spectacular. From almost nothing, the private sector would come to dominate these economies in a few short years. Western democratic systems took hold just as quickly. The majority of these nations would join the European Union in little more than a decade.

The developing world also moved in the direction of markets and capitalism. From Israel (under a young Benjamin Netanyahu) to India to Tanzania, nations founded on various forms of socialist doctrine in the post-war period transformed themselves. Government-led industrial policies were abandoned. Trade barriers were reduced. Deregulation and privatization became the norm. Foreign investment was encouraged rather than scrutinized. Most notably of all, even China's Communist Party embraced such reforms.

Back in the West, a new generation of dynamic centre-left leaders joined the market consensus. America's Bill Clinton, Britain's Tony Blair, and others would speak of a "third way" or a "middle way" between capitalism and traditional left-wing economics. This was, however, little more than political rhetoric. Clinton, Blair, and their cohorts fully accepted the basic pillars of a market economy, including fiscal discipline, low taxation, private control of the means of production, and globalized trade and commerce. It was, for all intents and purposes, a capitulation to conservative economic orthodoxy. In a reversal of Richard Nixon a quarter-century earlier, Clinton even used the 1996 State of the Union to proclaim that "the era of big government is over."[8]

It is worth mentioning that one important element of society never fully embraced the new economic consensus. Much of Western academia remained fixated on communism. Indeed, as the Berlin Wall fell, it became evident that communist true-believers persisted only on its Western side. In the educational establishment, Marxism lingered as the opiate of the intellectuals.

Not with all, of course. Among some academics, revised assertions of ideological finality came to the fore. Francis Fukuyama famously declared the new world of democratic capitalism and globalization to be "the end of history."[9] And economist John Williamson coined the term "Washington consensus." He confidently added that "we can now have developed far more consensus . . . because we now know much more about what types of economic policy work."[10]

In other words, the policy framework may have changed, but the old technocratic certainty was creeping back.

=

I view this period as largely successful. However, the growing ideological excitement overlooked some very real challenges that came with market reform and globalization. There were also cautionary experiences that should have attracted much more attention.

For instance, the overnight transformation of the Eastern Bloc countries was not without its challenges. In fact, it has been described as "the agony of reform."[11] The collapse and privatization of state-owned companies initially caused unemployment to spike. Output shrank. Inflation accelerated. Living standards fell. One Polish dissident's quip that "the worst thing about communism is what comes after" would resonate with millions of people.[12]

As market forces kicked in, there was inevitable improvement. Those countries that gravitated toward the European Union and its democratic political model fared well over time. This was especially true if they pursued swift and comprehensive economic reforms. Estonia and Poland stand out.

Not all the new market experiments turned out well, however. In Russia and the countries that have remained close to it, things went sideways. The process of "marketization" was slower and more painful. Unemployment remained high. Inflation and social dislocation persisted. Eventually, market transformation took on an extralegal character. Former political insiders effectively expropriated state assets for themselves and their cronies. These "oligarchs" would operate in semi-elective, authoritarian political environments.

Vladimir Putin, who came to power in 2000, is the quintessential example of this alternative model. A professed supporter of private enterprise, Putin's kleptocratic capitalism is a blurring of private business, political office, and organized crime. In many ways, it is actually the communist parody of market economics. Nevertheless, in the enthusiasm of the times, such profound differences were glossed over. Russia had already been added to the G7 group of Western nations in 1998 on the expectation of its inevitable transition to a democratic capitalist society.

Not all of the challenges of the era were linked to the legacy issues of communism. Others were much more directly attributable to the emerging system of global capitalism itself. This was especially true in Asian nations.

Some of the most impressive performances in the newly globalized economy came from Asia. However, in the mid-1990s, a series of financial crises began on that continent. Mixed economic results combined with opaque financial sectors to create panics. In 1997 in particular, what started as a run on the banks by foreign short-term depositors became a general capital flight from several countries and expanded into an assault on government currencies. Thailand's economy contracted by 8 per cent, Indonesia's by 14 per cent, and South Korea's by 6 per cent.[13]

The secondary effects of these actions were felt throughout the continent and across the world. Everyone, from the modest investor to the sophisticated institution, was affected. The risks of the special dynamics between large-scale globalization, deregulated financial markets, and cross-border contagion had been exposed.

Such experiences ought to have caused world leaders to rethink the rapid liberalization of financial markets. At the time, however, the episode was attributed to the nature of rapidly developing economies. This misreading of the 1997 Asian financial crisis was a huge mistake. It would also be a precursor to the events that hit the world eleven years later.

=

The term "bastardized Keynesianism" was coined in the early 1960s to describe how Keynes's ideas had come to justify any or all government interventions in the economy. A generation of technocrats and politicians had drifted far from the initial conception. Keynes's modest vision of macroeconomic stabilization had become shorthand for ever-expanding government.

One can argue that the same thing happened to Reaganism and Thatcherism in the 1990s and early 2000s. What had started as an effort to bring conservative insights to bear on contemporary problems became something else. A practical and timely response to stagflation—tax cuts, spending reductions, privatization, deregulation, and freer trade—became a fixed agenda no matter what the circumstances.

Nothing demonstrates this more clearly than the 2016 Republican presidential primaries. Leaving aside Donald Trump, there did not seem to be an economic problem the candidates could not solve by either cutting regulations or lowering corporate and top marginal tax rates. But many of the voters they were talking to had lived with stagnant wages and declining disposable income for many years, even after previous rounds of such GOP actions. Their health care costs were rising and their services declining. Post-secondary education was falling out of the reach of their children. How did any of these proposals address the problems they were actually experiencing?

Many conservatives had fallen victim to a broader market dogmatism. Capitalism had become an end rather than a means. Markets had ceased being viewed as a tool to solve problems and instead were described as a moral objective in themselves. How else can we explain, for example, an obsession with overregulation in the shadow of the financial crisis?

One especially peculiar trend among such conservatives is the equating of market dogmatism with the legacy of Ronald Reagan. No Republican race is complete without conservative politicians fighting over who is the Gipper's rightful heir. But this exercise has become detached from any substantive analysis of his policies or even his rhetoric. The Great Communicator did not measure his economic success by ever more market efficiency, by stock market indices, corporate endorsements, or even specific tax rates. He talked about economic opportunity, entrepreneurial freedom, good wages, better jobs, and families having more money to spend. These are all reasons why so many Democrats voted for Reagan—and why so many establishment Republicans of the day opposed him.

If anything, such errors have been compounded by "middle way" liberals. With their elite business connections and their predisposition to intellectual models and international institutions, centre-left office-holders moved to a distinctly corporatist version of market-oriented economic policy. This was reinforced in the clubs where business executives, bureaucratic policy-makers, and trendy politicians rub shoulders, of which the annual Davos gathering is the ultimate expression. Not surprisingly, many of the excesses of America's financial deregulation were carried out by Bill Clinton's Democratic administration.

====

This overconfidence in markets not only generated an irresponsible deregulation in banking and finance. It also created a world of economic interdependence where the consequences would spin rapidly around the globe to nations that lacked the means to avoid them or deal with them. In countries with collapsing banking sectors, the only option became the large-scale bailout of financial institutions, often with crippling effects on national budgets.

In the meantime, little was done to address the practical challenges facing working people and their families. After 2008, long-stagnant incomes for regular folks in many countries became declining ones. This was particularly notable in the United States.[14]

Yet, despite the global financial crisis, a theoretical moralism continued to reign supreme in the economic-policy talk of politicians, think-tanks, and policy-makers. Capitalism and markets, especially the rising stock market, would come to be viewed as ends in themselves. For most regular people, it might as well have been a different language. They were still hurting. They were angry. And they were being ignored. This is what Donald Trump heard that others did not.

The president may ultimately not deliver the change his people are looking for. But what has happened must serve as a wake-up call for how we think about markets and capitalism.

There is still a tendency on the part of some to have a romanticized conception of the market system. A typical characterization tends to be that of a localized economy, with small-scale transactions between familiar parties quickly bringing supply and demand into balance. This is not just a simplification; it misses much of the story.

Real capitalism, especially in its globalized form, is complex, dynamic, and aggressive. There is a reason it is described by economists as "creative destruction."[15] The enterprises and innovations that drive growth can broadly disrupt the marketplace. Social dislocation and economic imbalances can be large and sustained. Markets are not perfect, and those imperfections can make economic cycles much worse. These are truths that have to be acknowledged and understood.

It does not mean that we should swing the pendulum back to the government overreach of the 1970s. There is an important difference between sound yet limited rules and intrusive micromanagement. Still, the global financial crisis was a lesson that less intervention is not always the best intervention.

Markets are a powerful tool for allocating scarce resources, linking capital and customers, and producing huge sums of material wealth. But frameworks matter. It is up to government to establish an institutional framework that harnesses capitalism's productive capacity and constrains its destabilizing impulses.

It is also up to government to ensure the system serves broad public interests and not just those of big-market players. This means developing an agenda focused on getting good outcomes for working- and middle-class people, not on fulfilling intellectual abstractions. That includes, for example, the area of international trade, which I want to talk about next.

Too many lost sight of these things. That is why I found myself in the crisis meetings at the White House in November 2008. It is also why, almost exactly eight years later, as improbable a character as Donald Trump would be sitting in the same room.

3

GOOD DEALS AND BAD DEALS

E ight years before that fateful evening in the White House, I was running a Canadian conservative political action organization, the National Citizens Coalition. It was during my "retirement" from partisan politics. I had planned to use the management experience I was gaining in that new role to transition to a true private-sector career. As they say, so much for "the best laid plans of mice and men."

As NCC president, I attended an American conservative policy convention outside Chicago that spring. One of the issues swirling about was the congressional debate on President Clinton's push to have China admitted to the World Trade Organization. The discussion revolved largely around whether opening up U.S.–China trade would advance human rights and democratic reform in the People's Republic. Taken for granted, especially by most Republicans, was that the initiative meant unprecedented opportunity for the American economy. Indeed, without GOP support, the measure would never have passed.

It is long past time to come to the obvious conclusion on the human rights debate. President Xi Jinping may be an exceptional leader, but a liberal reformer he is not. Indeed, more than any Chinese leader since Mao, he is utterly committed to authoritarian governance. The central objective of his tenure to date has been to return China to a system in which one man governs for life.

Equally obvious, but less admitted, is that the economic argument has also proven to be wrong. The Clinton trade deal has been economically disastrous for much of the U.S. economy. The Chinese–American trade imbalance is four to one, with an outflow of $375 billion a year and rising.[1] Worse still, it has cost the United States millions of well-paying jobs.

Many continue to resist this negative evaluation. Their argument goes something like this: "Sure, the Chinese sell us lots of lower-end manufacturing goods. Yes, it has cost us some jobs. But Americans get cheaper products and that has kept down our cost of living." Seriously? What these people are describing is not even a trade relationship. "You sell me something and I get to buy it" is not trade. It is just a purchase.

For the most part, that is the Chinese–American economic relationship. The Chinese sell, Americans buy, and the jobs move one way—to China.[2] More problematically, these imbalances are funding the rise of a strategic rival to the United States. The enormity of the error of this policy is simply astounding.

Yet—and this is the important part—establishment voices in both U.S. political parties remain overwhelmingly supportive of the arrangement. This becomes particularly evident whenever Donald Trump attempts to do something about it. He is immediately condemned by a tirade of homilies about the benefits of trade and the sins of ever trying to limit it.

I am pro-trade. The fundamental arguments for free trade are clear enough to most economists, and the government I led concluded a record number of free-trade agreements. When we took office in 2006, Canada had such agreements with only five countries in the entire world. When we left office in 2015, we had concluded negotiations with fifty-one nations.

But one thing I know is this: trade is complicated. It has winners and losers. Trade negotiations require clear-eyed knowledge and in-depth assessment. It is as possible to get a bad deal as a good deal. And political leaders have a responsibility to know the difference.

From conservative think-tanks to the liberal crowd at Davos, many have lost this understanding. This is how we get columns and essays with titles like "There are no 'myths' or exceptions about free trade: It's always unrelentingly good,"[3] or "The blessings of free trade."[4] They assert a perspective based on theory alone—and a poor understanding of theory at that.

How did we get to the point where economic and political elites became more committed to trade principles than to trade outcomes? How did the geopolitics become unimportant? How did the actual impacts on working- and middle-class people become irrelevant?

===

Modern support for free trade goes back two hundred years, to the British classical economist David Ricardo. Ricardo's theory of comparative advantage showed that trade between two countries makes sense even if one of them produces all goods more cheaply than the other. In the example Ricardo gave, Portugal could produce both cloth and wine more efficiently than Britain. Still, Britain would be better off by producing cloth and trading with Portugal for wine. It would produce the quintessential win–win.[5]

This is the point where trade ideologues proclaim, "Ah ha! See. Trade is always good." And, yes, Ricardo's insight is a very important one. But it masks some complexities. Take something called the Stolper–Samuelson theorem.[6] Simplified considerably, it comes down to this: just because a country might be better off by trading, it does not follow that everyone in the country is better off.

Of course, this realization should be obvious, notwithstanding the many articles published to the contrary. Otherwise, trade deals would have no opponents at all. But how are we to weigh the gains of the winners in trade against the hardship that may be imposed on the losers?

In the Trump administration, it seems that the measure is often the size of the trade surplus or deficit. Trump has asserted that persistent trade deficits prove that the U.S. has a bad trade deal. Others have challenged this view, and they do so with some reason.

For example, a richer country is likely to have a trade deficit with a poorer country. Not always, but most probably. The reason is simple. A richer country buys more than a poorer country, simply because it is richer. Therefore, it is likely to buy more from a poorer country than it is to sell to that country.

The needs of the two countries may also have something to do with a trade deficit. I would argue that this helps explain the modest deficit the United States has tended to have with Canada. True, Canada is a somewhat poorer country than the U.S., but it is also America's largest supplier of energy. When that critical U.S. need is great and oil prices are high, Canada will tend to run a significant trade surplus with the U.S. At other times, not so much.

But what if a trade deficit is caused by the fact that one country has labour and environmental standards and the other country does not? Or, even more problematically, what if one country can sell its exports to another country, but the other one is not allowed to? Or what if the gains from trade are simply not worth the economic displacement caused in one's own country? These issues, not the theorems in textbooks, are the kinds of things at the centre of real-world trade negotiations.

=

The history of trade is also complicated.

There was spectacular growth in international trade in the late nineteenth and early twentieth centuries. It was actually the first era of what we now call "globalization." And it failed. National trade strategies were often closely linked to competitive empire-building. The system culminated in World War I. Then there followed more explicitly protectionist strategies. They exacerbated the Great Depression and ended with World War II.

As it became clear that the victory of the Allies over the Axis was assured, leaders began to put their minds to the post-war economic order. They obviously wanted to avoid the failures of both the globalization period before WWI and the attempts at autarky prior to WWII. Their plans took shape at the Bretton Woods Conference in July 1944.

Bretton Woods eventually led to the establishment of a series of international institutions that we know today as the World Bank, International Monetary Fund, and World Trade Organization. These would, respectively, provide international development finance, global stabilization capacity, and the ground rules for trade. The last would include a pegged but adjustable system of currencies, tied to the gold standard.

As the leading economist of the era, John Maynard Keynes played a significant role at Bretton Woods. Its system of "managed trade" reflected the same balance between the market and the state that Keynes sought through domestic macroeconomic management. This new world economic order was designed to both limit market fluctuations and discourage protectionism. It would encourage trade and attempt to prevent economic nationalism, imperial commercial rivalry, and competitive currency devaluations.

Like Keynesianism itself, this system was largely successful for some time, particularly in comparison with earlier periods. The greatest triumph was in Western Europe. The recovery of this region from the ravages of war and its emergence as an economic power-house were spectacular achievements. It had, however, considerable assistance along the way from the United States.

Beginning in 1948, America intervened directly in Western European reconstruction through the Marshall Plan. Sizeable resources were put into the effort—close to $150 billion in present-day funds.[7] The monies supported some top-down economic planning and helped underwrite some social welfare spending. However, the plan additionally included the breaking down of borders, the lowering of internal tariffs, and the development of a pan-European market. It also offered preferential trade access to the American economy.[8]

The United States underwrote post-war Western European reconstruction to contain Soviet expansionism. At a time when the region was economically fragile and facing large domestic communist movements, American aid kept it in the camp of the democratic capitalist world. The trade access advantages granted to struggling European states were seen as bound to benefit the larger U.S. economy over the longer term.

American support also laid the basis for later European integration. As the Marshall Plan came to an end, six countries—Belgium, France, West Germany, Italy, Luxembourg, and the Netherlands—created the European Coal and Steel Community. The ECSC paved the way for a series of European organizations of ever wider membership and scope. Following the collapse of the U.S.S.R., the Maastricht Treaty of 1993 created the European Union, a quasi-federal state. It stands in stark contrast to the economic competition and military conflicts that had marked the continent for centuries.

======

Just as the Keynesian domestic model came under stress in the 1970s, so too did its international version. In 1971, Richard Nixon had taken the United States off the gold standard, an act that effectively ended a critical element of the Bretton Woods system. As the problems of the decade worsened, spurts of protectionism and nascent autarky began to break out in different parts of the world.

In this environment, the impact of the Reagan–Thatcher revolution was bound to be felt. Just as free-market policies were being undertaken in various countries, so it was inevitable that free-trade initiatives would be pursued between them. The most consequential of these developments would occur in an unlikely spot—Canada.

It was unlikely because Canada had long seemed to be going in a very different direction. The left-wing economic nationalism and market intervention that dominated government policy through the 1970s had continued into the early 1980s, with increasingly worse results. By then, these policies had generated double-digit rates of unemployment, inflation, and interest. In 1984, the federal deficit hit an astounding 8 per cent of GDP, with the country barely recovering from a deep recession.[9]

In that year, a new Progressive Conservative government was elected. While generally aligned with the values of Reagan and Thatcher during the Cold War, that government turned out to be surprisingly tepid toward conservative economic reform. Its privatization and deregulation agendas were slow and wary. A timid approach to deficit reduction—limited spending restraint and modest tax increases—proved generally ineffectual.

The tax policies in particular began to drive young conservative activists, of which I was one, to other options. Most notable of those was the fledgling Reform Party. Its "populist" themes included attacks on deficit spending and tax hikes.

There was one area, however, in which the PC government embarked on consequential change—its approach to international economic policy. It began by scrapping the previous government's nationalistic restrictions on foreign investment. This created a largely open-door policy that has persisted to this day.

That initiative, the recommendations of a Royal Commission established by the previous government, and the growing personal rapport between Ronald Reagan and Brian Mulroney combined to create an even more important undertaking. It led our two countries to pursue free-trade negotiations, which were concluded successfully in late 1987.

In the Canadian federal election of 1988, the free-trade agreement polarized the debate. The deal was subject to near-hysterical attacks by opposition liberals and leftists who contended that a bilateral trade agreement would sacrifice the country's political independence. In making such a charge, the opponents could not have been more wrong.

Unlike post-war trade integration in Europe, the Canada–U.S. Free Trade Agreement proposed no increased political integration to parallel greater economic integration. The "governance" of the trade relationship, beyond a dispute-resolution mechanism, would be non-existent. It would be truly market-oriented.

The subsequent success of the Canada–U.S. deal utterly discredited free-trade opposition in Canada and led to another bold step: the North American Free Trade Agreement. Concluded at the initiative of George H.W. Bush and Brian Mulroney in 1992, the agreement essentially expanded the original deal to include Mexico. NAFTA instantly became the largest free-trade region in the world.[10]

The CUSTA and NAFTA agreements were outstanding achievements and a sign of things to come. As the Cold War came to a close, the era of managed trade was passing. Bilateral, multilateral, and regional trade negotiations broke out everywhere. The number of international trade agreements has since more than quadrupled.[11]

=

NAFTA was a harbinger in its inclusion of a major developing country in a trade pact. Indeed, the biggest developments in the new world of free trade were to come from emerging economies, particularly in Asia.

There was already an important post-war precedent for this—Japan. The Japanese model was, however, quite different from those in the United States and Western Europe. While business-driven, Japan's economy has been dominated by large conglomerates with close relationships to the government. As the Japanese economy was rebuilt, its bureaucracy worked closely with these corporations on research, finance, and marketing strategies. These strategies were export-oriented, and were often assisted by both an undervalued currency and a home market that has been difficult for foreigners to penetrate.

Significant frustration with the Japanese approach and its unequal trade access would develop in the United States. That said, the model was largely tolerated. Once again, the general (but not universal) American view was that the progress of Japan was in the United States' interest. After all, Japan had emerged from WWII as a democracy and a key U.S. global ally. Any sense that it might be an economic threat faded when Japan's growth slowed abruptly in the 1990s.

Other Asian nations came to the fore as the 1980s progressed and market-oriented policies swept the world. Some approaches were less driven by government strategy than Japan's. Others, like South Korea's, would emulate the Japanese model. But, in China, the quasi-market model would be taken to a new level.

The rapid transformation of China following the failures and death of Mao Zedong has been stunning. Beginning with the ascent of Deng Xiaoping in 1978, China underwent extensive market-oriented reforms. Competitive pricing, the de-collectivization of agriculture, some privatization, and a growing openness to foreign investment were introduced. Many state-owned enterprises remained major players but were pushed toward more genuinely commercial operations.

The result has been a spectacular liftoff. In thirty years, China has gone from being one of the world's poorest countries to being its second-largest economy. Since the financial crisis, it has become the linchpin of global economic growth.

The reality, however, is that the purpose of Chinese market reforms has always been to reinforce the power of its communist government. Economic liberalization, though wide-ranging, has remained careful, deliberate, and top-down, not spontaneous, organic, and business-driven. Whether we call China's economy "market socialism" or "state capitalism," it is not remotely a market economy in the Western sense. Elements of state ownership, central planning, and political direction remain important in all of the country's major industries.

This was all simply ignored when China was admitted to the World Trade Organization in 2001. As with the addition of Russia to the G7, the facts on the ground were disregarded. Actually, it was worse. Russia in the 1990s was developing some of the characteristics of a liberal democracy, a market economy, and a Western ally. Seeing these things in China was pure wishful thinking.

The practical problem for the West is that current arrangements effectively give Chinese goods and investment wide-ranging access to Western markets, except where this is explicitly blocked. But Western exports to China are admitted only when, where, and in what quantities China chooses. Not surprisingly, China has racked up enormous trade surpluses with key countries, particularly the United States.

===

There can be little doubt that trade flows are behind radically different views of globalization in the world. Polling shows that those in developing countries such as Vietnam, the Philippines, and India overwhelmingly believe it is a "force for good." Citizens in developed countries like the United States are less sure that is the case.[12]

Why such a gap? What happened to the triumphalism of the late 1990s? The truth is that the story of globalization in the twenty-first century is a mixed one. There have been both good and bad.

First, the good. Globalization has been a force for radically reducing poverty and inequality at the international level. In fact, integration of developing nations into the global economy has accomplished far more in a short period of time than decades of foreign aid and government planning.

As recently as 1990, nearly two billion people, one-third of the world's population, lived in extreme poverty. Today, that is true of only about one in ten.[13] This is an enormous and unprecedented reduction in human want and misery, and there can be no doubt that globalization is central to this achievement. One World Bank study concludes that "globalizing" countries in the developing world have seen income grow three and a half times faster than in "non-globalizing countries." Further, "higher growth rates in globalizing developing countries have translated into higher incomes for the poor."[14]

The upshot is that we have witnessed a narrowing of the income gap between advanced and developing countries. Per capita incomes in developing economies have grown almost three times as fast as in advanced ones. This trend began in earnest in the 1990s and has only accelerated in the 2000s.[15] This is a major social achievement, and open markets, free trade, and globalization are principally responsible.

=

And now the bad. Millions of workers in advanced countries have experienced wage stagnation, job losses, or both. As one example, manufacturing employment has fallen by one-third in the U.S. since 1980.[16] This has deeply affected individuals, families, and communities.

I recognize that various factors have contributed to this problem, and that technological innovation and automation have played a major role. In many cases, domestic manufacturing production has stayed steady, or even increased, as employment has fallen. I have toured many such factories.

But trade is also partly responsible for the loss of manufacturing jobs. It is silly to claim otherwise. Workers and communities can point to factories and jobs that still exist but are now located offshore.

This should not come as a surprise. Remember, the economic case for free trade is that we are better off in the aggregate, not that every single sector, community, or person is better off. Of course, there have been workers who have been dislocated by these trends. This is an unavoidable part of a globalizing economy.

Take NAFTA, for instance. Research finds that the agreement has generally produced positive results for U.S. workers. However, an "important minority" has experienced job and income losses. One estimate is that the surge of NAFTA imports has led to a loss of up to six hundred thousand American jobs over two decades.[17] Another study puts that figure at about fifteen thousand net jobs each year.[18]

More than any other Asian country, China has successfully leveraged its low-cost labour in this new era of globalization. In some cases, Western firms relocated operations—particularly labour-intensive manufacturing—to China. In others, old firms were simply displaced by new ones in the People's Republic. Ninety per cent of the growing mass of Chinese exports are now manufactured goods.[19]

Is it a coincidence that manufacturing jobs have plummeted in the U.S., Canada, and other advanced countries at the same time? Of course not. Trade with China cost America some two and a half million jobs between 1999 and 2011 alone. The figure for Canada is over a hundred thousand manufacturing jobs in roughly the same period.[20] Even more concerning, economic prospects for those people have remained depressed for many years.[21]

Some establishment voices may try to deny such impacts, but the fact is that they were utterly predictable. The most populous nation on earth with endless multitudes of low-skilled labour entered the global marketplace. What did they think was going to happen?

We are now seeing the political consequences. U.S. congressional districts exposed to large increases in imports, particularly from China, have tended to become more populist.[22] Likewise, there is a robust relationship at the district level between exposure to Chinese imports and a shift toward supporting Trump. Analysis suggests that Michigan, Wisconsin, and Pennsylvania would likely have elected Hillary Clinton in the absence of such developments.[23] Incidentally, a post-Brexit study similarly found that Leave votes were significantly higher in regions more affected by the ramping up of Chinese imports over the past three decades.[24]

Some will claim that these developments were "inevitable." We have to be clear about what the use of that term means. The general opening of global trade meant it was inevitable that low-skilled jobs in the West would go to lower-wage economies. However, no such opening was inevitable. And it was certainly not inevitable that the arrangement would allow China to largely shelter its own domestic marketplace. But that is what happened. And that is why the trade gap between China and many Western nations is persistent and growing.

So there really are good deals and bad deals. This is one of the major reasons why we have Trump. And it is why, even if Trump fails, this issue will not go away.

=

In retrospect, it is apparent that the post-war global trading order has been turned on its head by the emergence of China as an economic power. Its approach may make use of markets and private enterprise, but it also employs currency devaluation, industrial espionage, and intellectual piracy. The overall strategy is one of economic nationalism, commercial imperialism, and domestic protection. This is the very model the post-war order sought to avoid. Furthermore, it has had significant negative consequences for the well-being of many of our citizens.

You would think that both political and economic leaders in the West would be concerned about this situation. Instead, they have often been its apologists, if not its champions. This is particularly striking in the U.S. Republican Party.

Contrary to what some in the GOP try to claim, it is impossible to imagine Ronald Reagan embracing today's trade realities. Yes, he was a champion of free trade. His role in the original Canada–U.S. deal is proof enough of that. But, as with other parts of his legacy, his views have been simplified, caricatured, and distorted by his successors.

Known for his rhetorical flourishes about the benefits of globalized commerce,[25] Reagan was far from dogmatic on the issue. He supported open markets and free trade to the extent that he saw them as beneficial for working Americans. When this was not the case, and especially when he believed trade practices were unfair, he was not afraid to impose tariffs. He did so on Japanese goods, and even Canadian ones, at different times during his presidency.

Reagan put it this way in a 1985 speech: "I believe that if trade is not fair for all, then trade is free in name only. I will not stand by and watch American businesses fail because of unfair trading practices abroad. I will not stand by and watch American workers lose their jobs because other nations do not play by the rules. . . . Let no one mistake our resolve to oppose any and all unfair trading practices. It is wrong for the American worker and American businessman to continue to bear the burden imposed by those who abuse the world trading system."[26]

The evolution of the Republican Party's platform captures the extent to which it lost touch with Reagan's trade pragmatism. At the end of his time in office, the party stated in its 1988 platform that it "will not tolerate unfair trade and will use free trade as a weapon against it."[27] The 1992 platform still said that the Republicans were "tough free traders, battling to sweep away barriers to our exports."[28] Yet subsequent platforms were for unequivocal openness. Not until 2012 were any concerns raised about Chinese trade practices.

China is now on a trajectory to become the world's largest economy while also having preferential trade access to its competitors. This, combined with its renewed authoritarianism, its increasing foreign aggressiveness, and its military buildup, cannot be seen as anything other than a serious threat to the Western democratic model. It is ludicrous to argue that Reagan would not have been alarmed by this state of affairs. Yes, he would have understood that taking strong measures to deal with it is risky. But he would also have known that the path we are on is worse.

It would be grossly unfair, however, to ascribe the negative effects of the post-Keynesian trading system to Republicans and conservatives alone. The irony is that liberals, who resisted free trade for most of the twentieth century, are now among its biggest boosters.

Some conservatives may have underestimated the problems and challenges of contemporary trade arrangements. For the left, however, internationalism for its own sake has been an article of faith since at least Woodrow Wilson. This predisposed contemporary liberals to the new era of open markets and open borders. And, as we shall see, it has caused them to take it to new extremes.

4

SOMEWHERES AND ANYWHERES

M ost people in the world would not recognize the mild-mannered, eighty-year-old Klaus Schwab. He is, nonetheless, a major figure in global circles. In the 1970s, this business professor began work on a non-profit organization that became the World Economic Forum. Since 1988, it has hosted an annual meeting in Davos, Switzerland, that attracts corporate, political, and non-governmental leaders from all over the world.

How was someone as obscure as Schwab able to do this? Foresight, of course. And persistence. In my experience, Schwab decides who he wants to come and then repeatedly reminds them of the invitation. And each successful invitation has been leveraged to get the next.

During my time as prime minister, Schwab persuaded me to speak at Davos twice. On the first occasion, my purpose was to get out the story of Canada's successful economic management to an international audience. The second time, I wanted to convey some policy messages to the Canadian domestic audience. As Barack Obama once observed to me, when a leader has something of substance to say, the farther he or she can deliver it from the capital-city press corps, the more likely it is to be reported.

Schwab deserves enormous credit for what he has accomplished. The World Economic Forum is an outstanding organization. And Davos is a remarkable event. It is also, however, a bit disturbing.

In recent years, Davos has taken on an atmosphere of elitism that would be hard to surpass. Gathering at Davos' remote location and high elevation, many of its attendees seem to view themselves as some kind of supreme world council, casting judgments on whether nations and their leaders measure up. You can see it in the press reports.[1]

The one commonality in virtually all the new, populist, or disruptive political movements of recent years is their suspicion of such "globalism" and their appeal to nationalism and the national community.[2] The citizens who support these parties are not just frustrated with particular policies or economic outcomes; they simply do not trust the elites who support globalization. They believe such "globalists"[3] do not share their values and do not care about their interests. And, too often, they are right. In truth, policy-makers' stubborn adherence to market or trade theory frequently stems from an even greater abstraction, "the global community."

Globalists have been shaken by populism, particularly the "America First" rhetoric of both Donald Trump's campaign and his administration. It is true that U.S. leaders have often stressed American pride and American exceptionalism. But that was almost always tempered by a call to American leadership and American responsibility to the world. With Trump, the imagery of the "shining city on the hill" has vanished. What we see is a hard-headed nationalism rooted mostly in economic self-interest.

The response to this position has passed from surprise to outrage. Globalists have launched ongoing attacks on the notion of America First. Parallels have been drawn to historical episodes of American isolationism. Its nationalistic tone has been critiqued as exclusionary and divisive. There are allegations that it has given fodder to bigots and racists.

These critiques are not without merit. Excessive nationalism can be unproductive, even dangerous. A reversion to isolationism would be bad for the United States and the world. And there is little doubt that some fringe groups have chosen to interpret Trump's message in dark and illiberal ways.

All that said, Americans have every right to leaders who unequivocally put the interests of their country first. So, too, do the citizens of all nations. The anti-nationalism of today's elites is badly misguided, particularly out of step with U.S. public opinion, and in need of a serious rethink.

=====

Some dismiss Trump's clarion call to "Make America Great Again" as sheer jingoism, but to minimize the visceral embrace of his anti-globalist message is to miss its larger significance. It resonated with the core of the party that supported Ronald Reagan and George W. Bush and their robust internationalism. His message also had resonance with a considerable body of traditionally Democratic voters, many of whom crossed over to give him the presidency.

To my mind, this is perhaps the most easily understood part of the Trump phenomenon. America has been through a decade and a half of foreign-policy experiences that laid the groundwork for an America First approach.

To start with, there were the wars in Afghanistan and Iraq. Full disclosure: I supported both initiatives and still support the decision on Afghanistan. Nonetheless, enormous human and financial costs have been incurred through "nation-building," with very limited success. In the process, the idea of promoting America's ideals abroad was dealt a terrible blow.

Then came a new administration determined to avoid overextension. However, global security deteriorated further. And things like the "apology tour," "leading from the rear," and the "Syria red line" contributed to a view among many Americans that the country lacked confidence in itself.

Thus, the record of the recent past draws a pretty straight line to the orientation of the current U.S. administration. Still, it is only part of the story. It cannot fully explain the gut-level responses, both positive and negative, to the America First bent of the Trump administration.

═══

As a conservative, I confess to being more perplexed by those who fanatically oppose nationalism than by those who vehemently support it. Nationalism, or at least patriotism, seems to me a pretty normal state of human affairs in most places and at most times. And the idea that a country would put its own interests first was, I thought, a kind of fundamental maxim of international relations.

When and where did thinking so contrary to this emerge? As with modern views on economic and trade policy, it can be traced initially to the end of World War II, and then underwent a metamorphosis at the end of the Cold War.

Almost immediately following the victory of the Allied powers, the United Nations was founded. With the advent of the atomic bomb, the world's leaders faced an unprecedented urgency to prevent the recurrence of a major conflict. The UN would be not just a global forum but rather an organization with a wide range of international missions, including collective security. However, rivalry with the Soviet Union quickly undermined the concept of a global security architecture, causing the remaining Allies to form the North Atlantic Treaty Organization.

With the end of the Cold War, truly global security co-operation again became possible. This was demonstrated in the First Gulf War and the war in Afghanistan. The efforts had UN sanction, with American leadership and NATO providing the backbone of broad military coalitions. As I noted, the ideas that accompanied this American leadership, especially market economics and free trade, soon came to be seen as a universal model. With the simultaneous development of modern communications, especially the Internet and social media, this new state of world affairs made a distinct "globalist" orientation possible.

It is fair to say that all the victors of WWII had a desire to limit nationalism—certainly a desire to avoid its extremes. But it was more in Europe than in America that an explicit anti-nationalism first emerged. A generation of European leaders were rightly appalled by their continent's history in the preceding half-century. Their solution was a united Europe that would transcend its nation-states.

The product of this labour is impressive. The emergence of the European Union from the ashes of World War II is an unprecedented human achievement, on every level. There has been remarkably united economic, political, and social advancement after centuries of conflict.

═══

It would be a mistake, however, to downplay the weaknesses of the European project. Seven decades later, EU institutions still remain a work-in-progress, with populations often reluctantly pulled along and public opinion frequently ignored. In the process, EU behaviour has sometimes been not just undemocratic but badly disconnected.

Nowhere is this truer than in the U.K. Analysts can point to any number of campaign events or issues that produced the surprise Brexit vote. What they usually refuse to acknowledge is that the British simply never wanted a political, social, and legal union with Europe in the first place. They never looked for much beyond economic integration. In other words, they preferred—and are now seeking—a relationship with the European Union comparable with what Canada has had with the United States.

The British have inherited long and unique traditions of parliamentary sovereignty. They were never going to be fully comfortable in the intergovernmental, bureaucracy-led structures of Brussels. Moreover, the British have never regarded their nationalism as a cause of the continent's devastating conflicts. Indeed, they have seen it as part of what ultimately rescued Europe from fascism.

At the other extreme is Germany. No country has ever had its nationalism wreak such destruction on the world or, for that matter, on itself. This has defined the post-war German character to its core. And the Germans deserve enormous respect for assuming responsibility for their awful historical record and for charting an entirely new course. That said, Germany is truly an outlier in these matters. Nevertheless, its view of nationalism has spread not just in elite European circles but to similar ones everywhere. This has been especially true since the later stages of the Cold War.

I have mentioned how the various strains of Keynesianism and socialism were abandoned in the late 1980s and early 1990s. Likewise, we saw how conservative economic views were largely adopted by political parties of the centre left. To compensate, such parties increasingly differentiated themselves on non-economic issues. This is the origin of the "culture wars" and "identity politics." On cultural, social, and religious matters, contemporary left-liberal parties and elites have moved further and further to the left. Nationalism—or rather anti-nationalism—is one of those moves.

The problem for such liberals is that anti-nationalist views are just not that widely shared. Even after decades of European unity, national identity trumps continental identity in almost every EU country.[4] This is one of the things that makes an economically distressed Europe so vulnerable to political disruption.

The same is true, even more so, of the United States. A 2016 Gallup poll found that 52 per cent of respondents were "extremely proud"— not just proud, extremely proud—to be American. That is what Trump tapped into. He did not outperform Mitt Romney in thirty-eight states and pick up five more simply by bringing a few bigots out of the shadows. Clearly, racism could not have drawn the millions of Americans who voted for Obama in 2012 to instead pick Trump in 2016.[5]

Despite proclamations to the contrary, nationalism is alive and well almost everywhere. It is strong even in modest Canada. We saw this most vividly in 2008. With the onset of the global financial crisis, the Liberal Party tried to overturn my minority government. They had the virtually unanimous support of the mainstream media. However, driven by the necessity of the parliamentary numbers, they tried to include Quebec separatists in their efforts. They instantly faced a nationalist backlash in the rest of the country. It forced a chaotic retreat.

=

I do not want to reduce these different views of nationalism merely to philosophical shifts within political parties. As with the splits over global markets and international trade, something much deeper is going on. Trump, Brexit, and the European populist movements are exposing a fault line in modern Western societies.

The division is between what has been called those who live "any-where" and those who live "somewhere."[6] The rise of globalization in the past quarter-century has transformed an element of the population. Segments of urban and university-educated professionals have become genuinely globally oriented in their careers and personal lives.

Imagine yourself as someone who works for an international con-sulting firm or in a globally focused academic career. You can wake up in New York, London, or Singapore and feel at home. You may rent or even own regular accommodation in all of these places. Your work is not subjected to import competition or threat of techno-logical dislocation. You may attend (or aspire to attend) the Davos conference. You probably read *The Economist* and, like Thomas Friedman, believe that the world really is flat. Your spouse or partner has a similar professional background, although he or she is from somewhere else in the world. You are motivated by climate change and suspicious of religion. You are unequivocally pro–free trade and support high levels of immigration. Your values can broadly be described as "cosmopolitan."

Such cosmopolitans, or "Anywheres," or just plain "globalists" have an increasingly weak attachment to the nation-state. Their pro-fessional, personal, and even familial relationships are increasingly with people like themselves from a range of countries. The examples I give may be rooted in stereotypes, but there are many less extreme cases among people who work, study, or join online communities that cross boundaries.

There are a lot of these people, but there are still many more com-pletely unlike them. Maybe you are a manufacturing or retail worker, or even a small-businessperson. You probably do not live in the central areas of a major business centre. Your work can be, and is being, disrupted by import competition and technological change. You are motivated by steady work and a decent living. You and your spouse grew up in the same community in which you now live and work. Your children attend the local schools and your aging parent lives nearby. Your social life is connected to a local church, service club, restaurant-bar, sports team, or community group. You only leave your region for brief vacations. Your values can broadly be described as "localist."

Such localists or "Somewheres" are far more likely to be nationalists at heart. Social solidarity matters to them because their future hinges on the society in which they live.

==

For Somewheres, nationalism is more than just a strong emotional attachment (although it is usually that); it is critical to their lives. If things go badly, or if policy choices turn out to be wrong, Somewheres cannot just shift their lives to somewhere else. They depend on the nation-state.

Of course, Anywheres also depend on the nation-state, whether they admit it or not. It is, after all, the major nation-states that have made globalization possible. To the extent that there are global markets with rules and stability, it is agreements among nation-states that created them. Without these agreements, international commerce would be little beyond occasional exchanges and one-off transactions. Think about it. Anything more than that requires investments in transportation, communications, and logistics. It depends on enforcement of contracts, provision of information, and prevention of fraud. It needs stable, reliable, and exchangeable currencies. There must be arrangements that bring distributional outcomes into conformity with acceptable political norms. And so on.

It is fashionable for Anywheres to blame bad national policies—and especially populism—for the instabilities and uncertainties in the global economy. Sometimes they are indeed to blame, but not that often. The "global community" provides little or nothing in the wide range of institutions and practices that well-governed markets require. The critical functions of laws and regulations, monetary and fiscal stability, conflict management and resolution, and social services and redistribution have so far been provided almost exclusively by nation-states. Left to its own devices, globalization would be an economic world of massive and persistent instability—as it was in late 2008, until the major nation-states stepped in.

Incidentally, it is not self-evident what these institutions and practices would look like if they were pursued on a global basis. Given their distinctiveness, it is not surprising that nation-states address these issues very differently. The world simply does not agree on how to balance equality against opportunity, economic security against innovation, health and environmental risks against jobs and growth, or economic outcomes against social and cultural mores, let alone how to choose basic governance models.

In other words, the nation-state, with all its flaws, is a concrete reality. The "global community" is little more than a concept. People with something to lose are bound to be more beholden to an important fact than a mere notion.

This is where I part company with the Anywheres. I remember one occasion when an international automobile executive tried to tell me how Canadian policy for his industry should more closely match China's. Really? My gut reaction to this was more than just "it is not politically possible," which, of course, it is not remotely. I asked him, "Well, do you want to live in China?" Naturally, he does not. Neither do the Canadian people. But the Anywheres seem to believe they can pick from whatever national basket they like. Chinese economic outcomes, American legal protections, European governance, Panamanian taxes, you name it. And if they do not get what they want, they affirm a right to just pick up and leave—on a passport provided by their nation-state.

I do not quarrel with the Anywheres about the real and even greater potential benefits of globalization. My disagreement is more with this globalist mindset. I do not care how much of a globalist you fancy yourself. You have some responsibility as a citizen to Somewhere. And if you do not understand that, then you will behave as if you have no responsibilities at all.

=

Anywheres may be far from being a majority of the population, but in the era of globalization, they have come to dominate our politics. This is true on both the traditional centre left and the centre right. Democrats and Republicans, for instance, have not agreed on much in recent years. However, generally "open borders" for goods, services, and people have been a source of bipartisan consensus. The same is true in Europe.

Cosmopolitans have thus come to play an oversized role in our discourse. Only two thousand five hundred attend Davos each year— one of a tiny number of such conferences. Contrast that with just a single Donald Trump speech. In February 2017, the new president laid out his America First vision to the Conservative Political Action Conference in Washington. Some ten thousand people were present. But if you looked at our politics and the attendant media coverage, you might assume that these numbers were inverted.

Just as Anywheres have come to control all the main traditional political parties, Somewheres have also been split across the political spectrum. Some voted Democrat or Labour because of "progressive" economics. Others voted Republican or Conservative due to their cultural conservatism. But no political figures spoke to their collective circumstances, interests, or aspirations.

The Brexit referendum provides some insight into how such fault lines may manifest themselves. Cosmopolitan London voted Remain by a three-to-one margin. It was joined only by Scottish and Irish nationalists, for distinct (and diametrically opposed) reasons. Healthy majorities for Leave in the bulk of English, Welsh, and Irish unionist communities carried the day.

Similar dynamics have been apparent in American politics for some time. The Democrats are now a largely urban, coastal party with few congressional seats or governorships in middle America. The Republicans are increasingly shut out of big, cosmopolitan centres, but they are the clear majority party in most other places.

The upshot is that the success of Brexit and Trump points to a possible political realignment of much wider and longer-term significance. If underlying economic and social realities continue to diverge between elites and regular working people, such political patterns will get stronger. Ambitious and enterprising politicians more disciplined than Trump will effectively tap into populist values.

===

Which brings us back to where we started: the growing nationalist backlash to globalism. Few things have caused as much handwringing in establishment circles as America First. But regular people have generally liked what they have heard. One poll found that nearly two-thirds of the U.S. public had a positive reaction to the America First message.[7]

The public's response tended to line up with people's perceptions of the country's direction. If, on the one hand, you liked the economic and cultural trajectory of America, Trump's notions seemed like a threat. On the other hand, if you have been hurt by these economic and cultural trends, and felt ignored by the political system, his message represented a promising direction. These divergent perceptions also track pretty closely along cosmopolitan and localist lines.

What does this mean for American public policy and the U.S. role in the world? It is not yet clear. Trump's obvious talent is for messaging and marketing. Translating America First into a governing agenda requires plans, details, and determined execution. These have not been his strong suit to date.

However, we should also be leery of Trump's critics. As liberals have embraced some of the economic policy concepts behind globalization, these ideas have metastasized. They have been infused with an internationalism that not only is anti-nationalist but also has an ideological complexion.

Let us take one of the earliest and most outstanding advocates of this centre-left repositioning, Tony Blair. He said the following at the 2005 Labour Party convention: "I hear people say we have to stop and debate globalization. You might as well debate whether autumn should follow summer. . . . The character of this changing world is indifferent to tradition. Unforgiving of frailty. No respecter of past reputations. It has no custom and practice. It is replete with opportunities, but they only go to those swift to adapt, slow to complain, open, willing, and able to change."[8]

Bill Clinton used a similar formulation as his presidency came to a close in 2000. He stated: ". . . globalization is not something we can hold off or turn off. It is the economic equivalent of a force of nature, like wind or water. We can harness wind to fill a sail. We can use water to generate energy. We can work hard to protect people and property from storms and floods. But there is no point in denying the existence of wind or water, or trying to make them go away. The same is true for globalization. We can work to maximize its benefits and minimize its risks, but we cannot ignore it, and it is not going away."[9]

All of this is problematic for three reasons. First and foremost, it is not particularly inspiring. Are we really to simply accept that everything happening is just the natural order of things? A lack of human agency or national discretion in public policy is hardly a reassuring operating principle.

Compare this with what Donald Trump said about nationalism and globalism in a major campaign speech in April 2016: "No country has ever prospered that failed to put its own interests first. Both our friends and our enemies put their countries above ours and we, while being fair to them, must start doing the same. We will no longer surrender this country or its people to the false song of globalism. The nation-state remains the true foundation for happiness and harmony."[10]

Or take what leading Brexiteer Daniel Hannan declared in late May 2016, days before the referendum: "We are not just a random collection of individuals born to a different random collection of individuals. Being a nation means that we have a duty to keep intact the freedoms

RIGHT HERE, RIGHT NOW • 59

that we were lucky enough to inherit from our parents and pass them on securely to the next generation. My late father was prepared in 1944 to volunteer to defend with force of arms our right to live under our own laws, with our own people, in our own sovereign Parliament. . . . This is about self-confidence. This is about self-belief. It is about whether we think we are good enough to flourish in the world taking our own decisions. . . . This is a blessed country. . . . This is a great country whose song has not yet been sung."[11]

Which messages do you think resonated more with the Somewheres? With those folks who feel they are falling behind? With those who feel ignored and forgotten? I think you know the answer.

The second problem is that the central argument being made by Blair, Clinton, and others is simply not true. Open markets, open borders, and globalization are choices. Now, choices have real consequences. One cannot make bad economic choices—and many anti-market, anti-trade, anti-globalization policies are bad choices—and expect good results. But there are options, trade-offs, and nuances in such choices, and the consequences are often complex and uncertain rather than black and white.

The final problem is central to modern left-liberalism on all things. This is the tendency, once one has momentum behind one's argument, to declare the issue closed, to shut down debate, and to denounce all dissenters. Trump and Brexit have shown how that approach can completely backfire as an electoral strategy. In Western democracies, the public does have a decisive say. Telling them they have no choice is an invitation to a huge rebuke.

But more fundamentally, this tendency of modern liberals feels kind of pre-Enlightenment. After all, the reality of big issues is usually complicated, with reasonable elements of doubt. Such issues require more, not less, political debate. That is true for markets, trade, and globalization. And it is equally true in the single most controversial area of populist backlash—immigration.

5

WALLS AND DOORS

I feel considerable satisfaction about the immigration agenda that my government pursued. We had, in fact, the largest per capita immigration program in the world—over a quarter-million entrants per year, close to 1 per cent of the Canadian population.[1] This is not just a number. It represents individuals and families who came to Canada to make better lives for themselves and their children. In the overwhelming number of cases, they contributed to the economic needs of our country and brought dynamism to their communities.

I am also proud of the fact that, in a time of increasing discontent with immigration elsewhere in the world, our approach remained widely supported, including among New Canadians. The Conservative Party of Canada is one of the world's few centre-right parties to consistently win a substantial share of the immigrant vote. More on that later.

However, I also got a taste of how problematic bad immigration policy can be. I think in particular of my government's problems with the Temporary Foreign Workers Program. It remains by contrast one of my greatest sources of dissatisfaction from my time in office.

The TFWP had long been focused on filling gaps in labour-market expertise. However, in 2002, the previous government had expanded it to bring low-skilled workers into Canada.[2] From that moment forward, the number of TFWS grew steadily. Within a decade, it had more than doubled.[3] By 2014, the number of "temporary workers" in the country exceeded 175,000.[4]

Part of the reason I remain so unhappy about this is that I had a bad feeling about the policy from the outset. In Canada, we have always linked the idea of immigration with the aspiration of eventual citizenship. Why were we departing from this? As the numbers rose, and I repeatedly asked about them, I was assured that we faced unique circumstances from the commodity boom, especially in Western Canada. "Labour market impact assessments," I was told, had affirmed this.

With a hundred things on my plate at any given time, I did not pursue the matter. That is to say, I did not pursue it until some stories of blatant abuse began to surface in the media. The concerns were all true and they were only the tip of the iceberg.

In reality, there had been no substantive labour force assessments. Such assessments consisted of little beyond businesses simply affirming that they needed temporary foreign workers. Applications were not restricted to Western Canada, or booming sectors, or anything else. In fact, TFWs were increasingly being brought into some of the highest unemployment regions in the country. And they were not really "temporary" at all. When their terms expired, such workers often just rolled over to another admission period.

Some businesses had become so dependent on TFWs, and had so few experienced Canadians, that they were even asking for supervisory and management positions to be filled by them. They were, in effect, shifting to temporary foreign workers as their preferred labour model. The more we investigated, the more we encountered situations where companies would not even accept applications from Canadians—and would then claim they could not find Canadians to do the work.

Why did this happen? The evidence, put simply, shows that temporary foreign workers were helping companies keep wages down. Besides, it was easier for many businesses to have their workers recruited by the government and unable to search for any other job.

I recount this because immigration is high on the liberals' list of "settled" issues on which debate must be shut down and dissenters denounced. Any public concern, according to them, can be chalked up to racism and bigotry. It really is seen as that simple.

My experience is the opposite. If the public mood against immigration becomes so high that it is moving a lot of votes, then something is seriously wrong. Indeed, such widespread opposition likely occurs because the policies and their effects on people's lives have become very bad.

By and large, though, Canadians have had confidence in their immigration system. They believe it reflects their interests. The same simply cannot be said in the United States and many European countries.

=

Remember that one of the positive aspects of populism is its power to force onto the political agenda issues that elites do not want to talk about. There are few issues on which this has been truer than it has on immigration. Take Washington. Both Democrats and Republicans in the U.S. have been reconciled to higher immigration, including higher illegal immigration. And it was only in the context of this artificial "consensus" that they were prepared to entertain policy discussion.

The "Gang of Eight" bill of 2013 was the high-water mark of this approach. Sponsored by equal numbers from both parties, it would have, among other things, established a "pathway to citizenship" for illegal immigrants. Whatever you may think of the legislation's merits, it was a transparent, bipartisan plot to quietly put the issue to rest before the 2016 presidential election.

This effort was years in the making. You do not have to believe me. Just look at how the political parties' positions have evolved over time. Here is what the Democratic Party platform said in 2000: "Democrats believe in an effective immigration system that balances a strong enforcement of our laws with fair and even-handed treatment of immigrants and their families. The Clinton–Gore administration provided long overdue leadership in dramatically improving border management and law enforcement, including a major expansion of the Border Patrol and curbs on abuses of the asylum process. We also recognize that the current system fails to effectively control illegal immigration, has serious adverse impacts on state and local services, and on many communities and workers, and has led to an alarming number of deaths of migrants on the border. Democrats are committed to re-examining and fixing these failed policies."[5]

Here is what the same party said in 2016: "Democrats believe we need to urgently fix our broken immigration system—which tears families apart and keeps workers in the shadows—and create a path to citizenship for law-abiding families who are here, making a better life for their families and contributing to their communities and our country. We should repeal the 3-year, 10-year and permanent bars, which often force persons in mixed status families into the heart-breaking dilemma of either pursuing a green card by leaving the country and their loved ones behind, or remaining in the shadows. We will work with Congress to end the forced and prolonged expulsion from the country that these immigrants endure when trying to adjust their status."[6]

The change from the Bill Clinton administration to the Hillary Clinton campaign is not subtle. Democrats have gone from emphasizing the negative effects of illegal immigration to focusing on aiding illegal immigrants.

The same goes for the Republicans. The party's "autopsy" of its 2012 presidential election defeat recommended a move in the same direction. The party's opposition to illegal immigration was identified as a major problem. The report stated: ". . . among the steps Republicans take in the Hispanic community and beyond, we must embrace and champion comprehensive immigration reform. If we do not, our Party's appeal will continue to shrink to its core constituencies only. We also believe that comprehensive immigration reform is consistent with Republican economic policies that promote job growth and opportunity for all."[7]

This quickly became the overwhelmingly dominant view in Republican and even conservative circles. You basically could not turn on the television without a commentator talking about how the GOP needed to moderate its stance on immigration if it were to compete, starting with the 2014 mid-terms. Accordingly, the blunt term "amnesty" was adjusted to "a path to citizenship."

Driving this evolution was the fact that both parties had become ever more beholden to special interests within their respective coalitions. The Democrats were pulled by left-wing voices with "progressive" social agendas. The Republicans were pushed by corporate interests who sought both easier access to skilled foreign professionals and lower wages for unskilled workers. In practice, however, the parties' objectives were essentially the same.

Media reporting at the time even bragged that parts of the Gang of Eight bill had been "the product of [private] negotiations between the U.S. Chamber of Commerce and labor unions."[8] How exactly such a process would serve the public interest was never revealed. In any case, by the time of Trump's primary launch, there were few mainstream political voices prepared to challenge the status quo.

=

But as party elites were embracing each other on the subject of immigration, they were moving away from their own voters. The warning signs were there. On the ground, the Gang of Eight's bill was getting enormous kickback. This was especially true for the group's Republican members.

There is precious little evidence that the GOP's post-election analysis had looked at any public-opinion data. Polling showed that Americans in general and Republicans in particular were hardening in their opposition to illegal immigration and their anger over the government's failure to properly address it. Six in ten U.S. voters said they worried about illegal immigration a "great deal." The figure was 80 per cent for Republicans, but even half of Democrats felt the same way.[9] This was hardly a fringe position.

By the way, the same was largely true of the legal immigration system. A 2015 Gallup poll found that 60 per cent of Americans were "dissatisfied" with current immigration levels. Two in five wanted to see overall immigration decrease.[10] A 2017 poll similarly found that nearly 50 per cent favoured reducing legal immigration by half and less than 40 per cent would oppose it.[11]

The Republicans finally ditched the Gang of Eight bill. They also went on to make big gains in the mid-terms. But the obvious conclusion was not drawn. Maybe the 2012 electoral failure was not due to the opposition to illegal immigration. Maybe it happened because the proposed solution, "self-deportation," revealed that the GOP was not really serious about fixing the problem. In other words, maybe they got the wrath of the minority who like illegal immigration, but no support from the majority who wanted real change.

Thus, the groundwork had been laid for Trump. Ironically, those who decry him had laid it. They had created a flawed and failed policy. They had ignored public concerns about it. They had conspired to change it without real debate or public consensus. And, finally, they had failed to get even that done.

It is no exaggeration to say that this was a major differentiator for Trump. This was true in the Republican primary in particular and, to a significant degree, in the general election. Eighty per cent of Trump voters called illegal immigration a "very big problem." Close to 90 per cent believed it had worsened since 2008.[12] Six in ten of his voters also believed that legal immigration was too high.[13]

Trump's strong, blunt, and tactless language on immigration out of the gate was seen as politically fatal by virtually all commentators and the political establishment. They were wrong. His views turned out to be much closer to the sentiments of working- and middle-class voters than those of either Hillary Clinton or his own fellow Republicans. This is one reason why Trump has been called the "great disruptor."[14]

He recognized that the U.S. immigration system was unpopular and its advocates out of touch. In so doing, he realigned the political landscape. And he gave the public its voice back on immigration policy.

===

The United States, like Canada, Australia, and Israel, is one of a handful of countries in the world whose history and character has been substantially shaped by immigration. However, the size and composition of immigration has shifted considerably through the annals of American history. To be brief, there have been four distinct eras.[15]

The early immigration system was very open, but initially, inflows were low. This changed in the 1830s. From that point on, the levels increased steadily. The streams also broadened considerably, although they remained principally European in character. By the 1880s, over half a million immigrants per year were entering the country.[16]

This influx was not without controversy. In fact, an anti-immigration movement, the American Party or "Know-Nothings," briefly threatened to become a major political force. As the Whigs disintegrated in the 1850s, the Know-Nothings grew out of popular distrust of the widening immigration sources, in particular the rising number of Roman Catholics.[17] Of course, as political discourse shifted to slavery versus abolition and, ultimately, Confederacy versus Union, the new Republican Party emerged instead as the nation's major centre-right option.

By the 1890s, however, the new Populist Party and others were again demanding some central control over immigration. This cannot be dismissed as mere bigotry. The situation demanded change. Immigration had previously been necessitated by an ever-expanding frontier. But, by then, the supply of unbroken land was shrinking fast and farmers were facing new economic pressures. Reforms were necessary.

They began with the Immigration Act of 1891. The federal government asserted comprehensive authority over immigration control. The following year saw the opening of Ellis Island in New York harbour to serve as a central enforcement point.

Immigrants would still arrive with no prior visa or formal permission, but federal officials would now inspect them. They could enter the country as long as they did not fall under one of the explicit categories of exclusion. The list included any person "likely to become a public charge," as well as the diseased, criminals, anarchists, polygamists, those with low intelligence, paupers, and prostitutes. In 1917, a literacy test was added to the entry criteria, although it was conducted in the immigrant's native language.

There were also racial considerations. Asians were strongly discouraged and, of course, had there been African applicants, they would also have been. Canada, by the way, had exactly the same orientation. In 2008, I apologized to the remaining survivors of Canada's Chinese "head tax." The late Luke Yip was an example of the men isolated by this long-enforced policy. He was taken in by my wife's family for most of his life. Many were not so fortunate, and faced meagre, sad, and forgotten lives.

These failings aside, the policy remained quite open. U.S. immigration often exceeded one million entrants a year. Proportionately, this is still the largest immigration period in history. By 1910, 15 per cent of Americans were foreign-born.[18] In New York and Chicago, an amazing 80 per cent of the population consisted of either new arrivals or their children. But the policy did broadly serve the national economic interests—that is, the interests of a rapidly expanding, urbanizing, and industrializing society.

The Ellis Island regime lasted until the 1920s. Two world wars, the Great Depression, and increasing concerns about importing radicals (especially communists and fascists) led to the first sustained tightening of immigration policy. By the mid-1950s, America's immigration numbers were, on average, only about 250,000 to 350,000 per year. This period, from about 1925 to 1965, is regularly referred to as an immigration "pause."[19]

Arguably, this also made economic sense. The labour-force requirements of the post-war period were marked by a booming economy with increasing productivity and more diverse job prospects. The baby boom and expanded educational opportunities were meeting those needs. There were also, however, less enlightened measures. Quotas by country ensured that over two-thirds of immigrants were from just three countries—the U.K., Ireland, and Germany.

Starting in 1965, all this would change. Some changes would be for the better. But some of the changes have not been. From that moment forward, U.S. immigration policy has gradually become disconnected from the interests and views of Americans.

=

The Immigration Act of 1965 is a now largely overlooked part of Lyndon Johnson's Great Society agenda. But the president, unveiling it at Liberty Island in New York, called it "one of the most important acts of this Congress and of this administration."[20] He was not exaggerating.[21]

The legislation eliminated the discriminatory quota model. It substituted a new approach based primarily on family ties. This has been the central feature of the system ever since.

As an example, of the almost one million foreign nationals admitted into the U.S. as permanent residents in 2013, two-thirds were admitted on the basis of family relationships.[22] The comparable number in Canada was less than one-third. The principal result has been "chain migration." An immigrant can bring his or her spouse and children and then, once he or she is naturalized, also parents and siblings, who can then also bring their own family members.[23]

Under the 1965 law, immigration would take off once again. In the first decade, it rose by one-third. By the 1980s, it had doubled to more than six hundred thousand entrants per year. The flow has now stabilized at about one million per year.[24]

The 1965 reform also resulted in the growth of illegal immigration. Ironically, this was in large part driven by the new system's focus on "fairness." By eliminating country-specific quotas, the share of immigration visas from the Western Hemisphere was reduced. However, demand by and for these workers, including Mexicans, was actually rising. It has been described as yet another case of policy "set in some aspirational abstract . . . detached from real-world considerations."[25]

By the mid-1980s, there were an estimated three million illegal immigrants residing in the U.S., with another two hundred thousand entering every year.[26] The Immigration Reform and Control Act of 1986 sought to fix the problem with a mix of amnesty and enforcement. It was an unmitigated disaster.

The reform allowed migrants to legalize their status, and at the same time promised sanctions on employers who knowingly hired illegals. Large numbers of immigrants did take advantage of the new amnesty provision. However, the employer sanctions were never strongly enforced. Amnesty in conjunction with meaningless penalties was a powerful incentive for a new wave of illegal immigration. The decade from 2000 to 2010 alone saw an increase of roughly five million illegal immigrants in the U.S.[27]

The upshot is that a series of policy decisions—especially the 1965 and 1986 laws—have led to a huge increase in both legal and illegal immigration. There are now more than eleven million illegals in the U.S., with eight million of those in the workforce. About two-thirds of these people have been in the country for at least ten years.[28] But it is not only illegal migration that is problematic. Legal admissions remain focused almost entirely on family circumstances. Just consider that, in 2015, of the more than one million legal permanent residents admitted, only one in seven came through a job-based preference.[29] This is not an immigration policy rooted in the interests of a modern economy.

==

U.S. immigration policy is thus a failure not just because it ignores the rule of law. It is also a failure because it is not serving the interests of ordinary Americans, especially working-class Americans. These are the issues that both the Democratic and the Republican establishments have not wanted to talk about.

A poorly designed immigration system can have negative effects on labour markets. It is not really that complicated to explain how. When the supply of workers goes up, their value in the marketplace goes down. Wage trends over the past half-century suggest that a 10 per cent increase in the number of workers with a particular set of skills probably lowers the wage of that group by at least 3 per cent.[30] This is true even after the economy has fully adjusted.

Both low- and high-skilled workers can theoretically be affected by an influx of workers. However, because a disproportionate number of immigrants, especially illegal immigrants, tend to be less educated, it is low-skilled American workers who are most directly hit. And the monetary loss is sizeable. The typical non-high-school graduate in the U.S. will earn only about $25,000 annually. According to census data, immigrants admitted in the past two decades have increased the size of that workforce by roughly 25 per cent. As a result, their annual earnings have dropped by between $800 and $1,500.[31]

These basic facts about the impacts of immigration are generally accepted among economists. There is some methodological contention[32] and some dispute about magnitude. There is also debate about how those affected might respond.[33] But the argument that there is no relationship between immigration and labour market outcomes is an ideological mantra divorced from the evidence.[34] Even the left-liberal economist Paul Krugman has written that "Immigration reduces the wages of domestic workers who compete with immigrants. That's just supply and demand . . . the general point seems impossible to deny."[35]

It is easy for the more affluent to think about immigration policy in the abstract. They are not usually the ones directly affected. They are not the workers whose jobs or wages come under pressure. In their secure or even gated communities, they are also unlikely to be touched by the criminal side of illegal immigration. The immigrants they meet are likely to be Westernized, white-collar professionals, just like themselves.

It is therefore no surprise that different groups think and talk about immigration differently. In the U.S., nearly three-quarters of working-class whites think that immigrants drive down wages while less than half of college-educated whites do. Nearly 60 per cent of working-class whites believe that the government should aim to deport all illegal immigrants. Only one-third of the college-educated agree. Fifty-five per cent of the working class agree with President Trump on the necessity of a wall along the Mexican border, but more than 60 per cent of college-educated whites disagree.[36]

Some choose to dismiss all immigration concerns as just racism or bigotry. No doubt a few of them are. But the facts indicate that it is far more likely they are based on the real-world experiences of significant numbers of American workers.

It is interesting to note who joined Donald Trump in identifying these public opinion risks—Bernie Sanders. While far from identical to Trump's position, Sanders diverged from the hard left in embracing similar "populist" concerns about the interplay between immigration (legal and illegal) and working-class circumstances. When asked about immigration in a 2015 interview, Sanders dismissed the idea of "open borders" because, as he said, "it would make everybody in America poorer."[37]

==

These dynamics are not unique to the United States. We have witnessed them play out across the developed world. Ill-conceived and poorly managed immigration policies are causing citizens to push back. Simply dismissing these public concerns as hatred or ignorance belies the facts. It also lets elites off the hook for the problems they have created.

The United Kingdom is one example. There is compelling evidence that the Brexit vote was in significant part a rejection of the country's immigration policies.[38] Many voters had come to believe that successive governments—again, of both parties—had failed to protect the United Kingdom's immigration-policy interests within the European Union.

The irony is that the British government had the ability to deal with this issue itself. For example, it could have chosen to introduce transitional controls on the free movement of people into the U.K. Provision was made for just that when a slew of Central and Eastern European countries were admitted to the European Union. In the decade that followed, the influx from these nations exceeded eight hundred thousand—six times the initial estimates.[39]

Even European Commission president Jean-Claude Juncker recognized this was a mistake, noting, "In 2004, the U.K. did not use the transitional period that would have allowed it to phase in the right of free movement of the citizens of eight new member states. . . . As a result, over the past decade the U.K. attracted a record number of mobile EU citizens."[40]

This is part of the reason the U.K. witnessed a doubling of its foreign-born population between 1993 and 2015, when the number rose from nearly two million to more than five million. Poland was the most common source country of those who arrived.[41]

But the problem for the U.K. was not just the amount of immigration over this period. It was also its economic composition. Most of the immigrants were low-skilled and moved into sectors such as transport driving and food processing.[42] They have absorbed almost all net job creation over the past dozen years—filling three million positions out of a total increase of 3.5 million. One million of these would be unskilled or low-skilled workers from the EU cohort of 2004.[43]

This immigration influx has had economic consequences for U.K. citizens competing for work, especially for low-wage workers. Just one example: a 2015 paper from the Bank of England found that, in the service sector, a 10 per cent increase in the proportion of immigrants is associated with a 2 per cent reduction in pay.[44]

Similar situations can be observed elsewhere in Europe, most notably in Germany. Its opening to a massive "refugee" influx in 2015 was the subject of both elite praise and popular outrage. The German government has been pulling back from the policy ever since.

Nevertheless, in 2017, right-wing nationalists gained substantial representation in the Bundestag for the first time since World War II.

The effects of the German error have been felt beyond its borders. The move clearly contributed to the Brexit vote. It also led other European countries to reinstitute border controls during the same period. It was one thing to tell Europeans that the continental project aimed at free movement within the EU. It was another for them to find out it might mean free movement from outside the EU.

As in America, such developments have led to a divergence of opinion. According to a 2015 Gallup poll of 142 countries, people in Europe were on average the most negative toward immigration.[45] How does one account for this? Is Europe more racist than the rest of the world? Given the relative openness and racial diversity of the continent, that seems implausible. More likely, this view is a response to the unique "globalist" mindset of the European elite, which at times prides itself on its distance from national public opinion. In fact, a new major survey across Europe finds a growing chasm between elite and non-elite opinion on immigration questions.[46]

Again, the source of these two solitudes is probably life experience. The political and economic establishment are less affected by mass migration than the general voting public. Working- and middle-class Europeans are the ones facing the challenges this phenomenon presents. Wealthy and highly educated professionals are more likely to experience the benefits.

======

I started off this discussion by saying that my government was pro-immigration, as am I. But just as I am pro-market, pro-trade, and pro-globalization, mere sentiment is not sufficient to make good public policy. The policy-maker has to understand why something is good public policy and continually evaluate how it is playing out. And if it is not working out well for the public, in a democracy, you fix the policy; you do not denounce the public.

Many policy-makers in the U.S. and elsewhere do not seem to understand this. Immigration thinking has been at best about abstract "open doors," and at worst about commercial self-interest. Whatever the reason, it has resulted in policies frequently disconnected from the experiences, needs, and interests of working citizens. Even worse, a confluence of traditional liberal and conservative political interests has often conspired to shut down debate about the policy direction.

Not all the perceived problems with immigration are real. But many of them are. In some countries, immigration is often illegal or irregular, which is problematic in and of itself. In other cases, it may be legal but not serve clear economic or other national interests. Frankly, it should be obvious that, when economic and technological forces are creating severe pressures on low-skilled workers, the influx of large quantities of such labour is not in the public interest.

These are the ways immigration can become a flashpoint. The responsibility of governments is to avoid these pitfalls by developing immigration programs the public will support. If that is not done, it is policy-makers, not average citizens, who should be blamed for the backlash.

6

REDISCOVERING CONSERVATISM

I said I do not want this book to focus on Donald Trump. I also do not want it to focus on me. However, I do want to share my experience with leaders today. This is an age of increasing disruption of all sorts—one that is now having significant political impacts in even the most stable, advanced democracies.

My time as prime minister occurred largely during and after the global financial crisis. Under my government, Canada avoided the worst of the crisis and came out of it all the stronger. For Canadian Conservatives, it was the longest-serving government since 1891. By any measure, we left the country in good shape. No populist insurgency arose on our right, and as a consequence, since we returned to opposition in 2015, we have remained a strong and united party.

Through our numerous successes—and our occasional blunders— Canadian Conservatives were implementing many of the policies and strategies that are necessary to respond to the challenges that Western societies currently face. I call this approach "populist conservatism."

What is populist conservatism? It is about putting conservative values and ideas into the service of working people and their families. It is about using conservative means for populist ends. For me, it is a product of political experience.

As I mentioned, my economic conservatism was a conversion early in my adult life, as a witness to the failures of Keynesian intervention. It was filled out by many years of study in economics, particularly economic history and macroeconomic cycles. It left me both a proponent of market economics and a skeptic of market dogmatism. I saw that market approaches are unambiguously better at creating wealth than the alternatives. But, unlike libertarians, I could detect no self-evident blueprint for all policy at all times.

This led me to a more general conservatism—a conservatism of attitude. I came to be leery of large-scale change by edict and its inevitable, unforeseen consequences. In government, this was reflected in my (usual) incremental approach to policy change—small but constant steps. Incrementalism proved to be the best method of evaluating the effects of policy reform and of building political support for further change. In other words, it was both good philosophical conservatism and effective political pragmatism.

My populism was, I suppose, an outgrowth of a public-school, middle-class background. It took more shape during my involvement in the Reform Party, of which I was the founding chief policy officer. That experience taught me the importance of making policy relevant to regular working families. However, it also left me leery of the chaotic decision-making structures and unreflective political reform proposals that often bedevil populist movements.

My political entrepreneurship with Reform also shed light on how economic conservatism relates to non-economic issues. One quickly discovers that economic conservatives are generally (but, of course, not always) conservative on a range of other issues—faith, family, community, nation. This should really not be surprising. Markets depend on freedom, and freedom depends on underlying values, especially personal responsibility. Responsible people generally value the institutions that have nurtured and sustained them.

In short, I would describe populist conservatism as rooted not in abstract "first principles" but in real-world experience applied to the needs of regular people. In fact, this is not a branch of conservatism at all; this is the essence of conservatism.[1]

═══

Donald Trump's upset victory and tumultuous first eighteen months in office have produced plenty of predictions about our future politics. Some claim conservatism is "dead."[2] Others say the same about populism. That is certainly the view of most liberals and "Never Trump" conservatives. To wit, it is the opinion of those who were certain he could never win in the first place.

But none of this changes the forces that put Trump in office. Populism will be with us in one form or another for some time to come. That is to say, it will be with us as long as working men, women, and families continue to face current economic and social pressures, and conventional political parties do not adapt. And if they do not, troubling elements of the populist agenda could prove more potent in the hands of more focused political operators.

What does this mean for conservatives and conservatism? There are, in my view, three basic options.

One option is the old status quo: return with gusto to pre-Trump, *Wall Street Journal*, supply-side conservatism. This basically means forgetting everything of the past few years and getting back to advocating, among other things, lower taxes on the wealthy and high levels of unskilled immigration. Of course, that is a choice, as long as we remember this is partly what gave us the current moment of discord. Go down that path and we could well end up with left-wing populism and significant damage to our economies.

A second option is to double down on unbridled populism. That would also be a mistake. Not only would it produce unpredictable and frequently bad policy, it would have similar electoral consequences. Think of Roy Moore in Alabama, or Christine O'Donnell in Delaware, or Sharron Angle in Nevada, and so on. Attached to Republicans in the U.S. or conservatives anywhere else, such candidacies risk brand damage that can be substantial and lasting.

The third option is to reform conservatism to address the issues that are driving the populist upheaval. That is to say, adapt conservatism to the practical concerns, interests, and aspirations of working- and middle-class people. I believe this is the right path for our movement, our countries, and ultimately our citizens.

Conservatives are well placed to respond to populism. Real conservatism—a preference for the empirical over the theoretical, a predisposition to freedom and choice, a mistrust of large institutions and centralized planning—is especially important in the populist age. This means, however, getting away from both detached, elite conservatism and rootless, unprincipled populism. A new populist conservatism needs to bring conservative ideas to bear on the real-life challenges facing regular folks.

As I said, I am not proposing a new form of conservatism; this is about rediscovering conservatism. Conservatism is about drawing on the wisdom and insights of human experience. And it is about applying them to real problems in the interests of the wider society, including those of everyday people.

I told a Canadian journalist in 2006, "If you make conservatism relevant to ordinary working people, you make it the most powerful political philosophy in Western democratic society. Where conservative parties are successful, and successful on a sustained basis, that's what they do."[3] And that is how I tried to govern.

Whatever we choose, the key point is this: the stakes will only get higher. The alternative to getting conservatism back on track is much worse than anything about Trump. There may be much about the current administration's approach and agenda to disagree with. But its opponents on the left are the real threat to the future of our economies and the interests of our working citizens.

=

The process of recognizing the underlying conditions that led to Trump, Brexit, and other similar movements has been slow. Many are still in denial. There has been even less effort at figuring out how our politics ought to respond.

For liberals, the answer to populism is easy. Just denounce supporters of Trump, Brexit, and similar movements elsewhere as the stupid and bigoted people that liberals always thought they were. For the far left, it is even easier. Burn the whole economic system to the ground. It has been a mistake from day one, they say—or, to adapt Monty Python, "What has this wealth ever done for us?"

A lot of conservatives have not done much better. Some concentrate on screeds so denunciatory that they have become indistinguishable from the left. Others urge a return to the market mantras of the past quarter-century, simply refusing to believe that conservative-turned-populist voters will not come back.

There is a third group—those conservatives who have been trying to respond constructively to populist concerns. Indeed, well before the current upheavals, these people were warning of the economic challenges facing many middle- and working-class voters. And they were alarmed that traditional conservative dogma was failing to address their needs. The "reformicons,"[4] as they have been described, have done a good job diagnosing the problems. At times, they have even put forward compelling solutions.[5]

It is fair to say, however, that the reformicons have not made much progress in most countries. In the U.S., their ideas were largely ignored during the Obama years and had few political champions during the 2016 Republican primaries. The irony is that the Republican Party's failure to adopt their moderate correction to traditional conservatism ultimately created the political space for Trump. As *National Review* editor Ramesh Ponnuru put it, "We argued that if Republicans did not supply conservative answers to voters' economic anxieties, the political market would supply attractive, but non-conservative answers. We feared that the vacuum would be filled with mostly bad ideas by the Democratic nominee in a general election; it has instead also been filled with mostly bad ideas by Trump in the Republican primaries."[6]

One can debate about which of his ideas were "bad," but the point is basically correct. Trump's populism is in part an outgrowth of the intellectual and political failures of U.S. conservatism. Post-Reagan, American conservatism gradually ceased to address contemporary challenges facing everyday people. Instead it became about a finite set of doctrinaire policies, detached from many people's life experiences.

American conservatism fell victim to abstractions about markets, trade, globalization, and immigration. It may not have been as extreme as the liberal mix of corporatism, anti-nationalism, and cultural relativism, but it was still alien to millions of working people. In fact, much of the pre-Trump conservative agenda had become at best meaningless, and at worst deleterious, to those demographics.

President Trump won his improbable victory by filling this void. He presented ideas that spoke to the white working-class men and women who formed the core of his winning voter coalition.[7] His economic populism and cultural nationalism spoke to their anxiety, interests, and aspirations, and helped to deliver states such as Michigan and Ohio. Forced to choose between Trump's unrooted populism and the rest of the Republican field's disconnected conservatism, these voters opted for the former.

Incidentally, Trump's actions since his inauguration raise some doubts about the president's commitment to his populist agenda. Outside trade and foreign affairs, Trump's policies have thus far been fairly orthodox conservatism. The 2017 tax bill (which I will discuss later) is an example. In other words, it is possible that the lessons of 2016 have not really been learned, even in the White House itself.

What are those lessons? It is that we, conservatives, cannot make a fixed set of policies the essence of our vision. Conservatism is, by definition, contextual. It is an intellectual framework that draws on human experience to confront present challenges. It seeks to evaluate new developments by applying tried and true institutional and moral understanding. It does that in a way that reflects the broader, ongoing interests of society. It is, properly understood, a middle way between unrooted populism and disconnected elitism.

═══

The key point is this: conservatism begins with the issues it needs to address rather than the policies it wants to apply. Now that may seem logical. But there are a lot of voices in our politics that claim to know the answer before the question has even been posed. It is always more markets for some and more government programs for others. Just watch any political panel on television. It is all so predictable.

Incidentally, the liberals who purport to adhere to "evidence-based policy" are usually far worse practitioners of this type of ideological rigidity. Much of their "evidence" is little more than faith-like assertion from weak, non-empirical academic disciplines. Their desire to then use such "evidence" to shut down debate betrays the ideological nature of their policy preferences.

Conservatism, by contrast, is empirical. Properly understood, it is the opposite of dogmatism. It is about applying lessons of human experience and insights into human nature to new challenges as they emerge. As nineteenth-century British prime minister Benjamin Disraeli put it, conservatism is a "disposition to preserve" combined with an "ability to improve."[8]

Here is where conservatism—particularly in the United States—increasingly failed in the post-Reagan era. It became based on a fixed set of policy prescriptions that became the answer to seemingly every question. Reagan's application of conservative ideas to the problems of the late 1970s and 1980s was conflated with conservatism itself.

In fact, Reagan was applying conservative ideas about the limits of technocracy and state planning, the inherent dignity of work, the freedom of the individual, lower taxes, and decentralized governance to the particular challenges of his day. Those included a stagnant economy, high inflation, a sclerotic government, damaged incentives due to high personal tax rates, and weak competition due to protectionism. Lowering taxes, reducing regulations, and generally opening up markets were the right things in this context. It was the application of a conservatism relevant to the issues facing working people.

Of course, much of Reagan's agenda remains relevant. Limited government, low taxation, free trade, and sound money are all, properly applied, essential ingredients of conservative economic policy in the twenty-first century. But a lot has changed. The issues affecting working people and motivating voters are different than they were in 1980. Health care, immigration, unbalanced trade relationships, technological change, education, stagnant or declining wages, and growing income inequality loom larger than they did then. In fact, they loom larger than they did only a few years ago.[9]

A conservative governing agenda needs to adjust accordingly. This does not mean changing our core beliefs. It means applying them in ways that are relevant now. It means shifting from the macroeconomic issues of more than thirty years ago to the challenges emerging today.

An unyielding focus on Reagan-era solutions has caused U.S. conservatives to cede territory on a range of issues for which they ought to have persuasive answers. Conservatives need to get back into the policy game by learning more from Reagan's method of applied conservatism and less from his particular policy prescriptions.

=

I am going to talk a lot about my government's populist conservatism and how it addressed the modern challenges of markets, trade, globalization, and immigration. But I also want to spend some time talking about the other side. Because whatever differences I may have with other conservatives or quasi-conservative populists, they pale in comparison with the danger that modern left-liberalism represents.

Where conservatism needs to get back to empiricism and become more relevant to people's lives, modern liberalism is relentlessly headed in a very different direction. It is one purely about abstract intellectualism, not merely unrooted in experience but repelled by it. And, for all its protestations about "caring" about "the people," it means people in the abstract, not real people who fail to fit its model. For those, it has only condescension and insult, as its current response to populism so vividly demonstrates. We need to understand why it thinks like this.

Of course, we know how the modern left thinks about conservatives. You can witness it daily in the media. Conservatives are depicted as essentially non-intellectual—people who accept established institutions like business, the nation-state, family, and religion unthinkingly, if not bigotedly. In fact, we are today portrayed, for lack of a better term, as intellectually childish. This is why we get headlines like "The birth of the stupid party" or "Republicans are stupid" or research about the so-called "conservative syndrome."[10]

Now, in fairness, it is possible to think like that. It is possible to be naively accepting about the basis of one's life. And it is not inherently undesirable to question old ideas and established institutions. The thing about the modern left—both its conventional liberal and more extreme versions—is that it cannot get beyond doing only that.

The modern left is, again for lack of a better term, intellectually adolescent. Having discovered the shortcomings of old ideas and established institutions, it becomes all too willing to accept any argument for their denigration or even dismantlement. It does this without developing any parallel understanding of the history and strengths of older wisdoms and enduring structures.

The prototype for this type of thinking is still Karl Marx. I studied Marx and his work fairly extensively. In many ways, he was genuinely brilliant and insightful. He explored the workings of capitalism thoroughly, and gave some intellectual rigour to understanding various aspects of its functioning, especially its flaws.

Actually, Marx's study of capitalism was obsessed with its flaws. The real purpose was the promotion of his own intellectual blueprint—communism. But, here, any insight and brilliance ends. Marx's exposition of communism would not fill an intellectual thimble. For all his detailed analysis of the workings and "contradictions" of capitalism, he had almost nothing of substance to say about communism—how to transition to it, how it would work, what problems might have to be addressed.

This reality about Marxism permeated communism in power. Underlying its opposition to capitalism was a hollowness of substance, sustained only by an adolescent rage about wealth that defined its founder. It was a rage mixed with envy, one that saw virtually every relationship in Marx's own life dissolve in disputes over money.

The result was that there really was no concrete alternative on offer. Communist leaders, thus practising a philosophy divorced from any reference to human experience or human nature, responded to every problem with intolerance, denunciation, and, ultimately, violence on an extraordinary level. In fairness, they did also go to great lengths to try to create the system their founder had only imagined. In the end, however, the intricate production matrices of Soviet planners crumbled into dust.

Marxism has, nevertheless, become the inspiration for whole generations of intellectuals designing social blueprints.[11] This includes the complete modern raft of "deconstructionists," "post-modernists," "post-structuralists," and nihilists of every shape and form. Which is really all they are. These are the intellectuals who channelled the emotions of their adolescence into their studies, and then never left academia. For them, every flaw in an institution demands its overthrow. After all, how could the history of established structures and the wisdom of countless generations possibly teach us anything? And, if you do not agree, then the response is intolerance, denunciation, and, ultimately, violence, as we see on many university campuses today.

This is the essence of the modern left. It has an allergy to our society, its underlying ideas, and core institutions. On the hard left, it seeks their destruction. But even the centre left shares this trait. It may be reconciled to markets, trade, and contemporary globalization, but it is inclined to cast these as tearing down traditional institutions like family, faith, community, and, most notably, the nation-state. Its alternatives to the roles these things play in people's lives is rarely clear. Still, it is always willing to jump on the next trendy idea, however vacuous.

=

Conservatives can, and must, do better than that. First, we have to have the humility to admit that the traditions, institutions, experiences, and learning of human history have something to teach us. Because they are invariably richer and more complex than our own limited intellect and knowledge can presume.

But second, even knowing these things, we have to be able to evolve our policies in an age of ever more rapid change. Today's challenges are real, injustice does exist, improvement is possible, and the consequences of change are never fully knowable. Just as we cannot rely only on our present understanding, neither can we stick entirely to the past.

This is intellectual adulthood. This is conservatism. It understands that institutions like markets, nation-states, family, and faith exist for a reason and embody important lessons. Yet it also knows that policies have to be changed and, sometimes, even institutions themselves. This is how we should approach the political challenges that lie before us.

7

POWERFUL BUT NOT PERFECT

I t was inevitable that my fiftieth birthday would not be an entirely happy day. Turning fifty, you must face the undeniable reality that you are on the back end. That was compensated for by my good health, good fortune, and thousands of birthday greetings pouring in from across the country. As prime minister, however, I had one of my most difficult days.

On April 30, 2009, I forced through my government's final signoff on the bailout package for the North American automobile industry. With the premier of Ontario, Dalton McGuinty, agreeing to pay one-third of the cost, I pledged some thirteen billion dollars of tax-payers' money to what had been some of the wealthiest corporations in the world. In many ways, it defied what I had entered public life to do. Yet I had successfully cajoled the majority of my cabinet and caucus into supporting the action. Still, a small minority held out to the end. It was not pleasant.

Conservatives in the United States excoriated Barack Obama for the auto-sector bailout, of which the American government was contributing some 83 per cent of the funds.[1] It was grossly unfair. Obama was only carrying forward a policy that George W. Bush had locked the U.S. into on his way out the door. And Bush, like myself, had only done what he had to do.

The conservative critics like to say that the crisis in the automobile sector should have been dealt with in the market—between the companies and their creditors. And they are right, except that was a theoretical option only. In late 2008, there was no functioning financial sector in the United States capable of coming to such an arrangement. What loomed instead was a whole new level of mass unemployment in an economy that was already cratering.

That is why Bush decided he would bail out the industry. Because nearly one-fifth of that industry was located in Canada, I told the president that we would assist. Otherwise, the industry would have been relocated to the United States, costing our own economy at least another half a million jobs.

I recount this story to drive a moral. Conservatism is not, at its core, about markets. It is about making an economy work. Markets will generally do that. But when they do not, as a conservative, you do what will work. And if you fail to do that, then you create the kind of massive government intervention that I was compelled to deliver on my fiftieth birthday.

Markets are powerful, but they are not perfect. They gain their effectiveness from both human strengths, like freedom and ingenuity, and human weaknesses, like self-interest and greed. They require governance to control violence and prevent fraud, just as they need non-governmental institutions that breed personal responsibility and enable social attachments. In modern, advanced economies, markets are also complex. There are no easy formulas for creating successful, market-oriented policies. They require good judgment based on data, experience, and insight.

Understanding these things can give conservatives a huge advantage in an age of disruption. It can allow us to get beyond theoretical abstraction and to leverage the market's strengths, not for narrow state or private interests, but for the betterment of the broad mass of working families. It can help us better tackle some major issues, like economic stability, cost of living, entrepreneurship, consumer interests, and, most critically, the creation of jobs in an environment of rapid technological change.

===

Compared with the pure model found in introductory textbooks, markets in the real world almost invariably display some deviations and flaws. These can range from fairly normal situations—less than full information, for example—to more profound difficulties. In the latter category, I think of large players who may possess sufficient monopoly power to stifle competition on an ongoing basis.

Not every market imperfection demands a government intervention. In fact, such intervention should be cautious. Government action is itself subject to substantial imperfections that are usually far less self-correcting than those of the market. There is one area, however, where the inevitability of systemic failure needs to be fully appreciated and addressed—financial markets.

The markets that support investment, and ultimately capitalist growth, are unique. Here, the forces of supply and demand do not drive toward a price in the way we normally think about the value of an existing good or service. Instead, they are measuring expectations about future valuations. The future being unknowable, I would argue that such markets have an inherent bias toward significant levels of volatility.

Certainly, that is what we have observed historically. Unregulated financial markets have been given to extreme cycles of mood. Capitalist speculation has seen periods of wild optimism followed by mass panic, with broad economic consequences.[2] Fear and greed—emotions about the future—drive such markets as much as any hard economic data.

I am not making observations that are new. Among economic historians and empirically oriented economists, the dynamics of capitalist cycles have been broadly understood for a very long time. So has the need for sound regulatory frameworks. This is why, for instance, central banking came into existence. In fact, the U.S. Federal Reserve System was founded over a century ago, well before the Great Depression and Keynesianism.

Of course, financial regulation, like any government regulation, can go wrong. It can be used inappropriately, stifle innovation, come to protect incumbents, or just be plain ineffective. But we should be under no illusion. Without regulation of the financial sector, it is a certainty that advanced capitalist economies will suffer bouts of massive instability.

This, by the way, is even more true in this age of international capitalism, when the "contagion" of dysfunctional markets can rapidly spread around the world. That is what we witnessed in 2008, leading to massive state intervention on a global scale. So the choice that some present between intervention and non-intervention is a false one. The real choice is between modest intervention to avoid crises and large-scale intervention following them.[3]

In Canada, we eschewed much of the financial sector deregulation that took place in the United States. Our banking system did not experience any systemic domestic instability. No significant financial institution failed. None had to be bailed out by the government. It is a big part of the reason that we have had no populist backlash.

＝

I have said that good economic policy-making does not always reduce to simple formulas. For a pragmatic conservative, there are historical experiences. But there is no prescription that fits all illnesses.

As an example of the opposite approach, just consider the 2012 Republican Party platform on tax reform. For the umpteenth time, Reagan's proposals of 1980 were dusted off and brought down from the shelf. It did not matter that the economic context and household concerns had changed. The public was still offered the elimination of taxes on dividends and capital gains, reductions in top marginal rates on personal income, and the repeal of credits and deductions used by middle-class families.[4]

What would have been the result? According to the Tax Policy Center, the average after-tax income of those making over one million dollars per year would have been boosted. For those earning under two hundred thousand dollars, it would have been reduced.[5]

This is not merely an unappealing political message—"raising taxes on the middle class to cut them for millionaires"—its economic case is shaky. The supply-side benefits of further lowering top marginal tax rates are much smaller than in the 1980s when the rates were much higher.[6] It is small wonder that those with a below-median household income—under fifty-one thousand dollars a year—voted overwhelmingly Democratic in 2012.[7]

Even in 2017, after Trump's populist insurgency, some of the same mistakes are being made. Take the issue of corporate taxes in the most recent reform legislation. There is no question that the U.S. corporate tax rate needed to be made more competitive. And the bill includes some good structural changes to the U.S. business tax system. However, lowering the rate from 35 per cent to 20 per cent—it ultimately landed at 21—became a matter of simple dogma for some GOP lawmakers.

As a result, the package was quite imbalanced. Too little was dedicated to reducing taxes on working families. A modest increase to the Child Tax Credit was only grudgingly added to secure enough Senate votes following Roy Moore's defeat in Alabama. Even that revised bill encountered stiff resistance from those who considered it an unprincipled deviation from supply-side orthodoxy.[8]

But what, exactly, is the basis of such a position? Why, to parody *Wall Street Journal* terminology, is cutting taxes for business and the wealthy "good economics," but cutting them for workers, families, and consumers "just politics"?

Business investment and economic growth have been lagging in the United States and much of the developed world since 2008, despite near-zero interest rates. Maybe one of the reasons for this slump is ongoing weakness in consumer demand? Maybe one of the reasons is that workers and families have been falling behind?[9] Maybe, then, lowering taxes on working- and middle-class families can boost purchasing power and support greater investment and growth? Why not?

The recent tax bill suggests that such considerations continue to utterly elude some in the GOP. There is no inherent reason why tax cuts for ordinary people cannot make good economic policy. They can also help make the necessary parts of a supply-side agenda more politically viable.[10] We showed this in Canada.

Under Ministers Jim Flaherty and Joe Oliver, our Conservative government was a tax-cutter. We cut taxes every single year that we were in office. Federal revenues as a share of GDP fell to just 14 per cent, their lowest level in more than fifty years—and with a balanced budget.[11] To put that in perspective: in deficit-spending Washington, the tax burden is nearly 19 per cent of the economy and will remain higher even after the 2017 reductions.[12]

Our tax cuts were broad-based. We reduced taxes of all kinds— personal income taxes, corporate taxes, sales taxes, payroll taxes, taxes on capital, taxes on families, and so on. Not only did we create the lowest overall tax rate on new business investment in the G7, but we lowered taxes for people of all incomes and circumstances. In fact, low- and middle-income Canadians proportionately benefited the most.[13]

I recount this record to make a couple of broader points. First, its overall economic impacts were beneficial. Partly because of tax breaks for ordinary, hard-working people, income inequality actually fell,[14] and Canada became home to the world's richest middle class during our tenure.[15] Second, our reductions to business taxes encountered far less resistance than we see today in the United States. In fact, our Liberal successors have kept our corporate tax reductions in place.[16]

In other words, what we did was good economics and good politics. Properly done, there need not be a contradiction.

=

The conservative pragmatism we practised in financial regulation and tax policy was the same approach we brought to individual markets. Again, this requires a clear-eyed understanding about their strengths and limitations. In particular, it requires an appreciation of the difference between being pro-market and pro-business.

Corporatism is not conservative. A conservative should not conflate society's interests with those of particular industries or individual businesses. Of course, they frequently overlap, but it is up to policy-makers to also recognize where they do not.

My government undertook various initiatives to support markets and competition. Sometimes this involved intervening in the marketplace where competition was stymied. Naturally, these actions were not always in the interests of individual companies, but they were in the broader interests of a properly functioning marketplace.

Telecommunications policy, much of which was spearheaded by Ministers Jim Prentice, Christian Paradis, and James Moore, is a good example. Due in part to past government decisions, Canada has had a small number of incumbents with enormous market power. Consumers had few options and new entrants faced large barriers to entry. This has not been a trivial problem. Canada has been home to some of the highest wireless prices in the world, something that disproportionately affects working people[17] and ultimately harms the competitiveness of Canadian businesses.

A policy of non-intervention would just perpetuate this situation. Therefore, my government acted to cultivate and sustain new market entrants. We essentially earmarked the wireless spectrum for new entrants. The idea was to enhance competition, beginning with more competition in government auctions. We now have new players in the wireless market and there is evidence that prices have fallen.[18] And, despite their cries, the incumbents are still profitable.

Here is an example of where regulation or other forms of government intervention can assist the proper functioning of the market. There are countless others. This should hardly be a matter of controversy in principle. Unfortunately, so-called market advocates often vocally resist such reforms, which is partly why capitalism can get a bad rap.

The point is that, while regulation certainly imposes some costs on the economy, it is wrong to assume that all regulation is bad or that deregulation is always good. Regulation can be important in harnessing the profit motive to positive social ends. Unthinking deregulation has contributed to serious economic problems, the erosion of public trust, and the current rise of anti-market sentiment. We must be smarter. We must make judgments about deregulation based on evidence rather than ideology.

President Trump's adoption of a "regulatory budget" is a good step in this regard. New regulations are to be offset by the reform or repeal of existing ones. It is an approach that imposes greater prioritization and trade-offs. It is not just about deregulation as an end in itself, but about incentivizing bureaucracies toward reforms they would likely never undertake on their own.

I know a bit about this because Trump's plan is inspired in part by the one we adopted under Minister Tony Clement.[19] Canada was the first country in the world to legislate the "one-for-one" rule.[20] The end result can be fewer and smarter regulations with lower compliance costs, especially for small-business owners.

===

At most times, the most important economic issues confronting policymakers are those pertaining to job creation and unemployment. Few things are more fundamental to the prosperity and prospects of working people and their families. With the level of disruption that is already occurring, there is growing speculation about the negative impact of technological innovation on the "future of work."

We are hearing more and more about how automation, machine learning, and artificial intelligence are going to replace whole swaths of the labour force. We have already seen some evidence of this phenomenon. A November 2017 study by the global consulting firm McKinsey estimated that one-third of workers in the U.S., and some eight hundred million globally, could be jobless by 2030 due to these developments.[21] Polls show that working people are genuinely worried about these trends.[22]

Of course, this is not the first time that such alarms have been raised. The entire history of capitalism, from the late 1700s forward, has been marked by claims that machines will inevitably and imminently dislocate all workers.[23] John Maynard Keynes famously misdiagnosed the source of rising unemployment in 1930 as "a new disease . . . namely, technological unemployment." President Kennedy's economic advisers said that their major domestic challenge was "to maintain full employment at a time when automation . . . is replacing men." The 1973 Nobel Prize winner Wassily Leontief speculated that people would be permanently sidelined by technology, like horses were by vehicles.[24]

Ironically, precisely the opposite has taken place—the total number of jobs in capitalist economies has risen astronomically over the generations. The introduction of disruptive, labour-saving technology has led to large-scale economic growth and a greater diversity of occupations. To use the most dramatic example: two hundred years ago, almost all work was dedicated to the production of food; today, agriculture accounts for a tiny percentage of the labour force.

In other words, we have every right to be skeptical about predictions of labour market cataclysm. Skeptical, yes, but not complacent. History also shows that widespread and fast-paced employment dislocation can have very negative impacts on particular sectors, regions, and workers. The social and political consequences can be far-reaching and severe.

Conservatives need to have a sound policy agenda that speaks to this. Once again, a simple restatement of 1980s policies will not do the trick. This was not among the central challenges that Reagan, Thatcher, and the conservatives of their era were trying to address. Business tax cuts, deregulation, and other investment incentives may be good ideas, but they are not really fundamental to this set of worries.

If conservatives do not develop answers, we will not only seem disconnected, we will cede territory to the bad ideas of the other side. One of those is simple cash handouts, like a universal basic income or other unconditional transfers. True, these approaches can meet some basic economic needs. However, such proposals utterly fail to address the wider personal and social problems that arise in populations without meaningful employment.

Conservatives must be the champions of paid work. A huge body of thinking, writing, and evidence, dating as far back as Aristotle, shows that work brings dignity and self-worth. Besides, it is what anxious voters and insecure workers actually want.[25]

==

We cannot fully predict the effects of the coming wave of labour force pressures. But there are some things we can say with reasonable certainty. For example, education and training will be vitally important. This is because we know three things from the history of capitalist technological advancement: it will destroy some existing jobs; it should create many more new ones; and most of these new jobs will require higher levels of education.

Now, I guess I am speaking from a Canadian perspective, but I find the cost of post-secondary education in the United States shocking. When I see the price tags on even modest American college programs, I cannot understand how people of limited means are supposed to keep up, let alone get ahead. If we are to address the economic concerns that are driving populist politics, this is one issue that simply must be addressed.

I am not advocating the solutions of the left. I do not believe in free education paid for entirely by the government. And I do not believe in many of the subsidization schemes that exist in advanced countries. In truth, even in nations where there are huge public investments in education, much of that investment is increasingly off-track.

Post-war Western societies have encouraged access to higher education, often through increased government funding to educational institutions, especially universities. But they have also allowed these institutions to operate as private organizations. The result has been growing layers of non-teaching bureaucracy, an overexpansion of buildings, and general salary inflation in the sector.[26] Not surprisingly, the educational establishment directs students to the highest-cost options. Also, unsurprisingly, this appeals to policy-makers, both political and bureaucratic, who are generally graduates of such institutions.

Even more problematic, a significant percentage of this education bears little or no connection to present or future labour force needs and opportunities. So, if I were an American policy-maker, I would look not only at more ways of supporting post-secondary education, but also at linking funds to the likelihood of employment. I would tie loans and grants to such metrics.[27] And I would diminish direct payments to institutions.

In my government, we came to believe that a greater focus on technical and polytechnic education is advisable. First, it is easy to forget that only a minority of people in our societies possess a bachelor's degree or higher.[28] Policy-makers cannot afford to be disconnected from the majority of the population. But second, the elite consensus in favour of university education is not justified by the data. The numbers indicate pretty clearly that the job and income prospects of many vocational or technical careers are much better than believed.[29] It is simply social bias that presumes otherwise. Likewise, there are assumptions that university education is automatically valuable economically. In truth, it depends enormously on the program. There are many degrees that make it very likely that their recipients will earn a below-average income for life.[30]

Therefore, we sought to adjust educational priorities to promote vocational training and apprenticeships. We used limited grants, targeted tax policies, and some institutional funding.[31] Just as important as these actions was the validation it offered. My ministers and I regularly talked about the importance to our economy of "those who shower after work, not just those who shower before it." We wanted working-class people and those who wished to pursue a career in the trades to be respected and valued.

If enrolment numbers are a measure, we definitely moved the dial.[32] I believe our approach also helped better connect the Conservative Party to working Canadians. At a time of populist upheaval, this is not trivial. There is room for conservatives elsewhere to adopt similar policies and a similar perspective.

====

We also know that public policy must establish a good environment for job creation. Governments may be able to mandate the creation of individual jobs, but governments do not significantly raise overall levels of employment. It is economic growth that boosts employment over time. And it is the dynamics of markets and capitalism that create such long-term growth.

Many do not realize that the opposite is also true: without economic growth, we will see employment shrink. Capitalist innovation inexorably reduces the amount of labour required for a given amount of production. Thus, if growth fails to occur, the number of jobs will steadily decline in a market economy.

Governments can stifle growth. High taxes, excessive regulation, and anti-market intervention are all well-known ways this happens. One way that is not given enough attention today is long-term deficit financing.

Almost all Western governments are now going back down the road of so-called Keynesian expansionary policies—that is, ongoing deficit financing and monetary expansion through interest rate suppression. The problem is that these are not, and never have been, growth policies. They are, at best, short-term stabilization policies. Used continually, they are stagnation policies. I could simply point to the past thirty years in Japan, but let me say a little more about ongoing budgetary deficits.

Government borrowing takes money from investment markets. Over time, this will build up government spending (which is invariably consumption-oriented) and reduce the capital formation on which long-term growth depends. This is why effective economic leaders, like Germany's Angela Merkel and the U.K.'s David Cameron, refused to turn a blind eye to the long-term problems of deficits and debt as the global financial crisis faded.[33]

Incidentally, these things also exacerbate income inequality. Financing through borrowing means paying lenders, usually those of higher income, while financing through taxation tends to put the costs disproportionately on the wealthy.

Of course, I am not advocating tax hikes. I am preaching what I practised: sound public finances. But it is not easy. Eliminating relatively small Canadian deficits after the financial crisis was a Herculean task that took many years and much discipline. Reforms cannot be done quickly, but they must be done broadly and fairly. Those well connected to government and those working for it have a strong record of passing the burden of deficit reduction to the less fortunate and the private sector. That is all the more reason why conservatives need to take the job seriously.

====

Another way governments can encourage job creation and work is to borrow from the Hippocratic Oath and "do no harm." Onerous and heavy-handed regulations, mandates, and higher taxes that amount to a "war on work" are a perfect example. We are witnessing an escalation of such policies, especially those pursued in the name of the environment.

There are all kinds of legitimate environmental concerns. I had a series of strong environment ministers—Rona Ambrose, John Baird, Peter Kent, Leona Aglukkaq, and the late Jim Prentice—who pursued solid initiatives in conservation, pollution control, and the reduction of greenhouse gases. But they were careful that their actions did not throw ordinary people out of work.[34]

Unfortunately, there are many environmental crusades that do not care about this issue. They are causes funded by wealthy Anywheres that have their impacts on modest-income Somewheres. You might think that a heartfelt environmental crusade would start at home, not in someone else's backyard. If only.

As an Albertan, I obviously know about an example close to home—the oil and gas industry. I know lots of Somewheres who work in this business. Their industry faces growing levies and continual pressures from environmental groups to curtail production. These, in combination with energy commodity cycles, have cost many such Somewheres their jobs.[35] Of course, Anywheres who oppose this industry could just stop using their products. But not them. At best, they are going to pay "carbon offsets"—an exercise as meaningless as medieval indulgences.

There are dozens of cases like this. Affluent liberals expressing concerns about the fate of working people and then figuring out how to deliberately kill their jobs.

By the way, some conservatives have a version of this. It comes in some proposals for entitlement reform or welfare reduction. To be clear, these are good objectives, but, once again, we need to consider their impact on real people. The elimination of welfare will not automatically make a job appear.

An example of an alternative approach was the Working Income Tax Benefit developed by my late finance minister, Jim Flaherty, and inspired in part by the U.S.'s Earned Income Tax Credit. It provides wage supplements to those transitioning off welfare to ensure that all the benefits of obtaining paid work are not lost to reductions in social payments and services. In other words, it has sought, with some success, to promote paid work by ending the trap of the "welfare wall."[36]

===

I have spent this chapter laying out the case for a pragmatic conservative approach to market-oriented economics. I am convinced that, if we do not get this right, much worse awaits us. We will see the rise of a populism not of the right, but of the left. In fact, it is one virtually indistinguishable from old-fashioned communism or, as neo-communists prefer to call it, "socialism."

I must admit that, with communism's dismal record, I can hardly believe we need to talk about this. Even leaving aside its appalling legacy of tyranny and mass murder, its performance has been incredibly poor. "Socialist" command economies have, at their best, been able to bring about rapid early-stage economic development but only at staggering costs. After that, they utterly stagnate or, like Venezuela today, begin to decline.

Nonetheless, today's political reality indicates that we need to take this option seriously. I am not just referring to surveys that show growing support for socialism, especially among those too young to know anything of Soviet or Maoist history.[37] There are also concrete indications of socialism's rise in the political arena.

In the United States, all the energy in the Democratic Party is today in its far-left "progressive" wing. Indeed, might Bernie Sanders, a lifelong socialist, have won the 2016 nomination if not for the institutional bias in favour of Hillary Clinton? In the United Kingdom, Jeremy Corbyn is far to the left of any previous Labour Party leader, even the most unelectable of these. Yet he now has a real shot at winning the next general election.

How can we explain such developments in light of the historical record? As I have earlier alluded, it comes out of the only communist bastion of the post–Cold War era: Western academia. Through that channel, socialist thinking has been propagated first through education, and then via media, entertainment, and other cultural channels. But why do Marxism and its derivatives retain such a unique appeal to the intellectual mindset?

I believe it is precisely because of the market's strength—it is a pragmatic system that works. In other words, libertarian claims aside, it is one constructed on human nature, not lofty intellectual ideals. And it has been a spectacular success over the past couple of centuries. The poorest worker in an advanced capitalist economy today has a standard of living far beyond that of the richest rulers of earlier ages.

That said, to the committed socialist, the issue is not capitalism's successes. It is the fact that capitalism is just not perfect. To the non-empirical mind, this is everything. And, for one lacking an understanding of human nature, especially one's own, it is intolerable.

This intolerance, by the way, escalates whenever it gets power. We have seen it in all communist regimes. We see it on college campuses today when such people get control. Human failing, beyond that explained as purely the consequence of a "flawed system," cannot be tolerated. Exposed to the "correct" ideas, one must change and, if not, be re-educated and, if not that, be eliminated. The idea that human nature is flawed is impermissible, for it would imply that the socialist intellectual must be flawed.

This, by the way, is equally the nature of fascism. Fascism is just a variant of the socialist mindset focused on culture and race. That is why it called itself "national socialism." In practice, communist and fascist persecutions of large groups of people have often been indistinguishable. Many academics like to gloss over this, just as they conveniently forget that the two camps began World War II on the same side.

Of course, all of this is the antithesis of true conservatism. Conservatives advocate notions of morality not because we think they can always be fulfilled, but because we realize that they will not. We seek shelter in tradition and experience because we know that the human mind, left purely to its own devices, can never be fully trusted. We are suspicious of top-down change by edict because we understand it will never be fully successful, and that it is frequently not successful at all.

And true conservatives are not afraid to apply some of this critical thinking to markets themselves.

=

The upshot is this: conservatives need not lionize markets to advocate market-based policies. In fact, a good conservative understanding of how markets actually function is a useful tonic in a populist age. Adapting that understanding to develop a pro-growth, pro-work agenda that serves ordinary citizens should be the sweet spot for today's conservative policy-makers, both economically and politically.

Such an agenda is bound to have political resonance when juxtaposed with the economic policies of modern left-liberals. They are drawn to corporatism and the disconnected agendas of elitist Anywheres. They are prepared, for example, to kill jobs they see as dirty, monotonous, or stupid, believing that cash handouts from government can substitute for meaningful work.

Conservatives have a real opportunity to champion working people in general and paid work in particular. However, it will require that, in policy areas like regulation, taxation, education, and environmental protection, we find a space somewhere between free-market dogmatism and pure political expediency. The same is true for trade policy, which I will look at separately.

Such an approach is eminently doable. It is, in fact, what conservatives ought to have been doing all along.

8

THE ART OF THE DEAL

I consider October 18, 2013, one of my best days in office. I was in Brussels, standing with the president of the European Commission, José Manuel Barroso, to announce the agreement-in-principle on a free-trade pact, the Comprehensive Economic and Trade Agreement, between Canada and the European Union. Another year of technical work would be needed to produce the legal texts, and three more years to get the agreement implemented on the European side. Nevertheless, we had got the deal done.

As I stood on that stage, I knew that every single interest in the country would be drafting its response to the announcement. Literally thousands of industry lobbies, corporations, unions, think-tanks, subnational governments, and pressure groups would have their say. Most would be supportive, many strongly so. Some would not be, a few vocally. But in not one case would the reaction take my government by surprise.

We knew what we were doing. We knew what the response would be because we knew how the deal would play out. We knew who would win, who would struggle, and who would lose. We knew the deal inside out, and the likely effects it would have.

It is my conviction, borne out by polling data,[1] that most ordinary citizens understand that trade has benefits. They get that greater access to foreign markets and wider options for domestic consumers are good things. However, they want to be assured that the trade policies of their governments are firmly rooted in their interests.

This is the approach my government took, on every deal we negotiated. I believe it is why we had a successful record on free trade. We struck agreements all over the world and left Canada with the most extensive trade network among our peer countries. These free-trade efforts also maintained broad public support. That is, after all, what a populist conservative trade agenda is all about.

There is a presumption out there that a populist mandate is a protectionist mandate. It is just not that simple. In Canada, for example, populist movements have historically tended to be against tariffs and protection. Brexit is a more recent example. While self-evidently an expression of populism, that movement was not about protectionism. No leading Brexit voice was advancing the idea of becoming "closed." Indeed some, like MEP Daniel Hannan, are advocates of far-more aggressive approaches to trade than those currently being pursued by the European Union.

In other words, free trade is perfectly viable in an age of populist disruption. But trade advancement cannot rely on trade theory alone, or focus its attention only on a narrow set of large corporate interests. We have to do our homework and make choices based on a wide range of real-world economic considerations.

===

When I became prime minister in 2006, I was aware of two basic realities about Canada's trade situation. First, we were falling dangerously behind in global access. But, second, there was no guarantee that a free-trade agenda would be politically saleable.

Free trade has been a divisive political issue in Canada since our Confederation in 1867. There is a tendency to believe that this contentiousness ended in 1988 with the re-election of the Progressive Conservative government and the passage of the Canada–U.S. Free Trade Agreement. However, five years later, the Liberals swept the PCS from office, in part by campaigning against NAFTA. It is true that they later ratified the agreement, using some cosmetic changes as their justification. After that, however, they all but abandoned free trade. Only three small deals were concluded over the next thirteen years, and none of them risked any controversy at home.

The upshot is that we had no reason to assume that a renewed free-trade agenda was going to be popular. It would require careful analysis, large-scale consultations, considerable patience, the right choices, and, ultimately, effective communications. We would need to convince working Canadians that any deal was in their interests.

If you need to engage in any type of negotiation and want some initiation on the subject, Donald Trump's 1987 best-seller *The Art of the Deal* is not a bad place to start. It may not be the "second-best book" ever written,[2] but it does contain some useful advice. My own experience is that "aim high," "hold your ground," "never pay too much," and "hire the best people" are all good lessons. I was particularly fortunate to have our trade negotiations led by a series of capable ministers—David Emerson, Michael Fortier, Stockwell Day, Peter Van Loan, and Ed Fast—who were backed by large teams of smart and dedicated staff on both the departmental and political sides.

They spent considerable time and effort figuring out who the most promising partners were for trade deals, where the Canadian economy stood to gain from access to those markets, and which of them presented significant import risks to our own producers. They did not just rely on bureaucratic reports. Extensive consultations with our domestic industries were carried out behind the scenes to develop and validate our negotiating strategy.

The result was that we started each negotiation with a clear sense of what our offensive and defensive interests were, where trade-offs would be acceptable, and what our bottom line was. Indeed, we knew the kinds of deals we would accept or not accept before we even got to the table. We declined to even enter into free-trade talks with China after a pre-study. Canada is simply not in a position to get a good deal bargaining one-on-one with the People's Republic.

Trade negotiations are about careful evaluations of the real economic benefits and costs; they are not about academic theories.

Theory can indicate why trade deals might be beneficial, but it does not make any agreement automatically beneficial. Trade negotiators are not modelling free trade for a simplified, textbook economy. They are supposed to be acting on behalf of a complex, real-world economy that has both interests to advance and interests to protect.

I wish I could tell you that this is always the case. I have certainly dealt with many tough negotiators on the other side of the table. Yet I have also seen this kind of rigour lacking. The American decision to admit China to the WTO is just one example. Debate on that issue hinged largely around foreign-policy objectives. The benefits of opening trade seemed to have been just assumed, and a bad deal was the result.

=

Here is something else: when it comes to trade negotiations, one must let go of the artificial distinction many trade advocates make between "economics" and "politics." This is ideological thinking at its worst.

Let me give a Canadian example. We maintain a comprehensive system of supply management in the dairy and poultry sectors. Supply management provides for production quotas, high tariffs, and price controls in these industries.

Successive Canadian governments have defended this system in international trade negotiations, despite its negative impacts on consumer prices and secondary food processing. Trade advocates dismiss this as merely "politics," based on the power of the farm lobby. The implicit claim is that there is no "economics" case for such a position.

It is true that the dairy and poultry lobby is strong. But it is also small—maybe some sixteen thousand farms.[3] Yet its interests have been defended by every Canadian government to date. This includes governments with little parliamentary representation among such farmers. Therefore, the argument that this is just a case of successful lobbying should be taken with some very big grains of salt. There is clearly more to it.

For one thing, business investment in these sectors is very large.[4] This investment is based on quota ownership. For these farmers, it is the basis of their entire business, their family's wealth, and their long-term financial plans. Abandoning supply management in a trade negotiation would result in the destruction of this value—even if the farm could still compete.

The economic risk to these sectors is large as well. Ending supply management in an industry where products are so homogeneous could mean the wholesale swamping of domestic production. Cheaper imports from larger-scale farms in the United States, New Zealand, and elsewhere could devastate local farmers, virtually overnight. The industry's survival in Canada would indeed be in question.

Finally, such costs would have a wide impact. The effects would not be limited to supply-managed farmers. These businesses are often the core of the regional and local economies in which they operate. They are the basis of a whole set of supply and service chains. It is one thing for an industry to be dislocated in major centres with diversified economies. It is another for this to occur in rural communities where the sector is the backbone of the region. It is not hyperbole to say that whole communities would be negatively affected—some existentially so.

Thus, despite the costs of supply management at home and its complications in negotiations abroad, our governments have decided to support the system. They have concluded that the efficiency gains of scrapping it are not worth the costs. Of course, it is entirely reasonable to reach a different conclusion. But this is not a simple choice between "economics" and "politics."

Incidentally, the same trade advocates who argue so vociferously for the elimination of supply management do not argue—at least not loudly—for Canada to dismantle protections for its banking sector. Why not? Would doing so not lead to more diverse and cheaper options coming from New York and other world financial centres? Certainly.

But what if that meant our banking sector got clobbered? Or what if it were bought out by international firms and the head-office jobs moved abroad? This would have serious employment effects in the Greater Toronto Area and the other major cities where our financial sector is located. These urban centres are also where those same trade advocates usually live. So, suddenly those "end supply management" voices warn that reforms to banking protections are "complex," that we must "be very careful" and at best "go slow."[5]

So we need to begin any trade negotiation by dismissing the idea that one's own interests are all about "good economics" while the other guy's interests are "just politics." The truth is that these are complicated issues involving mixtures of broad and narrow economic interests, with impacts that hit some people more than others. They require careful assessment, and even then, they are not fully knowable. But it is trade negotiators' responsibility to understand them as best they can, not to rely solely on trade theorems.

==

In 2006, we inherited a number of trade negotiations, but almost all were pro forma. And none were on a path to a deal.

In the next decade, we concluded negotiations with forty-six countries. Some were difficult. We had to conclude an agreement with South Korea after the United States unexpectedly closed a not-particularly-strong deal there, undercutting our exports. The crowning achievements were the deal with the European Union and the Trans-Pacific Partnership. All gained widespread public support, so much so that our successors have pursued their implementation in every case.

Among the many lessons here is the necessity of rooting a trade strategy in the broad interests of working people and their families. We worked hard to outline the benefits in language they could understand and from a perspective they could relate to. As an example, we carried out joint studies with the EU to outline the type and scope of such benefits before even commencing negotiations.

We were also patient. We looked for continual progress, but we established no artificial deadlines. And, especially with the big players, we worked hard to figure out what their objectives and bottom lines really were.

We also did not blind ourselves to potential downsides. We did not fall victim to the globalist delusion that because trade is usually beneficial in overall terms, it must be beneficial under any terms and for everyone. There are going to be costs and there are going to be losers, and the public is smart enough to figure that out.

Knowing this, by the way, is the key to minimizing those costs. Our experience was that with an appropriately scoped agreement, phase-in options, and adjustment plans, even the most threatened industries will do surprisingly well. I can give an example from the original Canada–U.S. Free Trade Agreement. Doom was predicted for the relatively small Canadian wine industry. But with some adjustment assistance from government and new marketing directions in the industry, it would survive. Indeed, it ultimately thrived under free trade.

Part of a successful strategy is to use some of the gains from the "winners" of trade to help the "losers" adapt. This is a viable approach because the wins of trade are supposed to greatly offset its losses. Of course, there can be debate about what form this assistance should take, how it can be efficiently designed, what its generosity and duration should be, and so forth. But the basic principle strikes me as both good economics and good politics.

Speaking of which, I have never understood the U.S. conservative aversion to trade adjustment measures, especially as part of a pro-trade political bargain. It is true that the Trade Adjustment Assistance program has been around in different forms since the early 1960s. Yet its annual budget averaged only about $750 million per year between 2010 and the present.[6] This is a mere rounding error on the $3.8 trillion federal budget.

One can argue that this program ought to be reformed or improved to achieve better employment results for those affected.

My own government sought to make job training programs more market- and outcomes-focused. But I have little sympathy for those who reject such assistance as "wasteful" in principle or advocate "cutting it altogether."[7] That is a sure-fire way to further erode public support for free trade.

Again, Canada's supply-managed agriculture is a case in point. For both CETA and TPP, it would have been impossible to get any agreement without a significant opening of those markets. We therefore worked closely with the sectors to make the kinds of concessions they could most easily manage. We also consulted with them to develop adjustment programs. Admittedly, these programs were generous. But the sectors also broadly supported the agreements. This undercut any possibility of them forging an alliance with the ideological opponents of free trade and thus endangering the deals.

=

It is even harder to understand the reflexive opposition of some trade advocates to any form of action or remedy against unfair trade practices. These mechanisms exist in international trade law for good reason—systems without them have proven to be unstable. In many ways, they just parallel protections from anti-competitive behaviour in domestic jurisdictions.

The current U.S. trade remedy model does require some reform. For instance, there have been various congressional attempts to strengthen the regime around undervalued currencies.[8] This would be sensible. There is room for improved enforcement against counterfeit products as well. And there could also be better transparency and timeliness in intellectual property disputes.[9]

However, the most important issue will be how the U.S. government deals with China's status as a non-market economy. To explain briefly, when China joined the World Trade Organization in 2001, it agreed to be treated as a non-market economy for up to fifteen years. The practical importance of this requirement is that it lowers the threshold for proving unfair trade practices. The U.S. can look at costs in similar economies (such as Brazil) in determining whether Chinese exporters are selling below cost.

The fifteen-year term has since expired, and China now wants to receive its market-economy status.[10] The result would be to make action against China's trade practices more difficult. The Trump administration has so far strongly opposed this. In fact, it formally notified the WTO to this effect in November 2017, and has since worked with the EU and others to build support for its stance.[11]

The administration's position is that China's system of state-owned enterprises, direct and indirect subsidies, and other non-market practices ought to preclude market-economy status at this time. This is factually correct. Much deeper Chinese reform is necessary to justify such a designation.

We confronted the same issue in Canada. Our Liberal predecessors had attempted to slip special treatment of China into our regulations. I was shocked to discover in 2013 that market economy status for the P.R.C. would become automatic on December 31, 2018, effectively undercutting our trade remedy system. So, we changed it,[12] restoring Canada's right to make a determination based on the evidence.[13]

Trump needs to hold his ground here and continue to resist calls to change China's WTO status in the absence of sufficient reform. This is a clear source of leverage in the bilateral relationship, where too many others have been given away. The Chinese government wants market economy status badly. It needs to earn it.

====

This focus on evidence over accommodation should also apply to foreign direct investment. My government was broadly in favour of foreign investment. FDI in Canada doubled during our time in office.[14] This occurred in part because we raised the threshold for foreign investment reviews by nearly 75 per cent.[15]

However, we also toughened the system where it mattered. Frankly, the foreign-investment approval process had become a rubber stamp under our predecessors. We beefed up the process in a number of ways, including with enhanced national-security reviews. We ended up rejecting a small number of proposals that were unequivocally not in our country's best interest. We became the first Canadian government in three decades to do so.

One of the most challenging decisions we faced involved the prospect of increased state-owned-enterprise investment in Canada's energy sector. By 2012, we were faced with escalating purchases and the real possibility of wholesale Chinese SOE takeover of the Alberta oil sands. They constitute a huge part of the world's private-sector petroleum reserves. We ultimately approved the proposals on the table, but in the process, we established a new policy framework to render further SOE acquisitions difficult.

It was not an easy choice. However, in the end, we struck a balance between maintaining openness and protecting the country's long-term interests. The fact is that state-owned enterprises ought to be treated differently. In Canada, Conservative governments had spent years returning the energy sector to a market-based, private-sector orientation. It made no sense to see reduced Canadian government control replaced with control by foreign governments. One must acknowledge the fact that, with SOEs from countries like China, the line between commercial objectives and geopolitical goals are invariably blurred.

Critical to our approach was reintroducing a degree of flexibility into our judgments. Business consultants who specialize in foreign investment approvals did not like this. They preferred "certainty." They know that any set of crystal-clear rules can always be gamed. However, there are cases, especially in dealing with foreign governments, where countries should not surrender the option of discretion and, therefore, leverage.

Another area where we need to develop a less ideological view of foreign investment is residential real estate. Indeed, many governments are already implementing taxes and restrictions on foreign purchases, particularly for existing housing. Sure, the escalating prices being paid are good for the previous owners. But the broader effect can be to make home ownership inaccessible for local residents. This is another example of an area where we need to care a lot more about market outcomes than market principles. If we are to minimize negative political impacts in this age of disruption, surely people have to be able to live where they work, just as they must be able to work where they live.

My point is that, as with trade, we can be generally pro–foreign investment but also make selective judgments that safeguard the country's interests. This is not an inconsistent perspective. In fact, it is a profoundly conservative one. Conservatives in Washington, London, and elsewhere must not lose sight of it. In our trade and investment decisions, we must ultimately be accountable to our citizens' interests, not to abstract policy goals.

===

It would be odd to write on this subject and not say something about President Trump's trade targets, especially regarding NAFTA.

The promise to get better trade deals was a key element of Trump's electoral appeal. He has decried trade deficits, uneven market access, and the non-market objectives of some trade partners. None of these automatically make him a protectionist, although they could.

What we know for sure is that Trump's agenda and rhetoric emphasize the impact of trade on working- and middle-class people. If we are to overcome growing protectionist sentiment in the United States and other Western countries, this is the focus we must have. The challenge is to address legitimate concerns about trade flows and existing trade agreements without descending into a more general protectionism.

In this regard, Trump's decision to make NAFTA his first priority has been badly mistaken. NAFTA is the largest trade agreement in history and widely regarded as one of the most successful. The exports of all three parties have grown steadily and massively. Despite its ongoing security problems, Mexico has become more prosperous, more stable, and more closely aligned with the United States.

The administration has focused its anger on the trade deficits. With Canada, this deficit stood at US$17.5 billion in 2017, with imports outpacing exports by a mere 6 per cent.[16] With Mexico, the shortfall was US$71 billion, a gap of about 30 per cent.[17] Considering the superior wealth of the United States, this gap is not enormous, particularly given that it has been declining somewhat over time. As well, American investment in its NAFTA partners has significantly out-paced reciprocal flows, particularly from Mexico.

There is one area that can explain the administration's frustration—the automobile sector. It accounts for virtually the entirety of the U.S.–Mexico trade deficit.[18] And it is particularly annoying that the auto companies have been shifting production to Mexico since the govern-ment bailouts, in which Mexico did not participate. There also seems little doubt that unrelated issues, especially illegal immigration and drug violence, have clouded U.S. perceptions.

The NAFTA renegotiation came out of Trump's campaign commit-ments and was, at its heart, a U.S.–Mexico dispute. Given that Trump had indicated no grievance with Canada, and that our interests are much more closely aligned with the Americans, our government should have avoided being on the same side of the table as the Mexicans in this dispute. In any case, it has been an enormous and unnecessary distraction for all of us. This is because the three coun-tries largely share international trade interests.

Those interests converge on Trump's other big trade target—China. All three NAFTA countries have enormous trade deficits with the People's Republic in both relative and absolute terms.[19] These show no indication of shrinking. In fact, in the investment area, similar gaps are appearing. A coordinated pushback on the relatively closed Chinese market and its huge surpluses makes far more sense than NAFTA countries battling against each other over relatively tiny imbalances. U.S. membership in the Trans-Pacific Partnership similarly made sense. The Obama administration had pushed it forward to deal with the China problem.

That said, taking on China is easier said than done. Tariffs, no matter what their merit, do hurt consumers. The Chinese have also been clever in providing good access to their market for large, politically connected, Western corporations. They can be counted on to coordinate with China on resisting trade action.

So, if it really wants to level the playing field, this is where the U.S. should focus its energy. And it has enormous leeway. The risks of a "trade war" are grossly exaggerated. The superior access the Chinese have to the American market makes it in their interest to make great efforts to avoid one. In fact, because the Chinese are good economic pragmatists, this is one place where a "better deal" is begging to be had.

=

Notwithstanding the political fallout of the global financial crisis, leaders did do some things right. Most notably, the coordinated efforts of the G20 prevented a general descent into protectionism and global trade wars. Avoiding that was critical. It could have turned a relatively short-term financial crisis into a long depression, as happened in the decade following 1929.

Nonetheless, protectionism will continue to be a threat if obvious trade problems are not addressed. Even though the U.S. administration is wrong on some key trade matters, it is in everyone's interest that it have some success. If the status quo is not improved, far more radical voices are waiting to fill the void. The real dangers are "back to the future" socialist-protectionists.

The hard left ideologically abhors free trade because of its rejection of markets in general. Deep down, it wants to control all economic activity. But one thing we do know is that the top-down, closed-economy model is a sure-fire recipe for failure. It was so in the Soviet bloc and in Mao's China. Today's Venezuela is only the most recent disaster.[20]

But we cannot be complacent about this. More than one-third of the population was born after the collapse of the Berlin Wall.[21] These young people have grown up in a world without the Cold War or the Soviet Union. Left-wing education systems have sheltered these voters from understanding the real economic and human costs of economic collectivism.

Therefore, it is critical that conservatives do not play into this danger by defending the extremes of what some call "hyperglobalization."[22] Because that is precisely what modern liberals are doing. Their corporatism has made trade advocacy an article of faith. On this issue, they may come from the opposite perspective of the hard left, but both camps are arguing for ideological positions divorced from their real impacts on ordinary working people.

This disconnection was on full display at Davos in 2016. Chinese president Xi Jinping gave a spirited speech against protectionism. But the liberal globalists present failed to ask him when he would open his own market. Instead, they gave him a standing ovation. That is an example of why, in the next chapter, I will argue that conservatives must lead in the age of globalization.

9

NATIONALISM AND ALIENISM

Some of my best times as prime minister were when I was not the centre of attention. The Vancouver Winter Olympics and Paralympics of 2010 come to mind. British Columbia premier Gordon Campbell had done much of the heavy lifting in terms of Canada's preparations. Minister Gary Lunn had spearheaded most of the federal role.

But, along with my family, I did spend a good chunk of the Games in Vancouver and Whistler. It was an exhilarating experience. I watched Canadian athletes execute one gold-medal performance after another. Before it was over, Canada would set an all-time Winter Olympics record for gold medals, at fifteen. The fifteenth came in our men's hockey victory against the United States in overtime. The country's streets were deserted during the contest. After it, as throughout the week, Vancouver's downtown was filled with cheering and singing mobs of patriotic Canadians. Davos is interesting, but I would take displays of national pride like this over it seven days a week and twice on Sundays.

Some saw the big political upsets of 2016 as a return of nationalism. They are wrong. For most of us, the nation-state never went away. Most people found their political identity in geography and borders before 2016, and are going to do so for the foreseeable future.

For some in the political, media, academic, and business worlds, this was a shock. They had long anticipated, even welcomed, the "death" of nationalism.[1] The "post-national state" was supposedly the future.

They should have known better. Google "end of the nation-state." You will discover countless articles, books, columns, essays, speeches, and videos dating back decades. This narrative has been around for most of my lifetime, and it has been disproved regularly. The events of the past couple of years are only the most recent and spectacular manifestation.

Not only are nationalism and the nation-state far from dead, their relevance was never really in question. Claims to the contrary reflected nothing more than the detachment of Anywheres from how Somewheres live and think.

The question is not about whether the nation-state will survive any more than it is about whether globalization will survive. It is about how, in this age of disruption, we can balance the tensions of nationalism and globalization. The victories of Brexit and Trump are not indications of an impending collapse of the global order—at least they need not be—but rather a signal that we have failed to achieve such a balance. It is an example of where we need to ditch rootless paradigms in favour of Ronald Reagan's "new thinking rooted in old ideas."

Populism, nationalism, and the globalized exchange of trade, capital, and people are not incompatible. In fact, they can be complementary. They can draw on each other's strengths and safeguard against their own worst excesses. Nationalism taken too far can lead to protectionism and nativism and worse. Globalization taken too far can become elitist, anti-democratic, and dangerously disconnected. The balance between these forces is in the dynamism of global economics and the solidarity of national sovereignty. It is how we properly promote and safeguard the interests of working people.

More broadly, a new, positive nationalism requires promoting a shared sense of citizenship, restoring citizens' interests to the centre of government decision making, and championing a complex view of identity that draws on the strengths of civil society. In effect, it means rooting our global engagement in a healthy nationalism and our domestic politics in a healthy localism. Conservatives have unique insights to help lead the way.

And we have to get this right. Failure will mean a ramping up of the divisions between Somewheres and Anywheres. That can only lead to greater extremes in both elitism and populism, with a resulting increase in social, political, and economic dysfunction.

That said, the responsibility for the path forward falls on those in positions of power and privilege. They need to face the fundamental problem. That is not the natural nationalism of ordinary people. It is the anti-nationalist prejudices, the "alienism," of today's global elites.

=

It can hardly be a shock that populist anger in Europe has been directed against the European Union. That organization has played an increasing role in the lives of the citizens of its twenty-eight nation-states, but often with only their limited consent. Part of the problem remains the fundamental ambiguity around the basis of sovereignty in Europe. Is it national or continental? The answer has become so muddled that both the EU and its member states are seated at many international meetings.

In fact, the peoples of Europe have lost sovereignty to the EU bureaucracy in a wide range of policy areas. The myriad arbitrary and sometimes inexplicable regulations from Brussels are just one indicator. But the nationalist uptick across Europe is far from limited to regulatory matters.

Europe has a range of significant economic challenges, and some of those are attributable to the EU itself. Most notable has been the unorthodox decision to adopt a common currency. I say unorthodox because, at the outset, the euro lacked most of the key characteristics of a normal fiat currency—a dominant central government, a strong fiscal policy, common financial regulation, and a powerful central bank.

These deficiencies have had very serious consequences. With its nation-states lacking the option of independent monetary policy, there was bound to be pressure to socialize other matters at the EU level in the event of crisis. Thus, post–2008–2009, national fiscal problems have become EU-wide problems. The result has been the budgetary bailouts resented on both sides. Populations in lender countries, like Germany, do not understand why they should pay. Populations in recipient economies, like Greece, do not understand why other member states should dictate austerity measures. Several European populist movements are attributable to these dynamics alone.

There are other common-policy irritants, including foreign aid and immigration. The latter demands a separate discussion of its own. Most troubling, however, is the EU's reaction to the public upheaval, particularly its automatic call for "more Europe."

It was one thing to seek "more Europe" when continental integration seemed to be improving people's lives. It is another to demand it when, as with the euro, such integration is at least partly responsible for their problems. EU advocates have to come to terms with this reality: they cannot have greater integration without addressing the populist uprising. And that cannot be addressed without greater accommodation of democracy and nationalism.

This has been our experience in Canada in dealing over a long period of time with a similar phenomenon—the threat of Quebec separatism. During my time in office and before, both symbolic and substantive accommodations have been made for Quebec nationalism. I think of the parliamentary "Quebec nation" resolution and Quebec's seat at UNESCO as examples. These strengthened our hand in managing the core economic interests that all Canadians share.

In Europe, however, the continentalist–nationalist split continues to widen. Brexit is a perfect example. EU proponents somehow see the departure of a major economy as an opportunity for greater integration. They are right in observing that the U.K. was always an outlier—the country by far most likely to leave. However, there are now nationalists in power in Italy, Poland, Hungary, and Austria. In fact, since the Brexit vote, the share of the electorate supporting populist, nationalist, or Euroskeptic parties has risen in virtually every national election.

=

If the EU was bound to be a target of energized European populists, then foreign policy was almost certain to be a target of similar American anger.

I have talked here about the foreign policy actions taken by two U.S. administrations. I had the opportunity of witnessing both presidents and some of their decisions up close. I consider George W. Bush and Barack Obama to be among the most impressive leaders I have known. I was never at a meeting where the American president was not one of, if not the, best briefed and most articulate individual in the room.

These two presidents took very different approaches to "American leadership." One was assertive and bold. The other was accommodative and cautious. Yet both administrations are remembered much more for their foreign-policy difficulties than for their successes. It has led me to conclude that the concept of "American leadership" itself may be problematic. That is also what the American public seems to be saying.

Americans have for the past generation been told two things. One is that the United States has unique global leadership responsibilities. But the other is that the world is an increasingly multipolar place where the U.S. cannot lead alone. I do not think that both of these ideas can really be true. In fact, I have concluded that American administrations will continue to struggle in foreign affairs as long as they try to square these circles. That means they must accept what the second statement really means. If they cannot lead alone, then they cannot really lead. Not unless they are prepared to contribute most of the assets while sharing most of the decisions with others. Which is what has been happening, with less and less efficacy.

The American public is losing patience with that situation. The U.S. contributes nearly one of every four dollars of the United Nations budget. Yet it is regularly overruled or undermined by the vetoes and influence of those who simply do not share America's interests. The farcical results of international attempts to slow the Iranian and North Korean nuclear programs are only one example.

In the case of NATO, the U.S. spends three of every four dollars. But, even among allies, it seems frequently hamstrung by those who are as lavish in their opinions as they are stingy in their contributions.

It is not a reach to suggest that an "America First" foreign policy could provide a much clearer and more effective agenda of genuinely American priorities. In any case, given the evolution of the world and of U.S. public opinion, I believe that the days of foreign policy based on American leadership rather than national interest are numbered.

===

"America First" should not really be inherently objectionable. In my experience, it would simply give the United States the foreign-policy approach of almost every other country in the world. That would include Canada.

My approach in government, which was at its core "Canada First," could not be described as "Canada Only." We did take positions in international affairs based on our national interests. However, that reading of national interests recognized that our interests are often shared with or linked to those of others. It also understood that our ability to defend and promote those interests often requires the capacities of others (especially, in Canada's case, those of the United States).

In fact, what quickly struck me after I became prime minister was the degree to which so many key issues had a large international dimension. Economic impacts, security threats, health crises, and environmental challenges, among others, have ways of rapidly crossing borders today, even from great distances. They require international co-operation of varying degrees.

Thus, we tried to appreciate and accommodate the interests and values of other nations. But we always negotiated international agreements, spoke at world forums, or participated in global initiatives with a clear understanding of our own. We did so because it made sense for Canada and we could explain why. We knew that, otherwise, domestic support for outwardly focused actions would dry up.

I called this approach "enlightened sovereignty"—the application of enlightened self-interest to foreign affairs. The idea is that any government, including one rooted in a clear vision of national interest, will need to engage in the world. It must recognize that both immediate threats and long-term opportunities may reside far from its own borders, and will often need to be addressed in concert with others.

Unlike the concept of "American leadership," this does not mean that a country's interests are infinitely elastic, or that a major power like the United States should simply go along with some international consensus just because there is one. I refused to "go along to get along" with many bad ideas in the international community—attempts to isolate Israel, a naive embracing of the "Arab Spring," an IMF/G20 desire to bail out Europe, and environmental measures that would unilaterally damage our economy, among others. A country as powerful as the United States has considerable freedom of action—China demonstrates that every day.

My point is that there is a wide gap between unilateralism as an easy solution and internationalism for its own sake. Of course, liberals will criticize the approach I am advocating, because today they are on one extreme of this spectrum. But, to protect and promote the interests of our citizens, of the Somewheres, it is an extreme that conservatives must avoid.

Put another way, "America First," done properly, is the right way for the United States to go. In any case, this is where the U.S. is headed. An all-inclusive concept of America's international role is passing. Public sentiment, resource constraints, and a multipolar world will conspire to narrow U.S. focus, with or without Trump. Future foreign engagement by the United States will likely require direct and immediate implications to American interests, certainly more so than we have been accustomed to.

Many around the world will not like to hear this. They have grown accustomed to the United States assuming an overwhelming share of resources and responsibilities for global institutions and undertakings while they sit back, observe, and critique. It has been a good arrangement for them while it lasted, but Trump has ended it. And I believe his successors will follow his lead.

Leaders in the U.S. can refine this direction by undertaking a few of the following tactics. They should value shared interests and engage in collaboration where others are prepared to bring political will and hard assets to the table. When their contribution is little more than political advice and moral judgment, it should be filed accordingly. Similarly, the U.S. should put greater stress on ad hoc arrangements and coalitions than on permanent international institutions or structures. The latter are simply too prone to pro forma U.S. contributions and constraining U.S. options, with little upside. The Chinese are demonstrating that asking others to come to you often makes much more sense for a great power.

A foreign policy along these lines does not mean isolationism. It would instead point to a more focused, more strategic, and more effective approach for the United States. It is also more in line with the evolving views of the U.S. public. Americans see "American exceptionalism" as being largely about their own founding values and national institutions rather than about foreign relations. And they will expect their national interests in such relations to be clear and present.

═══

Of course, the nationalism/globalism divide is about much more than European structures or American foreign affairs. Indeed, it is about much more than even identity. Underlying it is widening social disunity and fracture.

Many have written about how modern societies are witnessing the weakening of the traditional web of human associations. For this there is a wide and diverse source of explanations. Those on the left tend to view it as an outgrowth of the individualism at the centre of capitalism and the market economy.[2] At its extreme is the mobility inherent in globalization. On the other side, conservatives see this social erosion as inherent in the welfare state. A host of modern, depersonalized, bureaucratic institutions has steadily marginalized, replaced, and even ridiculed traditional voluntary, community-based organizations.[3]

For those who grew up in an age before the Internet and the smartphone, it is the impact of technology that strikes us most. I am not talking just about the phenomenon of teenagers texting a conversation to each other even when in physical proximity. I am referring to the emergence of vast social-media associations, of their stars and their lynch mobs, of human interactions that range from enlightening to bullying.

In fact, we are seeing the transformation of much of society to web-based linkages, or "non-spatial associations." Do not get me wrong; there are new possibilities in these. I think of the Society for International Hockey Research, of which I am a member. On a bigger scale, I remember how my government's global child and maternal health initiative was effectively championed through Internet communities.

However, there is no guarantee such new associations will be positive. On one extreme, isolated numbers of pedophiles or terrorists have founded new "communities" through non-spatial association. But even in noble or at least non-harmful endeavours, this type of human interaction has limitations. Web-based association constrains deeper relationships. For instance, it is very limited in its ability to help build a school, or support a grieving parent, or assist a dislocated worker in getting back on his or her feet. And, of course, it can fuel the kind of narrowness of association that leads to tribalism or cause some to disengage from society entirely.

What can we do about this? I believe a healthy nationalism can be part of the ballast against these forces. It can reinforce common interests, a shared vision, and a wider purpose among large numbers of people. History, sport, and other non-political institutions can play an important role in enabling social solidarity.

We did this in Canada. We dedicated public resources to the commemoration of important milestones in Canadian history. We restored traditions to the Canadian Armed Forces. We championed our athletes' efforts and engaged thousands of volunteers in international athletic events. The left often sneered at such initiatives, but the public responded enthusiastically.

This is not to claim that national identity can be falsified or simply manufactured. It is also important to acknowledge historical failures, especially when they still have present-day impacts. I was the first prime minister to officially apologize for our historical system of Indigenous residential schools. Such things can be good steps if the goal is reconciliation, unity, and social progress. They are not if they just feed a grievance industry or promote "black-arm-band history" as an end in itself.

What too many globalists miss is that good human life, both individual and social, requires balance. Embracing national histories of military valour, athletic achievement, technological ingenuity, democratic progress, and the like need not be a threat to globalization. Such celebrations of nationalism are respites from its stresses and shared experiences to counteract its fragmenting pressures. This was a lesson I learned from former Australian prime minister John Howard—someone who was both a committed nationalist and an effective globalist.

Some people will be very happy in the world of global mobility, multinational connections, and international conferences. The truth is that most people's lives will never be lived in such a world. That is why shared citizenship and national identity matter. Because they should. And conservatives need to champion those things.

===

The recent backlash against the extreme globalism of the Anywheres gives us the opportunity to reassert national identity and shared history. It also provides the possibility of an antidote to their other excess—hyper-individualism. This involves a renewed commitment to what is often called "civil society"—relational institutions like family, volunteer, community, and faith organizations.

Think about your own daily life. Most of our actions or choices are made based on our roles as spouses, parents, children, teammates, members, and so on. Very few of us live out our lives thinking and acting merely as individuals. Those who do generally tend to be troubled or unhappy. All great faiths value the dignity of the individual, but they also teach that meaning in individuals' lives derives from healthy relationships.

Yet there is a tendency in our politics to assume a binary framework, to think about society as consisting only of the individual and the state. This is false. Insightful thinkers have long recognized that it is civil society—the institutions that occupy the space *between* the individual and the state—that sustains advanced social order.[4]

It is hard to argue, however, that civil society is not in decline. Institutional illness is evident in declining volunteerism, lower church attendance, widespread family breakdown, and a growing drug crisis.[5] It has been most acute in those parts of the West badly scarred by economic dislocation.[6] And it has its most disproportionate effect on working-class people.[7]

These trends not only hurt these communities, they exacerbate social inequality. The social capital that comes with civil society support is now disproportionately available to high-income citizens, while the lack of it transmits low income across the generations. In underdeveloped places, poverty is usually the cause of social and personal breakdown. But, in today's advanced societies, it is more likely to be the effect.[8]

I have thought and written about these challenges for most of my adult life. I have never believed that we could fully unwind the welfare state. The modern market economy and the society it has shaped leave family and community life too fragile to do entirely without it. Politically, there is little support for the notion beyond hard-core libertarians anyway. Nevertheless, as prime minister, I sought to bring a decentralizing agenda to our governance and our social policies.

I did this not only because of the long-term importance of a healthy civil society, but also because of the persistent underperformance of bureaucratic social policy. Civil society, harnessed creatively, can achieve things that the state cannot. It is notable, for instance, that refugees who are privately sponsored by church or community groups in Canada have much better economic and social outcomes than those supported by the government. And not just by a little bit.[9]

That was just one example. We also matched funds with diaspora communities and development agencies for major humanitarian assistance initiatives. We partnered with local homelessness groups to deal with the problems of housing and mental illness. We supported community-based organizations to promote literacy and education. We gave tax credits for children's athletic and artistic programs. We also made some progress with Social Impact Bonds, which provide capital to social-service non-profits and charities based on outcomes. In fact, where a case for social intervention exists, conservatives everywhere ought to make it the default position to use local and community service delivery.

Restoring civil society will not happen overnight or easily. One of the focuses has to be on younger generations. Research consistently shows that our "civic core"—that is, those who disproportionately donate and volunteer—is rapidly aging.[10] It should not be. These are activities that have great personal rewards—far beyond the kind of vapid virtue signalling that the left encourages among the young.

As I have said, I believe in the importance of nationalism, especially in the age of globalization. But the solution to the excesses of globalism is not a top-down, all-knowing, centralized nation-state. That would just substitute distant bureaucratic decisions with slightly closer, yet still distant, bureaucratic decisions. This is why conservatives need to support a positive role for civil society and localism as well.

=

Yet conservatives need to do more than just advocate for moderate nationalism and a healthy civil society. We also need to articulate a strong, principled opposition to one of the most extreme traits of modern left-liberal thought—alienism.

What is "alienism?" It is, in effect, the opposite of "nativism." Nativism is an extreme nationalism, championing an ethnocentric or even racial superiority. Alienism is an extreme anti-nationalism that, on the other side, reflexively identifies with other cultures and denigrates one's own society.

The term is not generally familiar, because this extremism is rather novel and bizarre. Nativism, though repulsive, is at least understandable—human self-centredness being what it is. Alienism is the unique by-product of modern circumstances, including a wealthy and disconnected global elite.

As we have seen, cosmopolitan Anywheres are partly attracted to globalism by the sense that it liberates them from responsibility toward national and local communities. Alienism helps justify such irresponsibility by disparaging such societies, their histories, their cultures, and the mainstream, the Somewheres, of their population.

To give an example: In 2007, Gordon Brown told the Labour Party conference that he would aim to "create British jobs for British workers." It immediately provoked a maelstrom in left-wing circles.[11] Why exactly? Is not one of the principal responsibilities of a leader to encourage economic policies that benefit one's own citizens? In the eyes of left-wing alienists, apparently not.

But the critics went much further. Brown was actually accused of "pandering to fascists"[12] by wanting to serve his country's citizens. Really? Setting aside the inherent nonsense of the accusation, I know Gordon Brown personally; he is a fine human being and public servant. No one who knows him would remotely consider the former prime minister a fascist.

The 2018 budget shutdown in Washington by congressional Democrats is another case of this ideology. Of course, there was miscalculation on both sides. That said, the refusal to extend spending on programs that served the wider population, in order to advance the interests of illegal immigrants, was just politically dumb.

The politics are so self-evidently bad that the act can only be explained by a deep-seated alienism.

An even more sinister example: Watch any left-liberal media coverage of a jihadist terrorist attack in the West. Then count the short number of minutes before the subject is changed to "Islamophobia." Think about that. We have a deadly example of Islamic extremism, but the inclination on the left is to come up with a concept that essentially blames our society, that blames the victim. This is a basic characteristic of much press coverage and political analysis. The underlying presumption is that Western, especially American, society is the source of all problems. It has no role but to be "fixed" and to learn from other, non-Western, cultures.

Such self-loathing (or, more accurately, loathing of everyone else in one's own society) is increasingly a fundamental element of modern progressivism. And it is just plain wrong. Openness to other cultures is a good thing, but we do have every reason to believe in our own. There are reasons why millions want to join Western societies. Our societies have made mistakes, but they also adapt in response to such errors, and learn from them in ways that are unique. And, of course, our mistakes are dwarfed by our achievements. Western populations, no less than any other, are right to be nationalistic, proud, and patriotic about our countries.

This alienism makes left-liberalism very vulnerable. This kind of thinking is way off-side with the vast majority of working people. Trump's victory was not just a reaction to the perceived apologetic tenor of the Obama years. It was also a backlash to the lectures that Americans—especially unemployed American workers and struggling American communities—receive regularly from well-heeled progressives. Yet modern liberals are deeply wedded to such narratives. They actually believe that a critical view of one's own society is a mark of moral superiority.

Conservatives do not have to do much to benefit from this. There is no need to embrace actual nativists or Trump's crudeness to distinguish ourselves from the left on such questions. We simply have to be proud of our own societies and actually like our own peoples. Because, frankly, too many on the other side just do not.

===

The key point is that nationalism and globalization need not be diametric opposites. They can, properly managed, be complementary. Contrary to what some claim, we do not have to reject one to embrace the other. It is not a case of take it or leave it.

For the foreseeable future, it will remain the role of the nation-state to weigh the policy choices that confront us. Whether those are about domestic economic policy, trade, or foreign affairs, how we respond should be rooted in national priorities, a healthy global orientation, and, above all, the interests of our working families.

The same is true of that most contentious element of all these current controversies—immigration.

10
THE PATH TO CITIZENSHIP

As a member of Parliament, well before I became prime minister, I attended Canadian citizenship ceremonies. They are inspirational events for new and old citizens alike. To see your country passionately embraced by newcomers from all corners of the earth is truly uplifting.

My views on the desirability of immigration are well known. Good immigration policy can support economic growth. It can also contribute much more. Immigrants can be an overwhelmingly positive source of social energy and cultural diversity. And immigration, done right, can attract strong political support.

Bad immigration policy and its cousin, bad multiculturalism policy, too often mask important truths. Immigrants want to succeed and immigrants want to belong. For the most part, they come to Western societies optimistically and enthusiastically. They do not wish to stagnate in segregated, old-world ghettoes, but to launch new lives for themselves and their future generations. In fact, whether we are talking about issues of security and crime, or family and faith, or hard work and entrepreneurship, the instinctive value systems of immigrants are often far closer to those of Western conservatives than to those of the liberal left.

We can enact immigration policies that unite those immigrant aspirations with the values of our citizens. Make immigration legal, secure, and, in the main, economically driven, and it will have high levels of public confidence. Politically, that was my experience.

My experience of the other side's approach is the opposite, whether we are talking about the low-wage corporatism of liberals or the "open-borders" alienism of the hard left. Reward illegal immigration, ignore real security threats, have no economic focus, encourage the kind of multiculturalism that fractures society, and two things will happen. Immigrants will often fail and immigration will be widely resented.

That is the direction in which too many developed countries have been going. That is why they are experiencing a backlash. It is time for policy-makers in those countries to stop pretending the backlash is all bigotry and to stop blaming the public for the mistakes they have made. Instead, it is time to use the populist uprising as an opportunity to undertake reforms that better serve our economies and our societies.

=

What should an immigration system look like if it is to be successful and popular? The answer, in short, is that it must be rooted in the broader interests of our countries and our citizens.

Under a series of able ministers—Monte Solberg, Diane Finley, Jason Kenney, and Chris Alexander—my government enacted a series of reforms to Canada's immigration system. The reforms were numerous and we were still making them at the end of our tenure. They contributed to a better functioning immigration system, but just as importantly, they created an environment in which a large part of the population was prepared to support one of the most open immigration policies in the world. Simply put: positive reforms enabled us to maintain relatively high levels of public support for relatively high levels of immigration.

There are some basic principles that ought to inform immigration policy. The first is the consent of the governed. Sovereign countries have a right and a responsibility to determine their own criteria for immigration, naturalization, and citizenship. Choices about who can join and under what conditions are among the most fundamental functions of a sovereign nation.

This is undoubtedly one of the principal reasons why the Brexit proposal was so powerful for many Britons. Successive U.K. administrations had relinquished more and more of the basic roles of sovereignty to the Brussels bureaucracy and its rules. The population simply wanted to regain control.

Indistinguishable from the consent of the governed is an affirmation of the rule of law. Immigration cannot be an exception to the principle that there be fair, firm, and equitable enforcement of the law. Entering a country illegally is an inherent act of bad faith, no matter what its motivations. And failure to enforce immigration laws is a dereliction of any office holder's basic duties.

Policy-makers from elsewhere have often asked me how they can get the public to accept the large-scale illegal or irregular migration they have experienced in their countries. My answer is simple: "You can't." One of the things that has made Canadians so accepting of immigration is that our system has always been overwhelmingly legal in character. Even if people do not like some aspects of immigration, they are likely to be tolerant of outcomes if the system functions according to the rules of a democratic society. Take that away and the most problematic aspects of immigration will colour the citizenry's perspective on all immigration.

This, by the way, is an area in which the views of citizens and most new arrivals are in sync. Illegal immigration is especially unfair to those who obey the law and go through the proper process to enter a country, a process that is rarely simple. Legal immigrants will be allies to conservatives who want to crack down on illegal migration. After all, as "nations of immigrants" we are mostly descendants of those who came in legally. And recent immigrants are among the most sensitive about and most opposed to those who break the rules and jump the queue.[1]

The second principle that should inform immigration policy is security. This is the core responsibility of any government and it must outrank any other economic, social, or humanitarian considerations. Of course, secure borders matter from the perspective of ensuring sovereignty. But the practical concern is much greater, especially in an era of global jihadism.

This issue is particularly acute in Europe, where migrant policies have sometimes had tragic results. The open-borders approaches in some countries have allowed the entry of bad actors, fuelling crime and, in France and Belgium, resulting in terrorist attacks. Other nations have toughened border measures in response. The escalation of conflict between elitist disconnection and populist reaction threatens to unravel decades of progress on continental mobility.

The third principle must be the economic interests of the country. Now, a wealthy and generous country will make certain judgments based on humanitarian or refugee considerations. Nevertheless, economic criteria must be paramount, and should never be disregarded or overridden. I am referring to the economic interests of the bulk of regular people, not to more narrow business, corporate, or investor interests. An immigration policy that becomes too far removed from its citizens' broader economic concerns will almost certainly lose public support over time.

As noted earlier, this is a central problem in the current immigration policies of the United States and many other Western countries. They are experiencing the large-scale importation of low-skilled labour just as wages for such labour have stagnated or are under sustained downward pressure. In these jurisdictions, there is a corresponding resistance to even the most in-demand, high-skilled immigrants. This should not be surprising. It is what happens when inappropriate immigration policies are pursued—support for all immigration plummets.

The final critical element for immigration policy is the effective integration of newcomers. Of course, this follows from some of the principles above. Immigrants who operate outside the law, or whose skills are not needed, are far less likely to successfully adapt to their new country. The opposite is also true. Where immigrants are willingly and lawfully accepted, where they embrace national values and institutions and learn the language, and where their relationships broaden beyond their own cultural communities, both they and the wider society profit immensely. Good public policy can encourage such outcomes.

═══

Canada is widely cited as a model for successful immigration and integration policies. Therefore, it makes some sense to look at our system and, in particular, how I believe it was strengthened during my government's decade in office.

Our system has long had three principal immigration streams— the economic class; the family class; and the humanitarian class, which broadly includes refugees. The first is a merit-based "points" approach and has been a significant part of the Canadian system for some time. The key objective of our reforms was to make this element more important than ever.

Our reforms took the economic class up to roughly 60 per cent of the immigration total. We wanted to make the system more economically sensitive, more clearly driven by longer-term labour-market demand. This explains why, when the global recession hit in 2008–2009, we had no need to radically cut immigration, as previous Canadian governments had done.

What specifically did we do? I will not go through the details of every reform and its underlying goals. But there are two key things that could easily transcend the Canadian context and have broader application.

One set of reforms shifted the system to a greater focus on jobs. The goal was to prioritize applicants who had already found and accepted a job. This involves a basic market test and ensures that newcomers will have the means to support themselves and their families.

Granting foreign students the ability to get relevant work experience helped us achieve this objective. Creating a job pipeline for people already pursuing advanced education in one's own country seems obvious. To this day, I remain amazed that we actually had to institute such a reform.

Another aspect of this job-related set of reforms was foreign credentials recognition. If we need an immigrant's skills and knowledge, we do not want that ability to contribute wrapped up in the red tape of accreditation processes. In Canada, much of the jurisdiction in this area belongs to the provinces and has been farmed out to professional bodies. Nevertheless, we established a federal Foreign Credential Referrals Office and worked with those other players. Much progress was made, just as plenty of work still needs to be done.

The second set of changes involved giving greater discretion to the provinces to select immigrants. Orienting decisions to immediate labour-market requirements is not as easy as it sounds. Devolving some of these decisions to lower levels of government can encourage a better understanding of the needs on the ground.

This decentralized portion of the process grew over time. Applications for this stream increased steadily and the criteria generally maintained a focus on work and citizenship. It is true that some provinces began drifting from economic immigration toward family considerations or temporary foreign workers. Such trends have to be monitored. Nonetheless, Canada's more regionalized system has served us well and could be adapted to other federal states.

These were important transformations that moved the system away from a growing emphasis on the family class (or what American debate would describe as "chain migration"). Our opponents were convinced that any kind of reduction to the family-class stream, even a relative cut, would be politically fatal. This stems from the belief that immigration policy must be rooted strictly in narrow ethnic politics, not wider economic or national needs.

Such naked political calculus proved to be largely false. Our Conservative government saw its support among New Canadians increase significantly over much of the tenure of our government. In fact, our majority government in 2011 was driven in large part by the Conservative Party's historic support in immigrant communities.

The prevailing political wisdom was wrong because it missed something big. Yes, individual newcomers may place a high priority on bringing in family members. But immigrants as a whole quickly come to identify with the general economic needs of the communities they move to. In fact, whether they are entrepreneurs or workers, immigrants are often disproportionately affected by economic and employment conditions and significantly more sensitive to them.

The point is, we could make these economic-oriented reforms and tighten the system's parameters without risking the political support of New Canadians. On the contrary, they were among the strongest supporters of many of our government's immigration reforms.

This is an important lesson—one that I will come back to. Many of the political fears conservatives have about immigration are based on our experiences with bad immigration policy—policy designed for narrow political ends. Change those policies and most newcomers will respond just as well as the native-born.

═══

Our immigration reforms had many other dimensions. For example, we also took steps to strengthen the system's integrity and place a greater emphasis on successful integration. These moves were certainly not incompatible with our economic emphasis, but they were distinct. They were driven by the understanding that support for immigration is enhanced by addressing problems, not denying them.

This is why, for instance, we acted quickly when Sri Lankan migrant smuggler boats started arriving in British Columbia in 2010. We had witnessed Australia's challenges and were determined that such problems would not come to Canada. Jason Kenney and others acted effectively to make sure Canada did not become a preferred destination for such irregular, mass migration. Australia had to wait for the arrival of Tony Abbott's government to finally do what was necessary there.[2]

I also talked earlier about our challenges with temporary foreign workers. As the magnitude of the problem became apparent, I moved to drastically reduce the size of the program. My intention was to phase out the low-skilled side of it altogether. Creating a category of low-wage workers who have no right to look for other jobs and no way of becoming members of society is not employment; it is servitude. It should be unacceptable in a country like Canada.

There were numerous, smaller examples of my government dealing with legitimate public concerns. We worked to detect fraudulent marriages, just as we cracked down on crooked immigration consultants. Again, these were steps that gave both our citizens and immigrants themselves greater confidence in the system.

One issue we tackled was restoring the value of Canadian citizenship. For reasons that no official could ever reasonably explain to me, Canada had embarked on a policy that encouraged the issuance of citizenship as an end in itself. Even today there are literally millions of citizenship holders around the world who have little connection to Canada and never did. Yet, when in jeopardy, they may well call upon the services of the Government of Canada. Thus, we changed the rules so that permanent residents who wished to obtain citizenship were required be in the country for four of the six years prior to application. This would demonstrate a clear and sustained commitment to Canada.

We also strengthened language requirements. Applicants between the ages of fourteen and sixty-four had to pass national language (English or French) tests. This dramatically increases the probability of successful integration. It is something virtually every serious organization agrees with—from the UN High Commissioner for Refugees[3] to the European Commission[4] to the Heritage Foundation.[5]

Shockingly, few Western countries are doing a good job at requiring language competencies or supporting language training. There is strong evidence, for example, that many U.S. immigrants speak English more poorly than those who immigrated in the past.[6] So such reforms make eminent sense even if (or perhaps because) our left-wing successors have watered them down.

We also rewrote the citizenship guide used for Canada's citizenship test, expanding the sections on Canadian history, institutions, and values. This change was more controversial than it ought to have been. Our "values" focus was on things that are almost universally accepted in Canada.

We included, for example, a passage about how female genital mutilation, honour killings, and other similar customs constitute "barbaric cultural practices." Alienism should not turn us away from being unapologetic about our basic societal expectations. Only politicians seeking support in the darkest corners object to stating such basic norms.

Another controversial move was curtailing public benefits for refugees where they had become more generous than those available to regular Canadians. This was done out of a basic sense of fairness. These are the kinds of actions we must take if we are to maintain public support for humanitarian-based migration, although the issue is bigger than that. Policy-makers in the developed world must ensure that their social-welfare programming does not become a magnet for bogus refugee claims. Lose sight of this standard and immigration consultants advocating "shopping around" strategies will quickly appear on the scene.

That is a long list of reforms—and there were plenty more. I have already mentioned, for instance, the greater emphasis we put on privately supporting refugees. But what is important about all these reforms is that they served broad Canadian interests. They were part of a pro-immigration policy.

The reforms were also generally supported by immigrants themselves. Part of the reason for this was that we had built credibility with immigrant communities. We met them. We talked to them. We knew what they would support and what they would not, just as they understood our objectives.[7]

===

Immigration needs and politics differ by country, but I believe some broader lessons can be gleaned from the Canadian experience. Even President Trump, who is frequently labelled as anti-immigration, cites Canada's fairly open approach as a model to emulate.[8]

The real key to a successful immigration system is not one particular policy or another. It is convincing the public that the system serves the national interest, that it is not injurious to working people, and that it is administered with integrity and consistency. Provide those assurances and the public can have trust and confidence in even fairly high levels of immigration. Without those things, immigration policy will be extremely challenging.

By contrast, the usual political methodology—asking legislatures to address particular problems in the system—is not effective. For instance, there may be legitimate issues pertaining to employer needs or well-established, long-term illegal residents. However, if the public does not trust the system, or the motives of those advocating specific reforms, such proposals will go nowhere.

Therefore, the only viable approach to such issues is a holistic one that addresses broader public concerns. To start with, illegal immigration simply must be confronted. It contributes to lawlessness, crime, and a lack of confidence in government in general and in the immigration system in particular. That leads me to Donald Trump's "wall."

A physical barrier to entry can be effective and may have its place. That said, we must understand that it alone will not remotely solve the problem. People go north to the United States, or to Europe for that matter, because opportunities there are so much greater than what they have at home. The vast majority of such people seek only to work and, often, to send money back to relatives in their native lands. But, in economic terms, the arrival of such immigrants is, for the destination countries, just a problem of "supply." It cannot be effectively addressed unless something is also done to address "demand."

The demand comes from employers who willingly hire illegal workers. If they do not suffer consequences for doing so, the problem cannot be fixed. Otherwise, the best scenario is that illegal workers will return almost as quickly as they are removed. Yet even Trump seems unwilling to face this issue. If conservatives are to be champions of immigration reform, the issue of illegal immigration, including the role of businesses big and small, must be tackled and it must be tackled honestly.

Yet conservatives must also advocate a vision of legal immigration. Such a vision needs to put skills, education, and language ability at the top of the list, and it must move family connections further down. More than anything, it must stop trying to tell the public that large-scale, low-skilled immigration makes sense in today's advanced economies. It simply does not.

==

There is perhaps nothing more illustrative of the problems of traditional approaches to immigration policy than the current U.S. debate about the "Deferred Action for Childhood Arrivals" policy.

As most people know, the "dreamers" are illegal aliens who were brought to America as children by their parents and who have grown up in the States. They are not only highly "Americanized"; they often have little or no connection or affinity to their country of citizenship.

To put it in context, the DACA issue essentially pertains to about 0.2 per cent of the U.S. population and around 7 per cent of total illegal immigrants.[9] Reasonable people can debate how to handle these individuals. But notice the time and energy dedicated to what is a relatively small and comparatively unusual aspect of the immigration issue. It speaks to the lengths to which the left will go to purposefully draw attention away from the core issue.

One of the central messages from the American electorate in 2016 was the need to rethink and reform immigration policy. Working-class citizens in particular were demanding that immigration better reflect their needs and interests. At the top of their list was the demand to do something to stop illegal immigration.

Nonetheless, as we approach the fall 2018 mid-term elections in the U.S., it looks like Washington has not listened. Instead, we have had an all-out attempt to put the focus on a side issue. True, we have witnessed some progress on the number of deportations from the U.S.[10] Beyond that, however, progress on strengthening enforcement has been limited. And, as the DACA debate shows, liberals have doubled down in prioritizing the interests of non-citizens over citizens.

Conservatives must not make the same mistake. The lessons of 1986 must not be forgotten. President Reagan's Immigration Reform and Control Act was a good-faith compromise aimed at strengthening the immigration enforcement regime in exchange for amnesty for illegal aliens. Roughly three million illegal immigrants were regularized as a result.[11] But commitments regarding enforcement, particularly those related to employers who use illegal immigration, failed to materialize.

Some have tried to minimize this problem. Former Pennsylvania senator Arlen Specter once declared that "since the '86 law did not succeed, people are understandably skeptical. But this time, things are different."[12] Yes, they are different, Senator—they are worse.

Fortunately, the White House has shown that it understands this. It has proposed to increase the number of DACA beneficiaries to two million in exchange for greater border enforcement and economically oriented changes to legal immigration. This approach is both generous and comprehensive.[13] It seeks the reforms real people want now while steering toward a better system in the future.

The key point is that dealing with the dreamers before, or without, sufficient measures to strangle illegal migration and reform the legal system would be a serious error. Whatever Trump and the Republicans do, they must not fall for that kind of a ploy again.

═══

As I have said, conservatives must also lead the way in building a strong and positive immigration system. If the liberal left leads the way—whether it is the low-wage liberalism of some business leaders, or the open-borders alienism of the hard left, or the no-welfare delusion of libertarians—the public will continue to become more categorically anti-immigration. We are seeing this in one developed country after another.

This is far from a strawman argument. We are witnessing the liberal left openly embrace extreme views on immigration as a matter of principle. The "open-borders" position is the clearest example. The U.S. Democratic Party's ever more explicit support for illegal immigration is another. Headlines such as "Everyone's wrong on immigration: Open borders are the only way to defeat Trump and build a better world"[14] and "The efficient, egalitarian, libertarian, utilitarian way to double world GDP" are evidence of this fixation.[15]

Even some moderate liberals are starting to see the dangers in such reckless approaches.[16] Frankly, it is remarkable how far and fast liberal views on these issues have moved left from even the positions of the Obama administration. This illustrates the rise in the power of elite globalism on the conventional left. It also demonstrates the decline in the influence of the labour movement and its working-class constituencies. Such radicalization should provide conservatives with a great political opportunity as the U.S. approaches the next presidential electoral cycle.

However, for that to be so, this radicalization on the left cannot be met by an inverse radicalization on the right. We no more need "closed doors" than we need "open borders." As in any other policy area, we conservatives need to draw on the sound lessons of human experience here. One of those is that a well-run immigration system generally attracts good, energetic, and ambitious people. That is how many of our countries in the West were built.

I have said it before, but let me say it again: I was struck throughout my political career by how conservative in character most immigrants are. They bring the family values and faith lessons of their older societies to the opportunities of a new world. They come to join and contribute. Some of the most powerful experiences I had as prime minister were in seeing the pride of New Canadians in their adopted country.

I also think that part of the problem is that the liberal left, through the media, has often managed to convince conservatives that their view of immigrants is the real one. They see immigrants as separate from the wider society, victims of its overwhelming bigotry, wanting to deconstruct it, unprepared to integrate, and forced to rely on their political sponsors for their rights. All of this reflects the left-wing world view—their take on our society, their dislike of it, their desire to fracture it, their obsession about tearing it down and rebuilding it from scratch. But, in my experience, that is rarely the vision of the immigrant.

Go to their communities. Yes, you will see differences. And, truthfully, even with the best of multiculturalism policies—ones that emphasize shared narratives and social solidarity—those differences will change our societies to some degree. But immigrants will change more. Because they want to succeed. They did not leave their age-old roots back home to be part of a small, isolated group at the other end of the world. They want to be part of our society.

That is what Canadian conservatives experienced when we met with immigrants. What immigrants experienced was equally good—respect. We did not try to tell them that they owed us their votes. Because we instituted meritorious immigration policies, we could not do that. We did not "let them in," as liberals often claim; they warranted admission. They have as much political choice as the rest of us.

==

I have spent much of this chapter talking about the dangers of, and the solutions to, illegal immigration. Let me end by emphasizing the most critical characteristic of a good immigration system. It is, as I experienced at those inspiring ceremonies, one that provides "the path to citizenship."

The term has been badly misused in the context of current American immigration debate. When people choose to enter the country illegally, they have not taken the citizenship path. Likewise, if our society offers a system of temporary foreign workers, which is often suggested as a substitute for illegal immigration, then we have not taken the citizenship path either. Those paths are the wrong paths.

Where immigration is successful, as it has been historically in countries like Canada and the United States, it is about the path to citizenship. The immigrant comes with a fundamental, life-altering aspiration. All the promise that our society has to offer is seen again through new eyes. In proving him- or herself through a bona fide process, the immigrant is accepted into the family. Our nations are not disrupted; they are enriched.

This has been, more often than not, our experience over the generations. It is true that abuse, dysfunction, and radicalism have overtaken a lot of immigration thinking and policy on the left. But we conservatives must never become blind to the tremendous nation-building possibilities that a sound, legal, and welcoming immigration system offers.

11

THE BUSINESS OF BUSINESS

I believe the current populist wave requires politicians and policy-makers to rethink how we are using markets, trade, globalization, and immigration. We need to understand that these things are not ends in themselves, but only tools. The goal must be to deploy their strengths in ways that further the interests of our working citizens. The past chapters have set out my thoughts on why and how we should do this.

But it would be wrong to think that this is only about politics or that other institutions have no role to play. The business sector is particularly crucial. A better environment for business cannot be created without the help of business. Yet the fact is that many present developments are being driven in part by the public's negative perceptions of business.

It is not uncommon for business leaders to decry populism. For instance, a late 2016 survey of chief financial officers found that 41 per cent believed that Brexit and the Trump election were negatively affecting their businesses.[1] Ray Dalio, the founder and co-chief investment officer at Bridgewater Associates, has described populism as "the most important issue globally."[2]

This is both right and wrong. The current populism is clearly disruptive to business. But a failure to respond constructively to it is the much bigger threat. Trump, the Brexiteers, and many populists may advocate policies that some businesses do not like. However, unlike their left-wing alternatives, they are not anti-business or anti-market in principle.

This is why it is so essential to get our response right.

———

The question then is this: What should business do in this era of upheaval to protect its interests and promote better outcomes? The answer starts with something that I was told early in my political career by my former minister Greg Thompson: "No one cares what you think until they think you care."

Many business leaders presume that their record of success will earn them the public's ear and the public's regard. This is only true, however, if the public believes these leaders care about them. If they do not, business executives may well get the public's attention, but they will get a reaction opposite to the one intended.

There are any number of cases of people in high-profile positions giving the public well-intentioned advice that is perceived as (or that actually is) condescending or threatening. The result is a public backlash. This, by the way, is far from strictly a business-related phenomenon. Celebrities are often the most notorious examples.

Therefore, the first lesson is this: if business leaders cannot articulate how their positions benefit the broader welfare of society, then they should not engage in public advocacy, period. Of course, CEOs must remain focused on their company's interests, but those interests must be clearly aligned with wider public interests whenever public advocacy is contemplated.

In this regard, Donald Trump's success deserves some study. He turned his business credentials into an effective tool of influence. He managed to convince many people to listen to him, especially on economic matters, because he talked in terms that convinced those people he cared about them.

Without a doubt, part of Trump's success was his television background. During the 2016 primaries, one Republican complained to me, "Trump is not really a great businessman; he just plays one on TV." But that missed the point entirely. It did not matter whether Trump was as rich or as successful as he claimed. He was richer and more successful than the people he was talking to. And he was talking to them, not at them.

====

The key, then, is trust. Rightly or wrongly, business is generally not trusted today. In fact, businesspeople are only slightly more trusted than politicians and the media.[3] This is hardly good company.

The turn of the current century marked the high point for trust and confidence in business and markets. A 2001 U.S. poll showed that Americans trusted business twice as much as government or the media. More than 60 per cent of respondents said that they trusted Microsoft to "do the right thing." That was nearly double the response in favour of Amnesty International.[4]

It has been downhill ever since. Trust in business declined in two-thirds of the twenty-seven markets covered in a 2015 World Economic Forum Survey. It is now below 50 per cent in fourteen markets.[5] The most recent survey is even more damning. Sixty-three percent said CEOs are not at all or only somewhat credible. Only government officials scored less trustworthy.[6]

I have already discussed some of the factors behind this decline in trust. The spark that lit the powder keg was the global financial crisis. A combination of banking malfeasance and corporate rescue packages badly tarnished the image of corporate leaders and the wealthy in many countries. For instance, five years after the crisis, three-quarters of Americans still said they opposed the Wall Street bailout.[7] As I have said, it is hard to overstate the effects of this episode on people's perceptions of business and markets.

The slow recovery from the crisis and longer-term negative trends for ordinary people have doubtlessly exacerbated this view. It is notable that as of 2014 more than 60 per cent of Americans believed that the economy had not yet recovered.[8] This way of thinking reflects realities like middle-income wage stagnation and labour's declining share of national income across the OECD.[9] Such factors account for growing public concerns about business behaviour and public anxiety about market forces. We see this in poll after poll, including in the overwhelming view that corporations pay too little tax.[10]

I should point out that, beyond even the financial crisis, there have been some spectacular examples of bad corporate behaviour fuelling some of these trends. They range from Enron at the beginning of the century, to the recent price-fixing of bread by grocery retailers in Canada, to the growing power and abuse of personal information by digital data companies. As a consequence of such events, the percentage of Americans who say that they have "very little" trust in large corporations is at its second-highest level since 1973, only slightly below the level during the 2007–2008 banking crisis.[11]

This decline in trust is hugely problematic. It ought to worry business leaders. It worries me because trust matters well beyond the confines of the corporation. High-trust societies are richer and happier. Why? Because a certain level of trust is an essential ingredient of prosperity. It enables efficient trade and commerce by allowing the market to function better. Low levels of trust generate more laws to regulate business activities and practices. The result is higher transaction costs. Think of lack of trust as an indirect tax on all forms of economic activity. Not surprisingly, low-trust societies tend to be poor.[12]

Put simply, there is an inverse relationship between trust and government intervention in the marketplace. Less trust leads to more rules and regulations, which have to be developed, implemented, litigated, and enforced. Think of the Sarbanes–Oxley Act following the Enron scandal, or the Dodd–Frank reforms after the U.S. financial crisis, or the recently launched Royal Commission into Australia's banking system. As laws, mandates, rules, and regulations multiply, investment, entrepreneurialism, innovation, and job creation suffer.

By the way, there is no point in getting angry with politicians who undertake these measures. In such circumstances, they are only and inevitably following public opinion. If the public is untrusting or even hostile toward business, then public policy is going to reflect that. Indeed, the risk is that this mutates into a much bigger problem, in the form of political leaders who are ideologically anti-business. For them, targeting untrusted corporations and their unpopular executives is like fishing with dynamite. It is easy, and it works.

So, my second lesson is this: be cautious about trying to lobby policy-makers on particular laws and regulations within a generally distrustful political environment. If the cause of the rules is a lack of public trust, such an approach will likely fail. Simply put, businesses must instead focus on the issue of declining trust.

===

Therefore, job number one for business is rebuilding trust. This is not about "making people listen." It is about behaving in a way that will generate confidence in business. And it is not a task that can be outsourced.

So, what should business be doing to rebuild trust and protect itself in increasingly volatile public-opinion environments? It starts with a realistic understanding of the situation. That is to say, business's image is a problem, but it is not a catastrophe. Even with the deterioration that has occurred, the private sector is still somewhat more trusted by the public than are government, politicians, or media.[13]

No doubt part of the problem has been communications. Many businesses have not been focused on it and, as a consequence, are not always adept at it. This will have to change. In the era of social media, public opinion can form very quickly and very unexpectedly. You have to be proactive and effective around your own messages, including your products, your services, and your motives.

Fortunately, the same forces that make public opinion so volatile also provide the means to get your own messages out quickly and to target them appropriately. And there is no excuse for not doing so. The tools at our disposal today are highly advanced. A business can have direct, immediate communication with everyone who matters or may potentially matter to it. Customers, suppliers, investors, communities of operations and their leaders, no matter where in the world, are keystrokes away from hearing directly from an enterprise. These are a business's networks, which it must turn into intimate relationships.

But just as close relationships can be developed with real partners through targeted, modern means of communication, it is also important, where possible, to avoid older, untargeted media. Now, I recognize that some business is so broad and public in nature that this may be unavoidable. However, generally speaking, just as close networks can assist in the modern age, unfocused communications are unlikely to do so. Traditional "public" media is dying. As it is doing so, its worst traits are becoming exaggerated—the escalation of conflict, the sensationalizing of speculation, opinion masquerading as news. None of this is about information, negotiation, and partnership—all of the things on which good business depends. Avoid these channels when possible. As the legendary hockey coach and manager Scotty Bowman once said to me about traditional media, "If you are doing well, you don't need them. If you are doing badly, they won't help you."

Once again, Donald Trump's stunning victories over the political establishments of both parties is a case in point. He broke with conventional wisdom on communications. He often avoided, and even deliberately antagonized, traditional media. Instead, his campaign focused on using technology to speak directly to his target populations.[14] Given the nature of Trump's coverage within traditional media, he could not have succeeded otherwise.

Ironically, many businesses looking to communicate better in this volatile age turn, if not to traditional media outlets, then to individuals whom they employed. I am frequently surprised to see former journalists, or even political or social activists, staffing key communications and outreach functions in corporations. Oftentimes their advice will be to reach out to the ideological enemies of business—"story"-seeking journalists, committed socialists, environmental fundamentalists, and the like. Nothing could be worse. These people will never be friends. They will, at best, take a business off its game.

The lessons here are clear. Immediate business networks, including customers, suppliers, investors, community leaders, and so on, matter immensely. A company must know them, serve them, and not betray them. Broader public opinion—of the vast "middle" who neither worship nor detest business—should also be kept in mind for appropriate communications. But, if a business's communications or public-relations or government-affairs people are telling it to focus on its opponents, then it should beware.

═══

This is the most important lesson about communications: it is not all about communications. There are some with my political background who think it is. As they like to say: "Perception is reality." In my experience, that may have some truth, but it is a short-term view. Over time, reality has a way of becoming perception.

In the long haul, to have good communications, the real, underlying business story needs to be a genuinely good one—successful, ethical, socially beneficial. If it is not, a communications strategy is probably not going to save it. There is no substitute for doing the things on which good business leaders build good brands and good reputations.

Let me return to an example I mentioned earlier—Canada's Temporary Foreign Workers Program. Having a policy of filling local jobs with foreigners instead of Canadians was not, substantively, a good story. No communications strategy was going to make it a good one. Episodes like this can be brand-damaging experiences.

I talked about the importance of relationships for doing business today. Like it or not, in an era of unprecedented disruption, relationships are indispensable for doing business. Market rules and contract legalities are not going to be enough. We have always understood this to be true in the developing world, but it is also becoming so in advanced economies. If, for example, you operate in a community, but you are unwilling to hire in that community, you risk suffering political and social consequences.

So, the lesson is that, in genuinely bad cases, do not fiddle with communications; change the policy. To return to my example, there are options for employers in tight labour markets. One is the good old-fashioned market way—paying people more. Another is to look at groups who are traditionally underrepresented in the job market.

Such a strategy can make for good business and good communications, especially where labour market outcomes for some groups continue to be relatively poor. For instance, even with the currently strong U.S. economic performance, the unemployment rate for African Americans remains more than double that of white workers.[15] Similar gaps exist in Canada among Indigenous peoples and others.[16]

Most governments put in place initiatives that target such groups for training and support, and that welcome business participation in these efforts.[17] As prime minister, I always found it rewarding to meet employees and employers who were benefiting from such measures. There are particularly positive examples of firms finding ways to accommodate workers with mental or physical disabilities.[18] The up-front costs of adaptation are frequently trivial compared to the value and loyalty of people who would not otherwise have such opportunities. Walgreens,[19] Northrop Grumman,[20] and Procter & Gamble[21] are just a few companies that have done this. But there are countless others.

===

We need to deal with business communications not only as they relate to a firm's activities, but also in the context of broader social and political advocacy. Business has a role to play with regard to public issues and public policy. Indeed, it is imperative that, as significant contributors to employment and the economy, companies and business groups contribute to discussion and debate on these matters.

That said, a business needs to think hard about its activism. Again, a company's public relations, government relations, and communications people—perhaps even its CEO—may well have strong views on certain issues. Still, some important questions need to be asked. Are those issues and the positions on them important to the interests of the business? Are they widely shared by its investors, workers, and customers? If the answer to these questions is not clearly "yes," then a business needs to ask itself why it would be speaking out on them.

The target markets matter. If such advocacy could alienate significant parts of a business's existing network, then it is foolish. Yet this kind of communications happens all the time. The better advice comes from Michael Jordan. When asked why he did not engage in political issues, he was direct: "Republicans buy sneakers too."[22]

In general, it is a risky business proposition to advocate on issues that divide and inflame the public. This is not just a matter of avoiding being on the wrong side of one's own people, of them seeing you as hostile or condescending or out-of-touch with them. It is also about recognizing the growing revulsion that many people feel, regardless of their personal political orientation, to the hyper-politicization of society. Ordinary folks do not live and think about politics every waking minute. They want to be able to turn on the television or have a conversation without being constantly subjected to political messaging or the latest manifestation of identity politics. Even the NFL has had to discover this the hard way.

The lesson here is that broader social and political advocacy should typically be focused on issues that are not divisive in an ideological or partisan sense. There are dozens of worthy causes that are widely supported across social, political, and religious groups. The fights against disease and poverty or support for local community projects are perfect examples. There is no shortage of such causes. In other words, if a company is intent on being in the public square, it would be better for it to reinforce social solidarity than to accentuate social division.

One particular area where business should be wary of activism is that of the environment. Needless to say, there are a lot of conservation and preservation initiatives that can garner non-contentious support. However, environmental groups who attack certain industries—and who therefore put people's jobs at risk—should be avoided like the plague. They may get kudos in the media, but one can bet that they are intensely disliked on the ground by many ordinary working people.

This leads me to mention carbon taxes. I am surprised by the number of businesspeople who believe it is a good idea to champion a carbon tax. Such thinking reflects a dangerous disconnect between elite consensus and regular citizens.

Carbon taxes are widely unpopular and become more so once people actually have to pay them. Political parties, including mine, have won elections just by opposing a carbon tax. The reason is simple. It is ordinary voters who pay carbon taxes. Worse, they are attractive to governments simply because they raise revenue reliably. In other words, they are not effective at reducing emissions.[23] For business, which is invariably seeking general or specific tax relief, there is little that can be more toxic for reputation than advocating higher taxes for others. It is the antithesis of rebuilding public trust.

=====

Of all the advice I want to convey here, this is the most important: a company must not lose sight of its central mission. The core value proposition of the commercial sector is its ability to make money by creating products, services, jobs, and growth. Social contributions should not be diminished, but business must not go too far down the path of social affirmation. Profits need to be made. And provided that laws are obeyed and ethics are practised, profits are a good thing. Businesses that stray too far from this fundamental purpose will fail regardless of their image. The saying that "the business of business is business" is ignored at one's peril.[24]

The most exciting business contributions to our society come through innovation—success at producing new industries, technologies, and employment possibilities. The profit motive drives these, creating a powerful incentive for businesses to produce things that contribute to our society. As a former adviser to the Bill and Melinda Gates Foundation puts it, corporate social responsibility activities "should not be a distraction from the business of making money, but rather a complement to it."[25]

The Gates Foundation is one of the most impactful social agencies in the world. But this adviser was not talking about the foundation; he was talking about business itself. Much commercial activity uses capital, expertise, and the marketplace to advance solutions to social challenges. There are many great examples of this today. Think of IEX—the "Flash Boys exchange"—which is attempting to reform the practices of stock markets in the aftermath of the global financial crisis. Look at Bristol Braille Technology, whose new e-reader, Canute, is the world's first multi-line Braille e-reader. Or consider Uber's efforts to involve deaf and hearing-impaired drivers in its business model. Such drivers have now completed over one million trips.[26]

I cannot emphasize this point strongly enough. Joe Lonsdale, a San Francisco–based venture capitalist whom I have gotten to know in recent years, frequently stresses that "many of humanity's most intractable challenges will only be solved through market-driven innovation."[27] He is right. From health care to the energy sector, we see, over and over again, that global innovation comes largely out of private companies pursuing profit in competitive markets.

As I said, markets are a tool. This is how we use that tool for success. The profit motive produces genius and agility. And it consistently proves itself to be a better and more productive motivator than coercion or centralized planning. It is what business does best.

======

I started this chapter by warning about the risks of not rebuilding the lost public trust in business and markets. I want to end there as well. A failure to constructively respond to contemporary populist concerns threatens serious consequences. It will lead to a more vola-tile and less hospitable public environment in the short-term. Longer-term, it could lead to much more fundamental challenges to the basic economic framework.

You do not have to take my word for it. Listen to what politicians like Bernie Sanders or Jeremy Corbyn are saying. They do not just think that markets require better governance. They believe that mar-kets are inherently corrupt and must be subordinated to government power. They advocate a return to the unapologetic socialism of the Cold War era—and we all know how that ended.[28]

Some may dismiss the ultimate political success of such actors as implausible. I bet they similarly dismissed the populist outcomes of 2016. The fact is that every piece of data since the last British election suggests Corbyn is in striking distance of becoming prime minister. Likewise, the U.S. Democratic Party is on a course to elect a far-left "progressive" as its candidate for president. Given Trump's uneven performance, such an individual also stands a good chance of winning. A "burn-it-all-down" message may have more resonance than analysts think, especially if the current pop-ulist insurgence from the right fails and mainstream conservatives do not adapt.

In such an environment, business needs to communicate its values, its benefits, and its concerns to the public. Business will, of course, have its own interests to defend. But it must also put effort into matters of wider public interest. It must also avoid doubling down on the liberal predisposition to corporatism.

What economists call "rent seeking" may seem like a good idea in the short-term. It can be difficult to resist the temptation to use the levers of government to access subsidies or exclude competitors through regulations. But these kinds of cozy business–government relationships inevitably serve to exacerbate public suspicions and dis-trust. This should be understandable. Corporatism can easily feed a perception of inequity between those who are rich and well con-nected, and those who are not.

Too often, when business and government get together, it is at the expense of taxpayers, consumers, or workers. Think of the Wall Street deregulation and subsequent bailouts. Remember the renewable-energy subsidy schemes. Look at the most unpopular aspects of immigration policy. The mixing of public policy and private interests may appeal to political actors and business leaders, but it usually ends up tarnishing both.

===

In many ways, the advice I am offering to business amounts to getting back to basics. Invest and hire, contribute positively to the communities in which you operate, and make sure the people you touch know about your enterprise and what you are doing for them. Also, of course, distance your own firm from unnecessary controversy and bad business behaviour.

In other words, take the lack of trust in the current business environment seriously. Fail to respond to it positively, and it will get worse. But act in a way that deserves trust, and trust will return.

EPILOGUE

There are many people who seem to believe that they can wish the events of 2016 away. Influential elements in the United Kingdom—those sarcastically labelled "Remoaners"—look to reverse the Brexit vote or, at a minimum, to get a deal with the European Union that apes the U.K.'s current relationship. In the United States, much of the anti-Trump narrative displays a desire to deny the simple reality that he won because enough people in enough places willingly voted for him. The underlying hope in both cases is that things will "go back" to the way they were.

But that is not the trend. Populist, nationalist, and anti-establishment movements are continuing to grow. Just look at Europe. A late 2017 analysis of twenty-two European countries revealed that support for such parties is at its highest level in at least three decades.[1] Recent votes in the Netherlands, the U.K., France, Germany, Italy, and elsewhere have seen such options make significant gains at the expense of the traditional centre left and centre right. In some cases, they are close to taking power. Even where they are not, they are often rendering the formation of government coalitions lengthy and laborious.

Despite the Trump administration's internal dysfunction and external enemies, its re-election remains plausible. Indeed, its grip on the Republican electorate has actually strengthened. The Democratic alternative is also drifting ever further from the party's establishment. Down-ballot, populist, and non-traditional candidates are making gains. And, outside the party structures, old "mainstream" commentators are being supplanted by new voices with large online followings.[2]

My diagnosis is simple: the populist trend will not stop until the issues driving it are being effectively addressed. True, these new populist alternatives may ultimately fall short in the eyes of many of their followers. But human nature teaches us that those so disappointed are unlikely to "go back." For the reasons they left in the first place, they will move on to the next new thing.

====

The more I have looked at these big political surprises, the less I think they should have been surprises. We are living in an age of disruption of unprecedented scale, scope, and pace. Whole industries are coming and going. New technologies are remaking jobs and communities. Cultural norms are shifting almost randomly. Seemingly no institution or aspect of traditional life is immune.

It is understandable—even predictable—that ordinary working people would be anxious under such circumstances. On top of that, the data indicates that significant numbers of them are experiencing serious, negative consequences. Thus, broad social disruption is morphing into widespread political disruption as night follows day. And this trend will continue if traditional political options, both conservative and liberal, double down on existing approaches.

This book has set out my views on how conservatives should respond. We must build an agenda that, while based on our enduring values, is focused on the issues that working people and their families are facing today. It must especially address populist concerns about market economics, trade, globalization, and immigration.

In addressing these things, conservatives should remain pro-market, pro-trade, pro-globalization, and pro-immigration at heart. Going in a completely opposite direction in any of these areas would be a big mistake with serious ramifications. But being pro-market does not mean that all regulations should be dismantled or that governments should never intervene. Being pro-trade does not imply that any commercial arrangement is a good one. Being pro-globalization should not entail abdicating loyalty or responsibility to our countries. And being pro-immigration should never mean sanctioning the erasure of our borders or ignoring the interests of our citizens.

In short, being pro-something is not an excuse for ideological tangents. It is about getting back to pragmatic applications of our values and away from theoretical abstraction in our actions. When it comes to public policy, it is about rolling up our sleeves, knowing the details, and monitoring the impacts on people's lives. Yes, we have a general orientation, but that does not render all choices obvious or easy.

One can call this "populist conservatism" or "applied conservatism," but, to my mind, it is really just conservatism. Conservatism, dating back to Edmund Burke, was never about ideological rigidity. In fact, Burke was rejecting the philosophical dogmatism that marked other thinkers and thinking in his era—including, by the way, those who reflexively defended the status quo. Conservatism is about seeing the world as it is and applying the lessons of experience to new challenges. It is inherently populist in the sense that it is necessarily concerned with people rather than theories.

This approach describes how many modern conservatives have governed, including no less a leader than Ronald Reagan himself. It has been modelled more recently by others, including the government I led, through many policies that can be adapted to other advanced countries. That applies not just to traditional conservative issues, but also to family policy, labour-market training, income inequality, homelessness, and numerous other contemporary challenges.

═══

While I know where I want our societies to go, I cannot predict with certainty what direction we will ultimately take. We can, however, make some reasonable guesses about what is possible and what is not. And that takes me back to this deepening social division between the Anywheres and the Somewheres.

It is commonplace to hear establishment voices—the Anywheres of today's world—muse that the political market frequently does not offer them what they desire. They want an option that is economically market-oriented, but strongly committed to being socially "progressive" on a wide range of values questions. So why does this choice so often fail to emerge?

There is actually a pretty clear answer to that question. The evidence shows that economically market-oriented, socially progressive voters do not really exist. More accurately, they are a small percentage of the population.[3] But they dominate much public debate and news analysis.[4]

The reason such people are small in number should be intuitive. In a world of rapid and unpredictable change, ordinary people are vulnerable. An economically market-oriented, socially progressive philosophy essentially proposes to dismantle all the certainties and protections of their lives. It is, on its face, the ideology of a wealthy, mobile elite—people who are not vulnerable or at least think they are not.

On the other hand, electors who are economically interventionist and socially conservative are numerous. They constitute a considerable portion of those whom we call the Somewheres. Yet, until Trump, the U.K. Independence Party, and the populists came along, *nobody* spoke for them. On the contrary, in those countries establishment conservatives ignored them and establishment liberals denounced them. That is what opened the door to the populists of the right. They have appealed to such voters by emphasizing their conservative social values while being less committed to market economics.

So, if today's political insurgency fails and conservatives have not adapted, the torch will likely pass to populists of the left. They will appeal to these Somewheres through socialist economics. They may come from new parties that abandon the extremes of social progressivism, like Italy's Five Star Movement. But, given the tiny numbers of elite liberals, they may be socialists who just take over traditional centre-left parties, as Jeremy Corbyn has done in Britain and Bernie Sanders almost did in America.

I have made my views pretty clear on that option throughout this book. A return to socialist economics in this day and age would take Western countries on a certain, irreversible, long-term decline.

So, the right path is the conservative path. And the right conservative path is not to condemn or bemoan today's populism. It is to listen to it and to learn from it.

═══

Conservative columnist Charles Krauthammer once wrote that "if we don't get politics right, everything else risks extinction."[5] It seems a tad hyperbolic, but bad human relations do have a way of wrecking everything else. Stable and responsive politics is an essential ingredient to a strong, dynamic society. Places where politics fail invariably experience broader economic and social challenges. Politics is not everything, but it is essential in providing a framework for individuals, families, and communities to succeed.

Politics today is exceptionally troubled. That is a great irony. This is an exciting time to be alive. We are in an age of greater wealth for more people than ever before. We are living longer and healthier lives. Technological developments are opening doors to human possibilities and choices that were science fiction only a short time ago. Objectively speaking, we have reasons for optimism that, compared with those of any previous generation, are truly without precedent.

But to seize these opportunities, we need to ensure that we get our politics right. Whether you accept the analysis and prescriptions in this book or not, I hope it will cause you to think about what we can do in this age of disruption to get it right—right here, right now.

NOTES

PROLOGUE

1   William Watson, "Who knew? Turns out the Harper government was actually terrific for wage growth," *Financial Post*, November 16, 2017. http://business .financialpost.com/opinion/william-watson-turns-out-the-harper-government-was-actually-terrific-for-wage-growth.

2   Trump posed this question following the December 2015 terrorist attack in San Bernardino, California. Tessa Berenson, "Donald Trump calls for 'complete shutdown' of Muslim entry into the U.S.," *Time*, December 7, 2015. http://time.com/4139476/donald-trump-shutdown-muslim-immigration.

3   Quoted in Craig Shirley, "The GOP has lost its way. Here's how it can return to its roots," *Washington Post*, November 9, 2012. https://www.washingtonpost. com/opinions/the-republican-party-must-go-back-to-go-forward/2012/11/09 /55947d9e-2a87-11e2-96b6-8e6a7524553f_story.html?utm_term=.3f5534d6bda4.

1. IN PLAIN SIGHT

1   Karlyn Bowman, "Who were Donald Trump's voters? Now we know," *Forbes*, June 23, 2017. https://www.forbes.com/sites/bowmanmarsico/2017/06/23/ who-were-donald-trumps-voters-now-we-know/#1f8290283894.

2   According to one survey, the odds a person who says he or she is struggling financially supports Trump are about twice as high as someone who says he or she is comfortable or moving up economically. Max Ehrenfreund and Scott Clement, "Economic and racial anxiety: Two separate forces driving support for Donald Trump," *Washington Post*, March 22, 2016. https://www.washingtonpost.com /news/wonk/wp/2016/03/22/economic-anxiety-and-racial-anxiety-two-separate -forces-driving-support-for-donald-trump/?utm_term=.b994dc5479d3. Similarly, another report found that Trump supporters might not be experiencing acute economic distress, but they are living in places that lack economic opportunity— including for the next generation. Max Ehrenfreund and Jeff Guo, "A massive new study debunks a widespread theory for Donald Trump's success," *Washington Post*, August 12, 2016. https://www.washingtonpost.com/news /wonk/wp/2016/08/12/a-massive-new-study-debunks-a-widespread-theory -for-donald-trumps-success/?utm_term=.1b277de31724.

3   Robert Putnam, *Our Kids: The American Dream in Crisis* (New York: Simon & Schuster, 2015).

4   Derek Thompson, "Who are Donald Trump's supporters, really?" *The Atlantic*, March 1, 2016. https://www.theatlantic.com/politics/archive/2016/03/who -are-donald-trumps-supporters-really/471714.

5   Daron Acemoglu et al., "Import competition and the great US employment sag of the 2000s," *Journal of Labor Economics*, Vol. 34, No. S1 (January 2016), pp. S141–S198. https://economics.mit.edu/files/9811; Susan Adams, "New job loss study: The less educated are the hardest hit," *Forbes*, August 16, 2012. https://www.forbes.com/sites/susanadams/2012/08/16/new-job-loss-study -the-less-educated-are-the-hardest-hit/#475fb2982aab.

6   Thompson, "Who are Donald Trump's supporters, really?" https://www.theatlantic.com/politics/archive/2016/03/who-are-donald- trumps-supporters-really/471714; Daniel Wright and Rachel Case, "Leave voters felt ignored and left behind as post-Brexit poll reveals extent of economic division across UK," Joseph Rowntree Foundation, July 15, 2016. https://www.jrf.org.uk/press/leave-voters-felt-ignored-and-left-behind-post -brexit-poll-reveals-extent-economic-division.

7   Jeff Stein, "The Bernie voters who defected to Trump, explained by a political scientist," Vox, August 24, 2017. https://www.vox.com/policy-and-politics /2017/8/24/16194086/bernie-trump-voters-study.

8   Bruce Newsome, "Stop blaming 'populism' for everything," Berkeley Blog, December 11, 2016. http://blogs.berkeley.edu/2016/12/11/populism-cant-be -blamed-for-everything.

9   Robert D. Atkinson and John Wu, "False alarmism: Technological disruption and the U.S. labor market, 1850–2015," ITIF @Work Series, May 2017. http://www2.itif.org/2017-false-alarmism-technological-disruption.pdf.

10 Charles Hirschman and Elizabeth Mogford, "Immigration and the American industrial revolution from 1880 to 1920," *Social Science Research*, Vol. 38, No. 4 (December 2009). https://www.ncbi.nlm.nih.gov/pmc/articles/PMC2760060.

11 Lawrence F. Katz and Robert A. Margo, "Technical change and the relative demand for skilled labor: The United States in historical perspective," in Leah Platt Boustan, Carola Frydman, and Robert A. Margo (eds.), *Human Capital in History: The American Record* (Chicago: University of Chicago Press, 2014). http://www.nber.org/chapters/c12888.pdf; Daron Acemoglu, "Technical change, inequality, and the labor market," *Journal of Economic Literature*, Vol. 40, No. 1 (March 2002), pp. 7–72. https://economics.mit.edu/files/4124.

12 Douglas A. Irwin, "Explaining America's surge in manufactured exports, 1880–

1913," NBER Working Paper, July 23, 2001. https://www.dartmouth.edu
/~dirwin/docs/Surge3wp.pdf.

13 Ruchir Sharma, "When borders close," *New York Times*, November 12, 2016.
https://www.nytimes.com/2016/11/13/opinion/sunday/when-borders-close
.html?mcubz=1.

14 Henry Littlefield, "*The Wizard of Oz*: Parable on populism," *American Quarterly*,
Vol. 16, No. 1 (Spring 1964), pp. 47–58. http://www.shsu.edu/his_rtc/2014
_FALL/Wizard_of_Oz_Littlefield.pdf.

15 Sean Speer, "Canada's participation rate could be the populist 'canary in the
coal mine,'" *Globe and Mail*, February 2, 2017. http://www.macdonaldlaurier.ca
/why-ottawa-should-worry-over-canadas-stagnant-labour-force-participation-
rate-sean-speer-in-the-globe.

16 Nicholas Eberstadt, *Men without Work: America's Invisible Crisis* (West
Conshohocken, PA: Templeton Press, 2016).

17 Eleanor Krause and Isabel Sawhill, "What we know and don't know about
declining labor force participation: A review," Brookings Institution, May 2017.
https://www.brookings.edu/wp-content/uploads/2017/05/ccf_20170517
_declining_labor_force_participation_sawhill1.pdf.

18 Josh Biven, "Using standard models to benchmark the costs of globalization
for American workers without a college degree," Economic Policy Institute,
March 22, 2013. http://www.epi.org/publication/standard-models-benchmark
-costs-globalization.

19 Gary Burtless, "New analysis turns up surprise on long-term wage trends,"
Real Clear Markets, May 17, 2017. https://www.brookings.edu/opinions
/new-analysis-turns-up-surprise-on-long-term-wage-trends.

2. SEEDS OF DISCORD

1 Author unknown, "The 2008 housing crisis displaced more Americans than
the 1930s Dust Bowl," National Center for Policy Analysis, May 11, 2015.
http://www.ncpathinktank.org/sub/dpd/index.php?Article_ID=25643; Sarah
Childress, "How much did the financial crisis cost?" PBS Frontline, May 13,
2012. http://www.pbs.org/wgbh/frontline/article/how-much-did-the
-financial-crisis-cost.

2 Author unknown, "G-20 declaration of the Summit on Financial Markets
and the World Economy," G20 Research Group, November 15, 2008.
http://www.g20.utoronto.ca/2008/2008declaration1115.html.

3 Thomas Kochan, "Wages and the social contract," *Prospect Magazine*, April 22,
2007. http://prospect.org/article/wages-and-social-contract.

4   Various factors contributed to the post-war boom, and most were outside the
    planners' control, such as post-war reconstruction, North America's post-war
    comparative advantage, technological advancements, large-scale demand for
    non-college educated workers, pent-up consumer demand, and the baby
    boom. Petros Milionis and Tamas Vonyo, "Reconstruction dynamics: The
    impact of World War II on post-war economic growth," Working Paper,
    August 2015; William H. Branson, Herbert Giersch, and Peter G. Peterson,
    "Trends in United States international trade and investment since World War
    II," in Martin Feldstein (ed.), *The American Economy in Transition* (Chicago:
    University of Chicago Press, 1980), p. 183; Martin Neil Baily and Jacob Funk
    Kirkegaard, *Transforming the European Economy* (Washington: PIIE, 2004), pp.
    35–36; Cecil Bohanon, "Economic recovery: Lessons from the post–World
    War II period," Mercatus on Policy, August 2012. https://www.mercatus.org/
    system/files/PostWWII_Recovery_Bohanon_MOP112-%281%29-copy.pdf;
    Livio Di Matteo, *A Federal Fiscal History: Canada, 1867–2017*, Fraser Institute,
    February 2017. https://www.fraserinstitute.org/sites/default/files/federal
    -fiscal-history-canada-1867-2017.pdf; and Brian Lee Crowley, *Fearful Symmetry:
    The Fall and Rise of Canada's Founding Values* (Toronto: Key Porter Books, 2009).

5   Stephen J. Harper, "The political business cycle and fiscal policy in Canada,"
    Master's thesis, University of Calgary, 1991. https://dspace.ucalgary.ca/bitstream
    /handle/1880/24345/1991_Harper.pdf;jsessionid=C57054E7BBF64754AF770
    E208D7FF590?sequence=1.

6   Ed Feulner, "Reagan's tax-cutting legacy," Heritage Commentary, July 24, 2015.
    http://www.heritage.org/taxes/commentary/reagans-tax-cutting-legacy.

7   Chris Edwards, "Margaret Thatcher's privatization legacy," *Cato Journal*, Vol. 37,
    No. 1 (Winter 2017). https://object.cato.org/sites/cato.org/files/serials
    /files/cato-journal/2017/2/cj-v37n1-7.pdf.

8   President William J. Clinton, "Address before a joint session of the Congress
    on the State of the Union," The American Presidency Project, January 23,
    1996. http://www.presidency.ucsb.edu/ws/?pid=53091.

9   As he observed: "What we may be witnessing is not just the end of the Cold
    War, or the passing of a particular period of post-war history, but the end of
    history as such: that is, the end point of mankind's ideological evolution and
    the universalization of Western liberal democracy as the final form of human
    government." Francis Fukuyama, "The end of history?" *National Interest*, No.
    16 (Summer 1989), pp. 3–18. https://ps321.community.uaf.edu/files/2012/10
    /Fukuyama-End-of-history-article.pdf.

10 Moises Naim, "Fads and fashion in economic reforms: Washington consensus
    or Washington confusion?" *Foreign Policy Magazine*, October 26, 1999. https://
    www.imf.org/external/pubs/ft/seminar/1999/reforms/Naim.HTM.

11 Daniel Yergin with Joseph Stanislaw, *The Commanding Heights: The Battle for the World Economy* (New York: Touchstone, 2002), p. 277.

12 I am referring to Adam Michnik. Michnik was raised as a communist in Poland, but had a long record of anti-communist activities before becoming involved in the replacement of the Soviet-backed regime by Lech Walesa's Solidarity movement in 1989. Andrei Shleifer and Daniel Treisman, "Normal countries: The East 25 years after communism," Working Paper, September 12, 2014. https://scholar.harvard.edu/files/shleifer/files/normal_countries _draft_sept_12_annotated.pdf.

13 International Monetary Fund Staff, "Recovery from the Asian crisis and the role of the IMF," International Monetary Fund, June 2000. https://www.imf. org/external/np/exr/ib/2000/062300.htm.

14 Jay Shambaugh and Ryan Nunn, "Why wages aren't growing in America," *Harvard Business Review*, October 24, 2017. https://www.brookings.edu/opinions/why -wages-arent-growing-in-america; Author unknown, "The big freeze," *The Economist*, September 6, 2014. https://www.economist.com/news/finance-and -economics/21615589-throughout-rich-world-wages-are-stuck-big-freeze.

15 Austrian economist Joseph Schumpeter popularized the concept of "creative destruction" in the twentieth century. Joseph A. Schumpeter, *Capitalism, Socialism and Democracy* (New York: Harper, 1975) [orig. pub. 1942].

3. GOOD DEALS AND BAD DEALS

1 Ana Swanson, "U.S.–China trade deficit hits record, fueling trade fight," *New York Times*, February 6, 2018. https://www.nytimes.com/2018/02/06 /us/politics/us-china-trade-deficit.html.

2 Lauren Carroll, "Trump: Since China joined WTO, U.S. has lost 60,000 factories," Politifact, March 24, 2017. http://www.politifact.com/truth-o-meter/statements /2017/mar/24/donald-trump/trump-china-joined-wto-us-has-lost-60000-factories.

3 John Tamney, "There are no 'myths' or exceptions about free trade: It's always unrelentingly good," *Forbes*, October 9, 2016. https://www.forbes.com/sites/ johntamny/2016/10/09/there-are-no-myths-or-exceptions-to-free-trade-its- always-unrelentingly-good/#37da139a26a1.

4 James K. Glassman, "The blessings of free trade," Cato Institute, May 1, 1998. https://www.cato.org/publications/trade-briefing-paper/blessings-free-trade.

5 Ricardo's theory of "comparative advantage" turned two hundred in 2017. His idea that every country, no matter how advanced or underdeveloped in its labour productivity, would benefit from trade with others is not self-explanatory and has been called a "difficult idea" by different trade economists. The description here does not capture all of its nuances. For more, see Douglas Irwin,

"Ricardo and comparative advantage at 200," Vox: CEPR's Policy Portal, April 19, 2017. https://voxeu.org/article/ricardo-and-comparative-advantage-200.

6   This theory, named after economists Wolfgang Stolper and Paul Samuelson, brought new economic models to better understand the welfare consequences of free trade. It basically finds that in a world with two goods and two factors of production, one of the factors—the one that is "scarce"—will end up worse off as a result of opening up to international trade. For more, see Dani Rodrik, "Populism and the economics of globalization," *Journal of International Business Policy*, 2018. https://drodrik.scholar.harvard.edu/files/dani-rodrik/files/populism_and_the_economics_of_globalization.pdf.

7   Curt Tarnoff, "The Marshall Plan: 70th anniversary," CRS Insight, April 18, 2017. https://fas.org/sgp/crs/row/IN10688.pdf.

8   Ibid.

9   Department of Finance Canada, "Fiscal reference tables," September 2017. https://www.fin.gc.ca/frt-trf/2017/frt-trf-17-eng.pdf.

10 Department of Foreign Affairs and International Trade Press Release, "January 1 marks 20th anniversary of North American Free Trade Agreement," Government of Canada, January 1, 2014. https://www.canada.ca/en/news/archive/2014/01/january-1-marks-20th-anniversary-north-american-free-trade-agreement.html. NAFTA was something else as well. It quickly became one of the best examples of highly integrated global supply chains. Put simply, modern trade is not just between say, British cloth and Portuguese wine. Instead, production may be subdivided into multiple parts and processes crossing many international boundaries. A North American car now moves between the three countries as many as six or seven times during the assembly process. In fact, in the era of multinational business, few products can be purely identified with one particular country. This is a feature of modern global trade that makes it distinctive from previous eras of globalization.

11 International Bank for Reconstruction and Development/World Bank Staff, *Global Economic Prospects: Trade, Regionalism, and Development*, International Bank for Reconstruction aand Development/World Bank Staff, 2005. http://siteresources.worldbank.org/INTGEP2005/Resources/gep2005.pdf.

12 Matthew Smith, "International survey: Globalisation is still seen as a force for good in the world," YouGovUK, November 2016. https://yougov.co.uk/news/2016/11/17/international-survey.

13 Author unknown, "Poverty overview," World Bank, accessed on May 24, 2017. http://www.worldbank.org/en/topic/poverty/overview.

14 David Dollar and Aart Kraay, "Growth is good for the poor," *Journal of Economic Growth*, Vol. 7, Issue 3 (September 2002), pp. 195–225.

https://siteresourcesqa.worldbank.org/INTRES/Resources/469232
-1107449512766/Growth_is_Good_for_Poor_Journal_Article.pdf; David
Dollar and Aart Kraay, "Trade, growth, and poverty," *The Economic Journal*,
Vol. 114 (February 2004), pp. F22–49. https://papers.ssrn.com/sol3/papers.
cfm?abstract_id=632684.

15 Kemal Derviş, "Convergence, interdependence and divergence," *Finance and
Development* (International Monetary Fund), Vol. 49, No. 3 (September 2012).
http://www.imf.org/external/pubs/ft/fandd/2012/09/dervis.htm.

16 Robert E. Scott, "Manufacturing job losses," Economic Policy Institute, Issue
Brief #402, August 11, 2015. https://www.epi.org/publication/manufacturing
-job-loss-trade-not-productivity-is-the-culprit.

17 Robert E. Scott, "Heading south: U.S.–Mexico trade and job displacement
after NAFTA," Economic Policy Institute, Briefing Paper #308, May 3, 2011.
http://www.epi.org/publication/heading_south_u-s-mexico_trade_and_job
_displacement_after_nafta1.

18 Gary Clyde Hufbauer, Cathleen Cimino-Isaacs, and Tyler Moran, "NAFTA at
20: Misleading charges and positive achievements," Peterson Institute for
International Economics, May 2014. https://piie.com/publications/policy-briefs
/nafta-20-misleading-charges-and-positive-achievements.

19 World Bank Staff, "Manufactures exports (% of merchandise exports)," World
Bank, accessed on April 2, 2018. https://data.worldbank.org/indicator/TX
.VAL.MANF.ZS.UN.

20 Alexander Murray, *The Effect of Import Competition on Employment in Canada:
Evidence from the "China Shock"*, Centre for the Study of Living Standards, July
2017. http://www.csls.ca/reports/csls2017-03.pdf.

21 David Autor, David Dorn, and Gordon Hanson, "The China shock: Learning
from labor market adjustment to large changes in trade," *Annual Review of
Economics*, Vol. 8, No. 1 (2016). https://www.annualreviews.org/doi/10.1146
/annurev-economics-080315-015041.

22 David Autor et al., "Importing political polarization? The electoral consequences
of rising trade exposure," David Dorn, December 2017. http://www.ddorn.net
/papers/ADHM-PoliticalPolarization.pdf.

23 David Autor et al., "A note on the effect of rising trade exposure on the 2016
presidential election," David Dorn, March 2, 2017. https://gps.ucsd.edu/
_files/faculty/hanson/hanson_research_TrumpVote-032017.pdf.

24 Italo Colantone and Piero Stanig, "Global competition and Brexit," Baffi
Carefin Centre, September 2016. https://papers.ssrn.com/sol3/papers.

cfm?abstract_id=2870313 and https://www.washingtonpost.com/news
/monkey-cage/wp/2016/07/07/the-real-reason-the-u-k-voted-for-brexit
-economics-not-identity/?utm_term=.a64991ce3566.

25 He famously called protectionism a form of "destructionism" in his 1988 State
of the Union. See transcript of his 1988 State of the Union Address, *New York
Times*, January 25, 1988. https://www.nytimes.com/1988/01/26/us/transcript-
of-reagan-s-state-of-the-union-message-to-nation.html.

26 Speech by President Ronald Reagan, September 23, 1985.
https://reaganlibrary.archives.gov/archives/speeches/1985/92385a.htm.

27 Republican Party Platforms, "Republican Party platform of 1988," The
American Presidency Project, August 16, 1988. http://www.presidency.ucsb.
edu/ws/index.php?pid=25846.

28 Republican Party Platforms, "Republican Party platform of 1992," The
American Presidency Project, August 17, 1992. http://www.presidency.ucsb.
edu/ws/?pid=25847.

4. SOMEWHERES AND ANYWHERES

1 Here are some examples: Author unknown, "President Xi's Davos speech receives
warm applause," *The Telegraph*, January 24, 2017. https://www.telegraph.co.uk
/news/world/china-watch/business/president-xi-davos-speech-receives-warm
-applause; Author unknown, "Laughed at and booed, Donald Trump spoke at
Davos," Euronews, January 26, 2018. http://www.euronews.com/2018/01/26
/laughed-at-and-booed-donald-trump-spoke-at-davos; and Mihir Sharma, "Modi
disappoints at Davos," Bloomberg, January 23, 2018. https://www.bloomberg
.com/view/articles/2018-01-24/modi-disappoints-at-davos.

2 It is important to note the rise of Emmanuel Macron and his new party, *La
République en Marche*. It is not nationalist or populist. Indeed, it is globalist and
elitist. Like the wave of other new parties in Europe, it has come about in part
because of the growing weakness of the traditional centre left and centre right.
However, it is principally a reaction to the rise of the extreme *Front National*.

3 "What do I mean by "globalism" and "globalists?" Harvard political scientist
Joseph Nye has described globalism as a "world which is characterized by networks of connections that span multi-continental distances." Globalists are
those who belong to such global networks and have commercial or personal
interests in the hyperglobalization that Harvard economist Dani Rodrik refers to.
I would extend the use of the term to those who may not belong to these networks but support the worldview of those who do. See Joseph Nye, "What are
the different spheres of globalism—and how are they affected by globalization?"
The Globalist, April 15, 2002. https://www.theglobalist.com/globalism-versus
-globalization/, and Dani Rodrik, "Populism and the economics of globalization,"

Journal of International Business Policy, 2018. https://drodrik.scholar.harvard.edu /files/dani-rodrik/files/populism_and_the_economics_of_globalization.pdf.

4 A 2017 Pew poll in France, Germany, Greece, Hungary, Italy, the Netherlands, Poland, Spain, and Sweden found that a median of 53 per cent of respondents across the nine European countries support having their own national referendums on continued EU membership. Bruce Stokes, Richard Wike, and Dorothy Manevich, "Post-Brexit, Europeans more favorable toward EU," Pew Research Center, June 15, 2017. www.pewglobal.org/2017/06/15/post-brexit-europeans -more-favorable-toward-eu. See also: Alina Polyakova and Neil Fligstein, "Is European integration causing Europe to become more nationalist?: Evidence from the recent financial crisis," Paper presented to the American Sociological Association, New York City, August 9–12, 2013. http://sociology.berkeley.edu /sites/default/files/faculty/fligstein/European%20Id%203.1.pdf. The authors find that "the number of people who have primarily a European identity is quite small and has not increased much in the past 20 years."

5 Alex Roarty, "Democrats say they now know exactly why Clinton lost," McClatchy DC Bureau, May 1, 2016. http://www.mcclatchydc.com/news /politics-government/article147475484.html.

6 David Goodhart, *The Road to Somewhere: The Populist Revolt and the Future of Politics* (London: Oxford University Press, 2017).

7 Rebecca Savransky, "Majority of Americans approves of Trump's 'America First' message," *The Hill*, January 25, 2017. http://thehill.com/homenews/ administration/316005-poll-majority-of-americans-approve-of-trumps-america -first-message.

8 Cited in Goodhart, *The Road to Somewhere*, p. 7.

9 President Bill Clinton, "Remarks at Vietnam National University in Hanoi, Vietnam," The American Presidency Project, November 17, 2000. http://www.presidency.ucsb.edu/ws/?pid=1038.

10 "Transcript: Donald Trump's foreign policy speech," *New York Times*, April 27, 2016. https://www.nytimes.com/2016/04/28/us/politics/transcript-trump -foreign-policy.html.

11 Daniel Hannan's EU Rally Speech, May 31, 2016. http://www.brugesgroup.com /events/10-events/1182-eu-referendum-rally-hammersmith.

5. WALLS AND DOORS

1 A.E. Challinor, "Canada's immigration policy: A focus on human capital," Migration Policy Institute, September 15, 2011. https://www.migrationpolicy. org/article/canadas-immigration-policy-focus-human-capital; Department of

Citizenship and Immigration, *Annual Report to Parliament on Immigration, 2014*. https://www.canada.ca/en/immigration-refugees-citizenship/corporate /publications-manuals/annual-report-parliament-immigration-2014.html.

2 Author unknown, "Temporary foreign workers being approved too easily, expert warns," CBC News, April 15, 2014. http://www.cbc.ca/news/canada/ temporary-foreign-workers-being-approved-too-easily-expert-warns-1.2609653.

3 Citizenship and Immigration Canada, "Facts & figures 2015: Immigration over-view—temporary residents—annual IRCC updates," accessed on August 12, 2017. http://open.canada.ca/data/en/dataset/052642bb-3fd9-4828-b608-c81dff7e539c.

4 According to Citizenship and Immigration Canada's "Facts and figures 2014: Immigrant overview—temporary residents," there were 76,786 TFWP work permit holders in 2002; 165,121 in 2012; and 177,704 in 2014. Citizenship and Immigration Canada, "Facts and figures 2014: Immigrant overview—temporary residents," accessed on August 12, 2017. http://www.cic.gc.ca/english/pdf/2014-Facts-Figures-Temporary.pdf.

5 Democratic Party Platforms, "2000 Democratic Party platform," August 14, 2000. Available at: http://www.presidency.ucsb.edu/ws/index.php?pid=29612.

6 Democratic Platform Committee, "2016 Democratic Party platform," July 8–9, 2016. http://s3.amazonaws.com/uploads.democrats.org/Downloads/2016_DNC_Platform.pdf.

7 Republican Party, Growth and Opportunity Project, March 15, 2013. http://apps.washingtonpost.com/g/documents/politics/republican -national-committees-growth-and-opportunity-project-report/380/.

8 Seung Min Kim, "Senate passes immigration bill," Politico, June 27, 2013. https://www.politico.com/story/2013/06/immigration-bill-2013-senate -passes-093530.

9 Jeffrey M. Jones, "In U.S., worry about illegal immigration steady," Gallup News, March 20, 2017. http://news.gallup.com/poll/206681/worry-illegal -immigration-steady.aspx.

10 Andrew Dugan, "In U.S., six in ten dissatisfied with immigration levels," Gallup News, January 29, 2015. http://news.gallup.com/poll/181313 /dissatisfied-immigration-levels.aspx.

11 Steven Shepard, "Poll: Voters support Trump-backed immigration bill," Politico, September 8, 2017. https://www.politico.com/story/2017/08/09 /trump-immigration-polls-241422.

12 John Gramlich, "Trump voters want to build the wall, but are more divided on other immigration questions," Pew Research Center, November 29, 2016. http://www.pewresearch.org/fact-tank/2016/11/29/trump-voters-want-to -build-the-wall-but-are-more-divided-on-other-immigration-questions.

13 David Lauter, "Trump's voters agree with him on cutting legal immigration levels," *LA Times*, October 1, 2016. http://www.latimes.com/politics/la-na-pol -immigration-poll-20161001-snap-story.html.

14 Michael Barone, "Trump the disruptor: Convention chaos may be a feature, not a bug," *New York Post*, July 22, 2016. http://nypost.com/2016/07/22/trump -the-disruptor-convention-chaos-may-be-a-feature-not-a-bug.

15 Much of this history is drawn from Vincent J. Cannato, "Our evolving immi- gration policy," *National Affairs*, Fall 2012. https://www.nationalaffairs.com /publications/detail/our-evolving-immigration-policy.

16 Michael Fix and Jeffrey S. Passel, "Immigration and immigrants," Urban Institute, May 1994. http://webarchive.urban.org/UploadedPDF/305184 _immigration_immigrants.pdf.

17 Carl Cannon, "Immigration and the rise & fall of the Know-Nothing Party," Real Clear Politics, February 18, 2015. https://www.realclearpolitics.com/ articles/2015/02/18/immigration_and_the_rise__fall_of_the_know-nothing _party_125649.html.

18 U.S. Census Bureau, "The foreign-born population in the United States," date unknown. https://www.census.gov/newsroom/pdf/cspan_fb_slides.pdf.

19 Cannato, "Our evolving immigration policy." https://www.nationalaffairs.com /publications/detail/our-evolving-immigration-policy. Michael Barone, "We've Been Here Before: America and the Dynamics of Immigration," Modern Age, No. 3, Vol. 58 (Summer 2016). https://home.isi.org/we've- been-here-beforebr-america-and-dynamics-immigration.

20 Lyndon B. Johnson, "President Lyndon B. Johnson's remarks at the signing of the immigration bill Liberty Island, New York," October 3, 1965. http://www.lbjlibrary.org/lyndon-baines-johnson/timeline/lbj-on-immigration.

21 Muzaffar Chishti, Faye Hipsman, and Isabel Ball, "Fifty years on, the 1965 Immi- gration and Nationality Act continues to reshape the United States," Migration Policy Institute, October 15, 2015. https://www.migrationpolicy.org/article/fifty -years-1965-immigration-and-nationality-act-continues-reshape-united-states.

22 William A. Kandel, "U.S. family-based immigration policy," Congressional Research Service, February 17, 2016. https://fas.org/sgp/crs/homesec/R43145.pdf.

23 U.S. Department of State, "Visa bulletin," No. 9, Vol. IX (June 2009). https://web.archive.org/web/20090603213642/http://travel.state.gov/visa /frvi/bulletin/bulletin_4497.html.

24 Cannato, "Our evolving immigration policy." https://www.nationalaffairs.com /publications/detail/our-evolving-immigration-policy.

25 Douglas Massey, "How a 1965 immigration reform created illegal immigration," *Washington Post*, September 25, 2015. https://www.washingtonpost.com /posteverything/wp/2015/09/25/how-a-1965-immigration-reform-created -illegal-immigration/?utm_term=.aae9fd899ae7.

26 Cannato, "Our evolving immigration policy." https://www.nationalaffairs.com /publications/detail/our-evolving-immigration-policy.

27 Ibid.

28 Jens Manuel Krogstad, Jeffrey S. Passel, and D'Vera Cohn, "5 facts about illegal immigration in the United States," Pew Research Center, April 27, 2017. http://www.pewresearch.org/fact-tank/2017/04/27/5-facts-about-illegal -immigration-in-the-u-s.

29 Priscilla Alvarez, "Is a 'merit-based' immigration system a good idea?" *The Atlantic*, March 11, 2017. https://www.theatlantic.com/politics/archive/2017 /03/trump-cotton-perdue-merit-based-immigration-system/518985.

30 George J. Borjas, "Yes, immigration hurts American workers," *Politico Magazine*, September/October 2016. http://www.politico.com/magazine/story/2016/09 /trump-clinton-immigration-economy-unemployment-jobs-214216.

31 Ibid.

32 George J. Borjas, "The wage impact of the Marielitos: Additional evidence," NBER Working Paper, January 2016. https://sites.hks.harvard.edu/fs/gborjas /publications/working%20papers/Mariel2015a.pdf.

33 Giovanni Peri and Chad Sparber, "Task specialization, immigration, and wages," *American Economic Journal*, July 2009. https://www.aeaweb.org/articles?id=10.1257 /app.1.3.135.

34 David Frum, "The great immigration-data debate," *The Atlantic*, January 19, 2016. https://www.theatlantic.com/politics/archive/2016/01/the-great -immigration-data-debate/424230.

35 Paul Krugman, "Notes on immigration," *New York Times*, March 27, 2006. https://krugman.blogs.nytimes.com/2006/03/27/notes-on-immigration/.

36 William Galston, "On immigration, the white working class is fearful," Brookings Institution, June 24, 2016. https://www.brookings.edu/blog /fixgov/2016/06/24/on-immigration-the-white-working-class-is-fearful.

37 Ezra Klein, "Bernie Sanders: The Vox conversation," Vox, July 28, 2015. https://www.vox.com/2015/7/28/9014491/bernie-sanders-vox-conversation.

38 M. Goodwin, H. Clarke, and P. Whiteley, "Yes, immigration really was to blame for Brexit," CapX, May 2, 2017. https://capx.co/yes-immigration -really-was-to-blame-for-brexit.

39 Nicholas Watt and Patrick Wintour, "How immigration came to haunt Labour: The inside story," *The Guardian*, March 24, 2015. https://www.theguardian.com /news/2015/mar/24/how-immigration-came-to-haunt-labour-inside-story; Author unknown, "The huge political cost of Blair's decision to allow Eastern European migrants unfettered access to Britain," The Conversation, November 16, 2016. https://theconversation.com/the-huge-political-cost-of-blairs-decision -to-allow-eastern-european-migrants-unfettered-access-to-britain-66077.

40 Adam Payne, "Tony Blair isn't the voice of Remainers—he's partly to blame for Brexit," Business Insider, October 29, 2016. http://uk.businessinsider.com /tony-blair-brexit-immigration-eu-referendum-2016-10.

41 Migration Observatory (University of Oxford), "Migrants in the UK: An over-view," February 21, 2017. http://www.migrationobservatory.ox.ac.uk/resources /briefings/migrants-in-the-uk-an-overview.

42 Migration Observatory (University of Oxford), "Migrants in the UK labour market: An overview," December 1, 2016. http://www.migrationobservatory .ox.ac.uk/resources/briefings/migrants-in-the-uk-labour-market-an-overview.

43 Michael Taylor, "Migration, productivity, living standards, and all that," Policy Exchange, August 7, 2016. https://policyexchange.org.uk/migration -productivity-living-standards-and-all-that.

44 Stephen Nickell and Jumana Saleheen, "The impact of immigration on occu-pational wages: Evidence from Britain," Bank of England, December 18, 2015. http://www.bankofengland.co.uk/research/Documents/workingpapers/2015 /swp574.pdf.

45 Neli Esipova, Anita Pugliese, and Julie Ray, "Europeans most negative toward immigration," Gallup News, October 16, 2015. http://news.gallup.com/poll /186209/europeans-negative-toward-immigration.aspx.

46 David Szabo, "As Germany heads to the polls, a growing split between European voters and elites," Fox News, September 22, 2017. http://www.foxnews.com

/opinion/2017/09/22/as-germany-heads-to-polls-growing-split-between
-european-voters-and-elites.html.

6. REDISCOVERING CONSERVATISM

1   Ronald Reagan said something similar in 1977: "If there is any political viewpoint
    in this world which is free from slavish adherence to abstraction, it is American
    conservatism." Reagan's CPAC speech, "The New Republican Party," February 6,
    1977. http://reagan2020.us/speeches/The_New_Republican_Party.asp.

2   Matthew Walther, "Conservatism is dead," The Week, November 27, 2017.
    http://theweek.com/articles/739147/conservatism-dead; Richard North
    Patterson, "Donald Trump and the death of principled conservatism,"
    Huffington Post, July 11, 2017. https://www.huffingtonpost.com/entry/donald
    -trump-and-the-death-of-principled-conservatism_us_5964b1dce4b09be68c005531;
    Jennifer Rubin, "The night Donald Trump killed conservatism," *Chicago Tribune*,
    December 13, 2017. http://www.chicagotribune.com/news/opinion/commentary
    /ct-trump-big-government-conservatism-dead-20170301-story.html; James
    Heaney, "Conservatism is dead; long live conservatism," The Federalist,
    August 6, 2016. http://thefederalist.com/2016/08/06/conservatism-is-dead
    -long-live-conservatism; Rod Dreher, "The death of movement conservatism,"
    American Conservative, September 1, 2016. http://www.theamericanconservative
    .com/dreher/death-movement-conservatism.

3   Brian Laghi, "Working class returning to fold, Harper says," *Globe and Mail*,
    January 16, 2016. https://www.theglobeandmail.com/news/national/work-
    ing-class-returning-to-fold-harper-says/article701725.

4   This is a group of young, policy-oriented, American conservatives. They are asso-
    ciated with a small number of conservative think-tanks, magazines, and journals.
    While they have lacked a champion among Republican politicians, Florida senator
    Marco Rubio now appears to be positioning himself in this space.

5   Sam Tanenhaus, "Can the GOP be a party of ideas?" *New York Times*, July 2, 2014.
    https://www.nytimes.com/2014/07/06/magazine/can-the-gop-be-a-party
    -of-ideas.html?mtrref=www.google.ca&gwh=C8E8B3EFA4B9757F4E5F9E4A
    3BE21A04&gwt=pay.

6   Ramesh Ponnuru, "What reform conservatives got right about the GOP,"
    National Review, April 21, 2016. http://www.nationalreview.com/article
    /434313/donald-trump-reform-conservatives-predicted-his-rise.

7   Nate Cohn, "Why Trump won: Working class whites," *New York Times*,
    November 9, 2016. https://www.nytimes.com/2016/11/10/upshot/why-
    trump-won-working-class-whites.html; Katie Rogers, "White women helped
    elect Donald Trump," *New York Times*, November 9, 2016. https://www.nytimes.
    com/2016/12/01/us/politics/white-women-helped-elect-donald-trump.html.

8 Jonathan Derbyshire, "The meaning of conservatism," *New Statesman*, October 8, 2009. https://www.newstatesman.com/uk-politics/2009/10/conservative-disraeli-burke.

9 Gregor Aisch and Alicia Parlapiano, "What do you think is the most important problem facing this country today?" *New York Times*, February 27, 2017. https://www.nytimes.com/interactive/2017/02/27/us/politics/most-important-problem-gallup-polling-question.html.

10 Noah Carl, "Verbal intelligence is correlated with socially and economically liberal beliefs," *Intelligence*, Vol. 44, May–June 2014. http://www.sciencedirect.com/science/article/pii/S0160289614000373.

11 Paul Johnson, *The Intellectuals: From Marx and Tolstoy to Sartre and Chomsky* (New York: Harper Collins, 1989).

7. POWERFUL BUT NOT PERFECT

1 http://www.oag-bvg.gc.ca/internet/English/parl_oag_201411_05_e_39963.html#hd5b

2 Financial markets are so central to the trajectory of capitalist economies that their instability has wide implications. This is in part because the activities of the financial sector—saving, lending, borrowing, and investing—effectively create money. Likewise, failures to realize the valuations behind debt creation can destroy money through bankruptcy, loan calling, account withdrawals, and hoarding. Thus, capitalist cycles can see both radical expansions and contractions of the money supply, driving even greater forces of instability.

3 As for the right scope and design for financial sector regulations, we should set a clear framework but not micromanage. We are now going down the path of more highly prescriptive rules, as mandated by the post-crisis Basel III approach. I am quite skeptical of this. Canada has, however, at least so far avoided putting all forms of financial regulation and oversight under the central bank. I believe that such a concentration of authority is more likely to make regulatory errors over the longer-term.

4 Republican Party, "We believe in America: 2012 Republican platform," The American Presidency Project, August 27, 2012. http://www.presidency.ucsb.edu/ws/?pid=101961.

5 Kim Dixon, "Romney tax plan helps rich, hurts middle class: Study," Reuters, August 1, 2012. http://www.reuters.com/article/us-usa-taxes-romney-idUSBRE8700PC20120801.

6 James Pethokoukis, "Supply-side economics needs a 21st century update: Responding to Cato's Dan Mitchell on middle-class tax cuts," AEI blog, August 21,

2014. https://www.aei.org/publication/supply-side-economics-needs-a-21st
-century-update-responding-to-catos-dan-mitchell-on-middle-class-tax-cuts/print.

7 Author unknown, "Presidential exit polls," *New York Times*, date unknown.
https://www.nytimes.com/elections/2012/results/president/exit-polls.html.

8 Chris Jackson, "Trump and the Republicans abandoned 'pocketbook populism,'"
The Hill, December 20, 2017. http://thehill.com/opinion/campaign/365801
-trump-and-the-republicans-abandoned-pocketbook-populism.

9 Alana Semuels, "Why is economic growth so lackluster?" *The Atlantic*,
October 21, 2016. https://www.theatlantic.com/business/archive/2016/10
/why-economic-growth-is-so-lackluster/504989.

10 The "supply-side agenda" is what you read about in the *Wall Street Journal*. It presumes that economic performance can always be improved by expanding "aggregate supply" through private investment, via such measures as tax reductions on
capital, lower marginal rates for high-income workers, regulatory reform, and
inflation control. The liberal left, by contrast, assume that poor economic performance is always a matter of a deficiency of "aggregate demand," which requires
government intervention in the form of deficit spending and monetary expansion.
The underlying belief is that, in a slow economy, existing productive capacity is
not being fully utilized and needs to be "stimulated." I actually tend to believe the
WSJ is right more often than not, especially when there is a well-regulated and well-
functioning financial sector. However, this is an empirical matter. In 2008–2009,
I concluded that we were facing the kind of systemic economic dysfunction that
made deficit financing and extraordinary monetary expansion unavoidable.

11 Department of Finance Canada, "Fiscal reference tables" (see Table #2—
Fiscal transactions (per cent of GDP)), September 2017. https://www.fin.gc.ca
/frt-trf/2017/frt-trf-17-eng.pdf.

12 "Table 1.2—Summary of receipts, outlays, and surpluses and deficits (-) as percentages of GDP: 1930–2022," White House Office of Management and Budget,
Historic Tables, accessed on January 3, 2018. https://www.whitehouse.gov
/omb/budget/Historicals.

13 Parliamentary Budget Office, *Revenue and Distribution Analysis of Federal Tax
Changes: 2005–2013*, May 27, 2014. http://www.pbo-dpb.gc.ca/web/default
/files/files/files/Fiscal_Impact_and_Incidence_EN.pdf.

14 Watson, "Who knew?" http://business.financialpost.com/opinion/william
-watson-turns-out-the-harper-government-was-actually-terrific-for-wage-growth;
Statistics Canada, "High-income trends among taxfilers, 1982 to 2012," *The
Daily*, November 18, 2014. http://www.statcan.gc.ca/daily-quotidien/141118
/dq141118b-eng.pdf.

15 As U.S. economist Raj Chetty put it, "You're twice as likely to realize the American Dream if you're growing up in Canada rather than the U.S." Sarah Rieger, "The American Dream is easier to achieve in Canada," Huffington Post, January 23, 2017. https://www.huffingtonpost.ca/2017/01/23/american-dream-canada_n_14350144.html; Ian Austen and David Leonhardt, "Life in Canada, home of the world's most affluent middle class," *New York Times*, April 30, 2014. https://www.nytimes.com/2014/05/01/upshot/canadians-have-plenty-of-concerns-but-also-a-sense-theyre-better-off.html.

16 They have, however, been willing to raise taxes on individuals, families, consumers, and small business. In combination with low corporate tax rates, this is a striking example of elite liberalism.

17 Peter Nowak, "Canadian cellphone rates among world's worst," CBC News, August 11, 2009. http://www.cbc.ca/news/technology/canadian-cellphone-rates-among-world-s-worst-1.800596; Peter Nowak, "Internet, phone bills in Canada too high, says consumer study," CBC News, March 23, 2015. http://www.cbc.ca/news/business/internet-phone-bills-in-canada-too-high-says-consumer-study-1.3005282.

18 Author unknown, "Canadian wireless prices still high by most standards but ISED sees positives," Canadian Press, December 13, 2017. https://www.ctvnews.ca/business/canadian-wireless-prices-still-high-by-most-standards-but-ised-sees-positives-1.3720238.

19 Justin Daniel, "Can Canada school Trump on regulatory reform?" *Regulatory Review*, January 26, 2017. https://www.theregreview.org/2017/01/26/daniel-canada-school-trump-regulatory-reform.

20 We legislated that new regulations needed to be offset by reforming and eliminating existing regulations of an equivalent economic cost—using a standardized costing model to measure the economic costs of regulations across the government. Departments were therefore responsible for weighing the benefits and costs of new regulations against existing ones and for setting out rules and regulations that minimized the cost burden on businesses and households. Sean Speer, "Regulatory budgeting: Lessons from Canada," R Street Institute, March 2016. https://www.rstreet.org/wp-content/uploads/2016/03/RSTREET54.pdf.

21 Thomas Franck, "McKinsey: One-third of U.S. workers could be jobless by 2030 due to automation," CNBC, November 29, 2017. https://www.cnbc.com/2017/11/29/one-third-of-us-workers-could-be-jobless-by-2030-due-to-automation.html.

22 Olivia Solon, "More than 70% of US fears robots taking over our lives, survey finds," *The Guardian*, October 4, 2017. https://www.theguardian.com/technology/2017/oct/04/robots-artificial-intelligence-machines-us-survey.

23 David Rotman, "How technology is destroying jobs," MIT *Technology Review*, June 12, 2013. https://www.technologyreview.com/s/515926/how-technology-is-destroying-jobs.

24 Philip Cross, "Our fears of job-replacing robots are long-held—and unfounded," *Financial Post*, March 21, 2017. http://www.macdonaldlaurier.ca/our-fears-about-job-replacing-robots-are-long-held-and-unfounded-philip-cross-in-the-financial-post.

25 The number of people working part-time but would prefer to work full-time has doubled in recent years. Drew Desilver, "What the unemployment rate does—and doesn't—say about the economy," Pew Research Center, March 7, 2017. http://www.pewresearch.org/fact-tank/2017/03/07/employment-vs-unemployment-different-stories-from-the-jobs-numbers. Nearly 60 per cent of unemployed Americans and 82 per cent of temporary unemployed in 2014 said that they wanted to work. Jennifer De Pinto, Sarah Dutton, Anthony Salvanto, and Fred Backus, "America's unemployed: Who are the Americans who are not working?" CBS News, December 11, 2014. https://www.cbsnews.com/news/americas-unemployed-who-are-the-americans-who-arent-working; Jim Tankersley and Scott Clement, "Among American workers, poll finds unprecedented anxiety about jobs, economy," *Washington Post*, November 25, 2013. https://www.washingtonpost.com/business/economy/among-american-workers-poll-finds-unprecedented-anxiety-about-jobs-economy/2013/11/25/fb6a5ac8-5145-11e3-a7f0-b790929232e1_story.html?utm_term=.a042ba4a1c8d.

26 Jon Marcus, "The paradox of new buildings on campus," *The Atlantic*, July 25, 2016. https://www.theatlantic.com/education/archive/2016/07/the-paradox-of-new-buildings-on-campus/492398; Paul Campos, "The real reason college tuition is so much," *New York Times*, April 4, 2015. https://www.nytimes.com/2015/04/05/opinion/sunday/the-real-reason-college-tuition-costs-so-much.html; Author unknown, "What's driving college costs higher?" NPR, June 26, 2012. https://www.npr.org/2012/06/26/155766786/whats-driving-college-costs-higher; Steve Odland, "College costs out of control," *Forbes*, March 24, 2012. https://www.forbes.com/sites/steveodland/2012/03/24/college-costs-are-soaring/#631d26d61f86.

27 Purdue University, under the presidency of former Indiana governor and conservative reformer Mitch Daniels, has had some success with a student financing program where the university receives a share of a student's funding earnings. These Income Sharing Agreements improves the incentives for colleges to focus on employability and future earnings. It is a model that looks to be effective and should be adopted and scaled up elsewhere. Richard Vedder, "Mitch Daniels has the right stuff for Purdue," James G. Martin Center for Academic Renewal, May 2, 2018. https://www.jamesgmartin.center/2018/05/mitch-daniels-has-the-right-stuff-for-purdue/.

28 Jeff Clabaugh, "If education counts, Americans have never been smarter," WTOP Business News, April 3, 2017. https://wtop.com/business-finance /2017/04/education-counts-americans-never-smarter.

29 Full-time jobs are more common in the trades and employees in the trades earn more on average than those in other occupations. Wendy Pyper, "Skilled trades employment," *Perspectives on Labour and Income*, Vol. 9, No. 10 (October 2008), Statistics Canada Catalogue No. 75-001-X. http://www.statcan.gc.ca/ pub/75-001-x/75-001-x2008110-eng.pdf.

30 ChangHwan Kim, Christopher R. Tamborini, and Arthur Sakamoto, "Field of study in college and lifetime earnings in the United States," *Sociology of Education*, Vol. 88, No. 4 (September 2015), pp. 320–329. https://www.ncbi.nlm.nih.gov /pmc/articles/PMC5198720.

31 Our measures were admittedly limited in scope. Remember that post-secondary education in Canada is largely under provincial jurisdiction.

32 Statistics Canada, "Table 477-0053—Registered apprenticeship training, registrations, by age groups, sex and major trade groups annual (number)." *The Daily*, October 26, 2015. http://www.statcan.gc.ca/daily-quotidien/151026 /t001a-eng.htm; Department of Finance Canada, *Jobs Report: State of the Canadian Labour Market*, 2014. https://www.budget.gc.ca/2014/docs/jobs -emplois/pdf/jobs-emplois-eng.pdf.

33 The IMF had to famously apologize to Cameron and his government for misreading how restraining spending would affect economic performance. See Sean Speer, "Christine Lagarde gives Trudeau just the spectacularly bad advice he wanted to hear," *Financial Post*, September 15, 2016. http://business.financialpost.com /opinion/christine-lagarde-gives-trudeau-just-the-spectacularly-bad-advice-he -wanted-to-hear.

34 This is in contrast with British Columbia's experience with the carbon tax that finds that carbon taxes "increase the unemployment rates of medium- and low-educated males by 1.4 and 2.4 percentage points, respectively. The policy is implemented mainly at the expense of the low-educated." Chi Man Yip, "On the labor market consequences of environmental taxes," *Journal of Environmental Economics and Management*, Vol. 89 (May 2018), pp. 136–152. https://www.sciencedirect.com/science/article/pii/S009506961730551X.

35 One estimate is that during recent years in the oil sands the loss of jobs among lower-income earners and blue-collar workers is nearly quintuple the losses among the highest-paid workers. See Sean Speer, "Natural resources are a win for rural communities," *Toronto Sun*, August 5, 2017. http://torontosun.com /2017/08/05/natural-resources-are-a-win-for-rural-communities/wcm /fd5af06b-a154-499d-afa6-eef6ac769b6a.

36 Department of Finance Canada, "The Working Income Tax Benefit: A profile of claimants, 2009–2012," *Report on Federal Tax Expenditures—Concepts, Estimates and Evaluations, 2016*. https://www.fin.gc.ca/taxexp-depfisc/2016/taxexp1608-eng.asp#_Toc442180658.

37 A recent Harvard poll found that 51 per cent of those in the U.S. aged between eighteen and twenty-nine said they opposed capitalism. Ben Steverman, "Get rid of capitalism? Millennials are ready to talk about it," Bloomberg, November 6, 2017. https://www.bloomberg.com/news/articles/2017-11-06/get-rid-of-capitalism-millennials-are-ready-to-talk-about-it.

8. THE ART OF THE DEAL

1 Alec Tyson, "Americans generally positive about NAFTA, but most Republicans say it benefits Mexico more than U.S.," Pew Research Center, November 13, 2017. http://www.pewresearch.org/fact-tank/2017/11/13/americans-generally-positive-about-nafta-but-most-republicans-say-it-benefits-mexico-more-than-u-s.

2 The first reference to the "second-best book" is from a Trump speech where he said it was his second favourite book after The Bible. See Tim Hains, "Trump: My favorite book is 'The Bible!'" Real Clear Politics, August 12, 2015. https://www.realclearpolitics.com/video/2015/08/12/trump_art_of_the_deal_is_my_second_favorite_book_first_is_the_bible.html. The second quotations come directly from *The Art of the Deal*. Donald J. Trump with Tony Schwartz, *The Art of the Deal* (New York: Ballantine Books, republished in 2004).

3 Khamla Heminthavong, *Canada's Supply Management System*, Library of Parliament, Publication No. 2015-138-E17, December 17, 2015. https://lop.parl.ca/Content/LOP/ResearchPublications/2015-138-e.pdf.

4 Janyce McGregor, "Supply management in Canada: Why politicians defend farm marketing boards," CBC News, July 26, 2015. http://www.cbc.ca/news/politics/supply-management-in-canada-why-politicians-defend-farm-marketing-boards-1.3166329.

5 Ian Vandaelle, "Canadian banks need some 'protectionism': Toronto mayor urges vigilance on NAFTA," BNN, July 19, 2017. https://www.bnn.ca/canadian-banks-need-some-protectionism-toronto-mayor-urges-vigilance-on-nafta-1.808223.

6 Tom DiChristopher, "Sizing up the Trade Adjustment Assistance program," CNBC, June 26, 2015. https://www.cnbc.com/2015/06/26/is-aid-to-trade-displaced-workers-worth-the-cost.html.

7 Nick Timiraos, "5 questions on Trade Adjustment Assistance," *Wall Street Journal*, June 15, 2015. https://blogs.wsj.com/briefly/2015/06/15/5-questions-on-trade-adjustment-assistance; David Muhlhausen, "Trade Adjustment Assistance: Let the ineffective and wasteful job-training program expire,"

Heritage Foundation, January 8, 2014. https://www.heritage.org/trade/report/trade-adjustment-assistance-let-the-ineffective-and-wasteful-job-training-program.

8   Vivian C. Jones, "Trade remedies: A primer," Congressional Research Service, March 6, 2012. http://www.aiis.org/wp-content/uploads/2015/02/CRS-Trade-Remedies-Primer.pdf.

9   Sasha Moss, "Trump's 'America first' agenda requires reform at international trade agency," *The Hill*, June 29, 2017. www.rstreet.org/op-ed/trumps-america-first-agenda-requires-reform-at-international-trade-agency.

10 David Dollar, "The future of U.S.–China economic ties," Brookings, October 4, 2016. https://www.brookings.edu/research/the-future-of-u-s-china-trade-ties.

11 David Lawder, "U.S. formally opposes China market economy status at WTO," Reuters, November 30, 2017. https://www.reuters.com/article/us-usa-china-trade-wto/u-s-formally-opposes-china-market-economy-status-at-wto-idUSKBN1DU2VH.

12 BJ Siekierski, "In Canadian anti-dumping regulations, China's market-economy status will have to wait," iPolitics, May 14, 2013. https://ipolitics.ca/2013/05/14/in-canadian-anti-dumping-regulations-chinas-market-economy-status-will-have-to-wait.

13 The regulatory backgrounder stated, "Without the amendment, prescribed countries under the Regulations would expire automatically and Canada's trade remedy regime would potentially not be able to take into account whether prescribed countries are operating according to market economy conditions."

14 Statistics Canada, "Table 376-0051—International investment position, Canadian direct investment abroad and foreign direct investment in Canada, by country annual (dollars x 1,000,000)," accessed on April 2, 2018. http://www5.statcan.gc.ca/cansim/a26?lang=eng&id=3760051.

15 Laura Payton, "Ottawa moves to limit foreign investment reviews," CBC News, May 25, 2012. http://www.cbc.ca/news/politics/ottawa-moves-to-limit-foreign-investment-reviews-1.1273789.

16 U.S. Census Bureau, "Trade in goods with Canada, 2017," accessed on April 2, 2018. https://www.census.gov/foreign-trade/balance/c1220.html.

17 U.S. Census Bureau, "Trade in goods with Mexico, 2017," accessed on April 2, 2018. https://www.census.gov/foreign-trade/balance/c2010.html.

18 Patrick Gillespie, "Remove car imports, and U.S.–Mexico trade deficit disappears," CNN Money, January 9, 2017. http://money.cnn.com/2017/01/09/news/economy/us-mexico-trump-cars-imports-trade-deficit/index.html.

19   The U.S. trade deficit with China is roughly US$375 billion. Mexico's trade deficit with China is more than US$60 billion. Canada's trade deficit with the P.R.C. is about US$50 billion. See Ana Swanson, "U.S.–China trade deficit hits record, fueling trade fight," *New York Times*, February 6, 2018. https://www.nytimes.com/2018/02/06/us/politics/us-china-trade-deficit.html; Ilaria Maria Sala, "Can China profit from Trump's hostility to Mexico? It's complicated," Quartz, September 4, 2017. https://qz.com/1068688/can-china-profit-from-trumps-hostility-to-mexico-its-complicated; Asia Pacific Foundation of Canada, "Canada's merchandise trade with China," accessed on April 2, 2018. https://www.asiapacific.ca/statistics/trade/bilateral-trade-asia-product/canadas-merchandise-trade-china.

20   James Kirchick, "Remember all those left-wing pundits who drooled over Venezuela?" *LA Times*, August 2, 2017. http://www.latimes.com/opinion/op-ed/la-oe-kirchick-venezuela-pundits-20170802-story.html.

21   The share of the population under 29 in Canada is 35.3 per cent. The share of the U.S. population under 29 is 39.4 per cent. See Statistics Canada, "Population by Sex and Age Group," 2016 Census, accessed on May 11, 2018. http://www.statcan.gc.ca/tables-tableaux/sum-som/l01/cst01/demo10a-eng.htm. U.S. Census Bureau, "Annual Estimates of the Resident Population for Selected Age Groups by Sex for the United States, States, Counties, and Puerto Rico Commonwealth and Municipios: April 1, 2010 to July 1, 2016, 2016 Population Estimates," accessed on May 11, 2018. https://factfinder.census.gov/faces/tableservices/jsf/pages/productview.xhtml?src=bkmk.

22   Dani Rodrik, "Put globalization to work for democracies," *New York Times*, September 17, 2016. https://www.nytimes.com/2016/09/18/opinion/sunday/put-globalization-to-work-for-democracies.html.

9. NATIONALISM AND ALIENISM

1   Gillian Tett, "Has the nation state had its day?" *Financial Times*, March 21, 2014. https://www.ft.com/content/3c14ccee-afc3-11e3-9cd1-00144feab7de; Daniel Martin, "Nation states are dead: EU chief says the belief that countries can stand alone is a 'lie and an illusion,'" *Daily Mail*, November 11, 2010. www.dailymail.co.uk/news/article-1328568/Nation-states-dead-EU-chief-says-belief-countries-stand-lie.html.

2   David Callahan, *The Moral Center: How Progressives Can Unite America Around Our Shared Values* (Wilmington, MA: Mariner Books, 2007); Callahan, "The biggest problem with capitalism that nobody talks about," Demos, January 31, 2014. http://www.demos.org/blog/1/31/14/biggest-problem-capitalism-nobody-talks-about.

3   David Beito, *From Mutual Aid to the Welfare State: Fraternal Societies and Social Services, 1890–1967* (Chapel Hill: University of North Carolina Press, 2000).

4   Yuval Levin, "The solution: A conservative governing vision," in *Room to Grow: Conservative Reforms for a Limited Government and a Thriving Middle Class* (YG Network, 2014). http://conservativereform.com/wp-content/uploads /2014/05/Chapter-2-Introduction-The-Solution.pdf.

5   The decline of civil society has been the subject of considerable scholarship and analysis ever since Harvard sociologist Robert Putnam's path-breaking book *Bowling Alone*, in 2000 (New York: Simon & Schuster).

6   Joint Economic Committee, "What we do together: The state of associational life in America," Social Capital Project No. 1-17, May 2017. https://www.lee .senate.gov/public/_cache/files/b5f224ce-98f7-40f6-a814-8602696714d8 /what-we-do-together.pdf.

7   Putnam's latest work, *Our Kids*, documents how these trends have come to disproportionately affect poor and working-class people and created a "social capital" gap that is as deterministic as different financial endowments. J.D. Vance's best-selling book, *Hillbilly Elegy*, also brings expression to this breakdown of civil society and how it has affected working-class people in the rust-belt states.

8   Richard Reeves, "Trickle-down norms," *National Affairs*, Winter 2018. https://www.nationalaffairs.com/publications/detail/trickle-down-norms.

9   Department of Citizenship and Immigration Canada, *Summative Evaluation of the Private Sponsorship of Refugees Program: Final Report*, April 2007. http://www.cic.gc.ca/ english/resources/evaluation/psrp/psrp-summary.asp.

10 Paul B. Reed and L. Kevin Selbee, *Patterns of Citizen Participation and the Civic Core in Canada*, Statistics Canada, undated. http://www.publications.gc.ca /Collection/Statcan/75F0048M/75F0048MIE2002003.pdf; Paul B. Reed and L. Kevin Selbee, "The civic core in Canada: Disproportionality in charitable giving, volunteering, and civic participation," *Nonprofit and Voluntary Sector Quarterly*, Vol. 30, No. 4 (December 2001). https://www3.carleton.ca/casr/civic.pdf.

11 John Rentoul, "'British jobs' blows up in PM's face," *The Independent*, November 4, 2007. http://www.independent.co.uk/voices/commentators /john-rentoul/john-rentoul-british-jobs-blows-up-in-the-pms-face-398892.html.

12 Simon Walters, "Ed Miliband hires the former Trotskyite who claimed Gordon Brown 'pandered to fascists' as his new aide," *Daily Mail*, January 13, 2013. http://www.dailymail.co.uk/news/article-2261520/Ed-Miliband-hires -Trotskyite-claimed-Gordon-Brown-pandered-fascists-new-aide.html.

10. THE PATH TO CITIZENSHIP

1   Sabrina Tavernise, "Sanctuary bill in Maryland faces a surprise foe: Legal immigrants," *New York Times*, May 8, 2017. https://www.nytimes.com /2017/05/08/us/legal-immigrants-who-oppose-illegal-immigration.html.

2   Australia witnessed a large spike in unauthorized boat arrivals in 2009. The number of people went from 161 in 2008 to 2,726 in 2009 and more than 20,000 in 2013. Tony Abbott's government took concerted action to stem the flow in 2013. The number of people fell to 160 in 2014. Author unknown, "Statistics relating to Migrant Smuggling in Australia," University of Queensland (TC Beirne School of Law), accessed on May 11, 2018. https://law.uq.edu.au/research/our-research/migrant-smuggling-working-group/resources-menu/statistics-relating-migrant-smuggling-australia.

3   Kitty McKinsey, "Learning language key to integration, say young refugees," UNHCR, January 30, 2018. http://www.unhcr.org/news/stories/2018/1/5a6b3af64/learning-language-key-integration-say-young-refugees.html.

4   Author unknown, "EU policy framework for migrant integration," European Commission, July 2017. https://ec.europa.eu/migrant-integration/the-eu-and-integration/framework.

5   Israel Ortega and Matt Spaulding, "Immigration reform: The need for upholding our national language," Heritage Foundation, June 5, 2007. https://www.heritage.org/immigration/report/immigration-reform-the-need-upholding-our-national-language.

6   Author unknown, "Close to half of new immigrants report high English-language speaking ability, Census Bureau reports," US Census Bureau, June 10, 2014. https://www.census.gov/newsroom/press-releases/2014/cb14-105.html.

7   Many contributed to this outreach. Long-time member of Parliament Deepak Obhrai comes to mind. Of course, so does former minister Jason Kenney, who has rightly earned an international reputation as a conservative who knows how to build policy and political bridges to minority communities.

8   Alex Panetta, "Canada's immigration policy inspired Donald Trump's new plan: White House," Canadian Press, August 2, 2017. https://globalnews.ca/news/3643835/trump-immigration-canada/.

9   Gustavo Lopez and Jens Manuel Krogstad, "Key facts about unauthorized immigrants enrolled in DACA," Pew Research Center, September 25, 2017. http://www.pewresearch.org/fact-tank/2017/09/25/key-facts-about-unauthorized-immigrants-enrolled-in-daca/; Jens Manuel Krogstad, Jeffrey S. Passel and D'Vera Cohn, "5 facts about illegal immigration in the United States," Pew Research Center, April 27, 2017. http://www.pewresearch.org/fact-tank/2017/04/27/5-facts-about-illegal-immigration-in-the-u-s/.

10 Miriam Valverde, "Have deportations increased under Donald Trump? Here's what the data show," Politifact, December 19, 2017. http://www.politifact.com/truth-o-meter/article/2017/dec/19/have-deportations-increased-under-donald-trump-her.

11 Author unknown, "A Reagan legacy: Amnesty for illegal immigrants," NPR, July 4, 2010. https://www.npr.org/templates/story/story.php?storyId=128303672.

12 Rachel Swarns, "Failed amnesty legislation of 1986 haunts the current immigration bills in Congress," *New York Times*, May 23, 2006. http://www.nytimes.com/2006/05/23/washington/23amnesty.html.

13 Editors, "The White House's welcome proposal on immigration," *National Review*, January 26, 2018. http://www.nationalreview.com/article/455837/white-house-immigration-proposal-welcome.

14 Anis Shivani, "Everyone's wrong on immigration: Open borders are the only way to defeat Trump and build a better world," Salon, March 15, 2017. https://www.salon.com/2017/03/15/everyones-wrong-on-immigration-open-borders-are-the-only-way-to-defeat-trump-and-build-a-better-world.

15 Bryan Caplan, "The efficient, egalitarian, libertarian, utilitarian way to double world GDP," EconLab, August 20, 2011. http://econlog.econlib.org/archives/2011/08/the_efficient_e.html.

16 Peter Beinart, "How the Democrats lost their way on immigration," *The Atlantic*, July/August 2017. https://www.theatlantic.com/magazine/archive/2017/07/the-democrats-immigration-mistake/528678.

11. THE BUSINESS OF BUSINESS

1 David Spiegel and Anthony Volastro, "As global populism rises, so does fear among corporate elites: Survey," CNBC, December 14, 2016. http://www.cnbc.com/2016/12/14/populism-increases-fears-of-elite-global-corporations-cnbc-cfo-survey.html.

2 Matt Clinch, "The CEO of the world's largest hedge fund says populism is now No. 1 market concern," CNBC, January 18, 2017. http://www.cnbc.com/2017/01/18/populism-is-number-one-market-concern-ceo-of-largest-hedge-fund.html.

3 Author unknown, "2017 Edelman trust barometer—Canadian results," Edelman Insights, February 14, 2017. https://www.slideshare.net/EdelmanInsights/2017-edelman-trust-barometer-canadian-results.

4 Strategy One and Edelman PR Worldwide, *The Relationship among NGOs, Government, Media and Corporate Sector*, January 2001. https://cms.edelman.com/sites/default/files/2017-03/2001-Edelman-Trust-Barometer.pdf.

5 Jo Confino, "Public trust in business hits five-year low," *The Guardian*, January 21, 2015. https://www.theguardian.com/sustainable-business/2015/jan/21/public-trust-global-business-government-low-decline.

6 Matt Harrington, "Survey: People's trust has declined in business, media, government and NGOs," *Harvard Business Review*, January 16, 2017.

198 · STEPHEN J. HARPER

https://hbr.org/2017/01/survey-peoples-trust-has-declined-in-business
-media-government-and-ngos.

7   Allison Kopicki, "Five years later, poll finds disapproval of bailout," *New York Times*, September 26, 2013. https://economix.blogs.nytimes.com/2013/09/26
/five-years-later-poll-finds-disapproval-of-bailout.

8   Kathy Frankovic, "Looking back at the 2008 financial crisis," YouGov, September 11, 2014. https://today.yougov.com/news/2014/09/11/2008
-financial-crisis.

9   International Labour Organization and the Organisation for Economic Co-operation and Development, *The Labour Share in G20 Economies*, Report prepared for the G20 Employment Working Group, Antalya, Turkey, February 26–27, 2015. https://www.oecd.org/g20/topics/employment-and-social-policy
/The-Labour-Share-in-G20-Economies.pdf.

10 Christine Filner, "Two-thirds say large corporations pay too little in federal taxes (poll)," ABC News, September 26, 2017. http://abcnews.go.com/Politics/
thirds-large-corporations-pay-federal-taxes-poll/story?id=50082215.

11 Author unknown, "Big business" (polling data). Gallup News, accessed on September 1, 2017. http://news.gallup.com/poll/5248/big-business.aspx.

12 Francis Fukuyama, *Trust: The Social Virtues and the Creation of Prosperity* (New York: The Free Press, 1995).

13 Author unknown, "Trust in business vs. government," *Wall Street Journal*, August 15, 2016. https://www.wsj.com/articles/trust-in-business-vs-
government-1471304776.

14 Author unknown, "Trump uses Twitter to bypass media," PBS NewsHour Extra, December 8, 2016. http://www.pbs.org/newshour/extra/daily-videos
/trump-uses-twitter-to-bypass-media.

15 Bureau of Labor Statistics, "Table A-2: Employment status of the civilian population by race, sex, and age," accessed on September 1, 2018. https://www.
bls.gov/news.release/empsit.t02.htm.

16 Statistics Canada, "Aboriginal people and the labour market," *The Daily*, March 16, 2017. http://www.statcan.gc.ca/daily-quotidien/170316/dq170316d-eng.htm.

17 Department of Finance Canada, "Jobs report: The state of the Canadian labour market," 2014. https://www.budget.gc.ca/2014/docs/jobs-emplois/pdf/jobs-
emplois-eng.pdf.

18 Elizabeth Piccutio, "Hiring people with disabilities isn't just the right thing to do—it's good for business," Daily Beast, November 27, 2014. http://www.thedailybeast.com/hiring-people-with-disabilities-isnt-just-the -right-thing-to-doits-good-for-business.

19 Joseph Erbentraut, "How these 4 major companies are tackling the autism unem- ployment rate," Huffington Post, May 7, 2015. http://www.huffingtonpost.ca /entry/autism-employment_n_7216310.

20 Sarah Blahovec, "Why hire disabled workers? 4 powerful (and inclusive) companies answer," Huffington Post, February 24, 2016. http://www.huffingtonpost.com /sarah-blahovec/why-hire-disabled-workers_b_9292912.html.

21 Tavia Grant, "Working wisdom: How workers with disabilities give companies an edge," Globe and Mail, February 27, 2015. https://www.theglobeandmail.com /report-on-business/working-wisdom-how-workers-with-disabilities-give -companies-an-edge/article23236023; David Bartage, "We can all be change leaders: Employing people with many abilities," The White House, October 20, 2014. https://obamawhitehouse.archives.gov/blog/2014/10/20/we-can-all -be-change-leaders-employing-people-many-abilities.

22 Callum Borchers, "Wary of fan anger, athletes largely avoid political fray," Boston Globe, May 25, 2012. https://www.bostonglobe.com/news/nation /2012/05/24/wary-fan-anger-athletes-largely-avoid-political-fray /qhGWfwl2cRIGwbbHzZwobN/story.html.

23 Energy resources are among what economists call "inelastic" goods, meaning that consumption of them will not vary significantly with price changes. This is what makes a carbon tax appealing from a revenue stand- point, but it is the same thing that ensures such a tax will produce little reduc- tion in emissions, unless its rate is astronomical—well over $100 per tonne. As a 2015 study by Manhattan Institute scholar Oren Cass points out, this means that a carbon tax can either reduce emissions or preserve economic activity but not both. Oren Cass, "The carbon-tax shell game," National Affairs, Summer 2015. https://www.nationalaffairs.com/publications/detail/the -carbon-tax-shell-game.

24 It is usually attributed to economist Milton Friedman. What Friedman actually said was ". . . there is one and only one social responsibility of business—to use its resources and engage in activities designed to increase its profits so long as it stays within the rules of the game, which is to say, engages in open and free competition without deception or fraud." Friedman, "The social responsibility of business is to increase its profits," New York Times Magazine, September 13, 1970. https://www.colorado.edu/studentgroups/libertarians/issues/friedman -soc-resp-business.html.

25 Nick O'Donohoe, "What is the business of business?" World Economic Forum, February 26, 2016. https://www.weforum.org/agenda/2016/02/the-business-of-business-is-what.

26 Andrew Hawkins, "Uber will teach you sign language to better communicate with deaf drivers," The Verge, September 29, 2017. https://www.theverge.com/2017/9/29/16384384/uber-sign-language-teach-deaf-driver.

27 Joe Lonsdale, "Don't just donate, innovate," Medium, October 5, 2017. https://medium.com/8vc-news/dont-just-donate-innovate-808c7cfe82e7.

28 To make the philosophy of these individuals crystal clear, consider the following: Bernie Sanders said in 1995, "I personally happen not to be a great believer in the free enterprise system for many reasons," in James Pethokoukis, "Just how much of a socialist is Bernie Sanders?" AEI Ideas, January 22, 2016. www.aei.org/publication/just-how-much-of-a-socialist-is-bernie-sanders/; and Jeremy Corbyn has specifically committed to end the "failed model of capitalism," in Rob Merrick, "Jeremy Corbyn vows to end UK's 'failed model of capitalism' as he promises new deal for tenants and women workers," The Independent, September 27, 2017. https://www.independent.co.uk/news/uk/politics/jeremy-corbyn-speech-labour-leader-capitalism-conference-renting-grenfell-tower-fire-theresa-may-a7970441.html.

EPILOGUE

1 Andre Tartar, "How the populist right is redrawing the map of Europe," Bloomberg, December 11, 2017. https://www.bloomberg.com/graphics/2017-europe-populist-right.

2 Bari Weiss, "Meet the renegades of the intellectual dark web," New York Times, May 8, 2018. https://www.nytimes.com/2018/05/08/opinion/intellectual-dark-web.html.

3 Jonathan Chait, "New study shows what really happened in the 2016 election," New York Magazine, June 18, 2017. http://nymag.com/daily/intelligencer/2017/06/new-study-shows-what-really-happened-in-the-2016-election.html.

4 Incidentally, this electoral reality makes Emmanuel Macron and his new party in France extremely vulnerable. With the right opponent, they could be obliterated as quickly as they skyrocketed.

5 Charles Krauthammer, "Alone in the universe," National Review, December 30, 2011. https://www.nationalreview.com/2011/12/are-we-alone-universe-charles-krauthammer.

BIBLIOGRAPHY

Acemoglu, Daron. "Technical change, inequality, and the labor market." *Journal of Economic Literature*, Vol. 40, No. 1 (March 2002): 7–72. https://economics.mit.edu/files/4124.

Acemoglu, Daron, David Autor, David Dorn, Gordon H. Hanson, and Brendan Price. "Import competition and the great US employment sag of the 2000s." *Journal of Labor Economics*, Vol. 34, No. S1 (January 2016): S141–S198. https://economics.mit.edu/files/9811.

Adams, Susan. "New job loss study: The less educated are the hardest hit." *Forbes*, August 16, 2012. https://www.forbes.com/sites/susanadams/2012/08/16/new-job-loss-study-the-less-educated-are-the-hardest-hit/#475fb2982aab.

Aisch, Gregor, and Alicia Parlapiano. "What do you think is the most important problem facing this country today?" *New York Times*, February 27, 2017. https://www.nytimes.com/interactive/2017/02/27/us/politics/most-important-problem-gallup-polling-question.html.

Alvarez, Priscilla. "Is a 'merit-based' immigration system a good idea?" *The Atlantic*, March 11, 2017. https://www.theatlantic.com/politics/archive/2017/03/trump-cotton-perdue-merit-based-immigration-system/518985.

Asia Pacific Foundation of Canada. "Canada's merchandise trade with China." Accessed on April 2, 2018. https://www.asiapacific.ca/statistics/trade/bilateral-trade-asia-product/canadas-merchandise-trade-china.

Atkinson, Robert D., and John Wu. "False alarmism: Technological disruption and the U.S. labor market, 1850–2015." Information Technology & Innovation Foundation @Work Series. May 2017. http://www2.itif.org/2017-false-alarmism-technological-disruption.pdf.

Austen, Ian, and David Leonhardt. "Life in Canada, home of the world's most affluent middle class." *New York Times*, April 30, 2014. https://www.nytimes.com/2014/05/01/upshot/canadians-have-plenty-of-concerns-but-also-a-sense-theyre-better-off.html.

Author unknown. "The 2008 housing crisis displaced more Americans than the 1930s Dust Bowl." National Center for Policy Analysis, May 11, 2015. http://www.ncpathinktank.org/sub/dpd/index.php?Article_ID=25643.

Author unknown. "2017 Edelman trust barometer—Canadian results." Edelman Insights, February 14, 2017. https://www.slideshare.net/EdelmanInsights/2017-edelman-trust-barometer-canadian-results.

Author unknown. "Big business" (polling data). Gallup News, accessed on September 1, 2017. http://news.gallup.com/poll/5248/big-business.aspx.

Author unknown. "The big freeze." *The Economist*, September 6, 2014. https://www.economist.com/news/finance-and-economics/21615589-throughout-rich-world-wages-are-stuck-big-freeze.

Author unknown. "Canadian wireless prices still high by most standards but ISED sees positives." Canadian Press, December 13, 2017. https://www.ctvnews.ca/business/canadian-wireless-prices-still-high-by-most-standards-but-ised-sees-positives-1.3720238.

Author unknown. "Close to half of new immigrants report high English-language speaking ability, Census Bureau reports." U.S. Census Bureau, June 10, 2014. https://www.census.gov/newsroom/press-releases/2014/cb14-105.html.

Author unknown. "EU policy framework for migrant integration." European Commission, July 2017. https://ec.europa.eu/migrant-integration/the-eu-and-integration/framework.

Author unknown. "G-20 declaration of the Summit on Financial Markets and the World Economy." G20 Research Group, November 15, 2008. http://www.g20.utoronto.ca/2008/2008declaration1115.html.

Author unknown. "The huge political cost of Blair's decision to allow Eastern European migrants unfettered access to Britain." The Conversation, November 16, 2016. https://theconversation.com/the-huge-political-cost-of-blairs-decision-to-allow-eastern-european-migrants-unfettered-access-to-britain-66077.

Author unknown. "Laughed at and booed, Donald Trump spoke at Davos." Euronews, January 26, 2018. http://www.euronews.com/2018/01/26/laughed-at-and-booed-donald-trump-spoke-at-davos.

Author unknown. "Poverty overview." World Bank, accessed on May 24, 2017. http://www.worldbank.org/en/topic/poverty/overview.

Author unknown. "Presidential exit polls." *New York Times*, accessed on August 4, 2017. https://www.nytimes.com/elections/2012/results/president/exit-polls.html.

Author unknown. "President Xi's Davos speech receives warm applause." *The Telegraph*, January 24, 2017. https://www.telegraph.co.uk/news/world/china-watch/business/president-xi-davos-speech-receives-warm-applause.

Author unknown. "A Reagan legacy: Amnesty for illegal immigrants." NPR, July 4, 2010. https://www.npr.org/templates/story/story.php?storyId=128303672.

Author unknown. "Statistics relating to migrant smuggling in Australia." University of Queensland (TC Beirne School of Law), accessed on May 11, 2018. https://law.uq.edu.au/research/our-research/migrant-smuggling-working-group/resources-menu/statistics-relating-migrant-smuggling-australia.

Author unknown. "Temporary foreign workers being approved too easily, expert warns." CBC News, April 15, 2014. http://www.cbc.ca/news/canada/temporary-foreign-workers-being-approved-too-easily-expert-warns-1.2609653.

Author unknown. "Trump uses Twitter to bypass media." PBS NewsHour Extra, December 8, 2016. http://www.pbs.org/newshour/extra/daily-videos/trump-uses-twitter-to-bypass-media.

Author unknown. "Trust in business vs. government." *Wall Street Journal*, August 15, 2016. https://www.wsj.com/articles/trust-in-business-vs-government-1471304776.

Author unknown. "What's driving college costs higher?" NPR, June 26, 2012. https://www.npr.org/2012/06/26/155766786/whats-driving-college-costs-higher.

Autor, David, David Dorn, and Gordon Hanson. "The China shock: Learning from labor market adjustment to large changes in trade." *Annual Review of Economics*, Vol. 8, No. 1 (2016): 205–240. https://www.annualreviews.org/doi/10.1146/annurev-economics-080315-015041.

Autor, David, David Dorn, Gordon Hanson, and Kaveh Majlesi. "Importing political polarization? The electoral consequences of rising trade exposure." December 2017. http://www.ddorn.net/papers/ADHM-PoliticalPolarization.pdf.

———. "A note on the effect of rising trade exposure on the 2016 presidential election." March 2, 2017. https://gps.ucsd.edu/_files/faculty/hanson/hanson_research_TrumpVote-032017.pdf.

Baily, Martin Neil, and Jacob Funk Kirkegaard. *Transforming the European Economy.* Washington: PIIE, 2004.

Barone, Michael. "Trump the disruptor: Convention chaos may be a feature, not a bug." *New York Post*, July 22, 2016. http://nypost.com/2016/07/22/trump-the-disruptor-convention-chaos-may-be-a-feature-not-a-bug.

———. "We've been here before: America and the dynamics of immigration." *Modern Age*, No. 3, Vol. 58 (Summer 2016). https://home.isi.org/we've-been-here-beforebr-america-and-dynamics-immigration.

Bartage, David. "We can all be change leaders: Employing people with many abilities." The White House, October 20, 2014. https://obamawhitehouse.archives.gov/blog/2014/10/20/we-can-all-be-change-leaders-employing-people-many-abilities.

Beinart, Peter. "How the Democrats lost their way on immigration." *The Atlantic*, July/August 2017. https://www.theatlantic.com/magazine/archive/2017/07/the-democrats-immigration-mistake/528678.

Beito, David. *From Mutual Aid to the Welfare State: Fraternal Societies and Social Services, 1890–1967.* Chapel Hill: University of North Carolina Press, 2000.

Berenson, Tessa. "Donald Trump calls for 'complete shutdown' of Muslim entry into the U.S." *Time*, December 7, 2015. http://time.com/4139476/donald-trump-shutdown-muslim-immigration.

Biven, Josh. "Using standard models to benchmark the costs of globalization for American workers without a college degree." Economic Policy Institute, March 22, 2013. http://www.epi.org/publication/standard-models-benchmark-costs-globalization.

Blahovec, Sarah. "Why hire disabled workers? 4 powerful (and inclusive) companies answer." Huffington Post, February 24, 2016. http://www.huffingtonpost.com/sarah-blahovec/why-hire-disabled-workers_b_9292912.html.

Bohanon, Cecil. "Economic recovery: Lessons from the post–World War II period." Mercatus on Policy, August 2012. https://www.mercatus.org/system/files/PostWWII_Recovery_Bohanon_MOP112-%281%29-copy.pdf.

Borchers, Callum. "Wary of fan anger, athletes largely avoid political fray." *Boston Globe*, May 25, 2012. https://www.bostonglobe.com/news/nation/2012/05/24/wary-fan-anger-athletes-largely-avoid-political-fray/qhGWfwl2cRIGwbbHzZwobN/story.html.

Borjas, George J. "The wage impact of the Marielitos: Additional evidence." NBER Working Paper, January 2016. https://sites.hks.harvard.edu/fs/gborjas/publications/working%20papers/Mariel2015a.pdf.

———. "Yes, immigration hurts American workers." *Politico Magazine*, September/October 2016. http://www.politico.com/magazine/story/2016/09/trump-clinton-immigration-economy-unemployment-jobs-214216.

Bowman, Karlyn. "Who were Donald Trump's voters? Now we know." *Forbes*, June 23, 2017. https://www.forbes.com/sites/bowmanmarsico/2017/06/23/who-were-donald-trumps-voters-now-we-know/#1f8290283894.

Branson, William H., Herbert Giersch, and Peter G. Peterson. "Trends in United States international trade and investment since World War II." In *The American Economy in Transition*, edited by Martin Feldstein, 183. Chicago: University of Chicago Press, 1980.

Bureau of Labor Statistics. "Table A-2: Employment status of the civilian population by race, sex, and age." Accessed on September 1, 2017. https://www.bls.gov/news.release/empsit.t02.htm.

Burtless, Gary. "New analysis turns up surprise on long-term wage trends." Real Clear Markets, May 17, 2017. https://www.brookings.edu/opinions/new-analysis-turns-up-surprise-on-long-term-wage-trends.

Callahan, David. "The biggest problem with capitalism that nobody talks about." Demos, January 31, 2014. http://www.demos.org/blog/1/31/14/biggest-problem-capitalism-nobody-talks-about.

———. *The Moral Center: How Progressives Can Unite America around Our Shared Values*. Wilmington, MA: Mariner Books, 2007.

Campos, Paul. "The real reason college tuition is so much." *New York Times*, April 4, 2015. https://www.nytimes.com/2015/04/05/opinion/sunday/the-real-reason-college-tuition-costs-so-much.html.

Cannato, Vincent J. "Our evolving immigration policy." *National Affairs*, Fall 2012. https://www.nationalaffairs.com/publications/detail/our-evolving-immigration-policy.

Cannon, Carl. "Immigration and the rise & fall of the Know-Nothing Party." Real Clear Politics, February 18, 2015. https://www.realclearpolitics.com/articles/2015/02/18/immigration_and_the_rise__fall_of_the_know-nothing_party_125649.html.

Caplan, Bryan. "The efficient, egalitarian, libertarian, utilitarian way to double world GDP." EconLab, August 20, 2011. http://econlog.econlib.org/archives/2011/08/the_efficient_e.html.

Carl, Noah. "Verbal intelligence is correlated with socially and economically liberal beliefs." *Intelligence*, Vol. 44, May–June 2014. http://www.sciencedirect.com/science/article/pii/S0160289614000373.

Carroll, Lauren. "Trump: Since China joined WTO, U.S. has lost 60,000 factories." Politifact, March 24, 2017. http://www.politifact.com/truth-o-meter/

statements/2017/mar/24/donald-trump/trump-china-joined-wto-us-has-lost-60000-factories.

Cass, Oren. "The carbon-tax shell game." *National Affairs*, Summer 2015. https://www.nationalaffairs.com/publications/detail/the-carbon-tax-shell-game.

Chait, Jonathan. "New study shows what really happened in the 2016 election." *New York Magazine*, June 18, 2017. http://nymag.com/daily/intelligencer/2017/06/new-study-shows-what-really-happened-in-the-2016-election.html.

Challinor, A.E. "Canada's immigration policy: A focus on human capital." Migration Policy Institute, September 15, 2011. https://www.migrationpolicy.org/article/canadas-immigration-policy-focus-human-capital.

Childress, Sarah. "How much did the financial crisis cost?" PBS Frontline, May 13, 2012. http://www.pbs.org/wgbh/frontline/article/how-much-did-the-financial-crisis-cost.

Chishti, Muzaffar, Faye Hipsman, and Isabel Ball. "Fifty years on, the 1965 Immigration and Nationality Act continues to reshape the United States." Migration Policy Institute, October 15, 2015. https://www.migrationpolicy.org/article/fifty-years-1965-immigration-and-nationality-act-continues-reshape-united-states.

Citizenship and Immigration Canada. "Facts and figures 2014: Immigrant overview—temporary residents." Accessed on August 12, 2017. http://www.cic.gc.ca/english/pdf/2014-Facts-Figures-Temporary.pdf.

———. "Facts & figures 2015: Immigration overview—temporary residents—annual IRCC updates." Accessed on August 12, 2017. http://open.canada.ca/data/en/dataset/052642bb-3fd9-4828-b608-c81dff7e539c.

Clabaugh, Jeff. "If education counts, Americans have never been smarter." WTOP Business News, April 3, 2017. https://wtop.com/business-finance/2017/04/education-counts-americans-never-smarter.

Clinch, Matt. "The CEO of the world's largest hedge fund says populism is now No. 1 market concern." CNBC, January 18, 2017. http://www.cnbc.com/2017/01/18/populism-is-number-one-market-concern-ceo-of-largest-hedge-fund.html.

Clinton, William J. "Address before a joint session of the Congress on the State of the Union." The American Presidency Project, January 23, 1996. http://www.presidency.ucsb.edu/ws/?pid=53091.

———. "Remarks at Vietnam National University in Hanoi, Vietnam." The American Presidency Project, November 17, 2000. http://www.presidency.ucsb.edu/ws/?pid=1038.

Cohn, Nate. "Why Trump won: Working class whites." *New York Times*, November 9, 2016. https://www.nytimes.com/2016/11/10/upshot/why-trump-won-working-class-whites.html.

Colantone, Italo, and Piero Stanig. "Global competition and Brexit." Baffi Carefin Centre, September 2016. https://papers.ssrn.com/sol3/papers.cfm?abstract_id=2870313.

———. "The real reason the U.K. voted for Brexit? Jobs lost to Chinese competition." *Washington Post*, July 7, 2016. https://www.washingtonpost.com/news/monkey-cage/wp/2016/07/07/the-real-reason-the-u-k-voted-for-brexit-economics-not-identity/?utm_term=.a64991ce3566.

Confino, Jo. "Public trust in business hits five-year low." *The Guardian*, January 21, 2015. https://www.theguardian.com/sustainable-business/2015/jan/21/public-trust-global-business-government-low-decline.

Cross, Philip. "Our fears of job-replacing robots are long-held—and unfounded." *Financial Post*, March 21, 2017. http://www.macdonaldlaurier.ca/our-fears-about-job-replacing-robots-are-long-held-and-unfounded-philip-cross-in-the-financial-post.

Crowley, Brian Lee. *Fearful Symmetry: The Fall and Rise of Canada's Founding Values*. Toronto: Key Porter Books, 2009.

Daniel, Justin. "Can Canada school Trump on regulatory reform?" *Regulatory Review*, January 26, 2017. https://www.theregreview.org/2017/01/26/daniel-canada-school-trump-regulatory-reform.

Democratic Party Platforms. "2000 Democratic Party platform." The American Presidency Project, August 14, 2000. http://www.presidency.ucsb.edu/ws/index.php?pid=29612.

Democratic Platform Committee. "2016 Democratic Party platform." July 8–9, 2016. http://s3.amazonaws.com/uploads.democrats.org/Downloads/2016_DNC_Platform.pdf.

Department of Citizenship and Immigration Canada. *Annual Report to Parliament on Immigration, 2014*. https://www.canada.ca/en/immigration-refugees-citizenship/corporate/publications-manuals/annual-report-parliament-immigration-2014.html.

———. *Summative Evaluation of the Private Sponsorship of Refugees Program: Final Report*. April 2007. http://www.cic.gc.ca/english/resources/evaluation/psrp/psrp-summary.asp.

Department of Finance Canada. "Fiscal reference tables." September 2017. https://www.fin.gc.ca/frt-trf/2017/frt-trf-17-eng.pdf.

———. "Jobs report: The state of the Canadian labour market." 2014. https://www.budget.gc.ca/2014/docs/jobs-emplois/pdf/jobs-emplois-eng.pdf.

———. "The Working Income Tax Benefit: A profile of claimants, 2009–2012." *Report on Federal Tax Expenditures—Concepts, Estimates and Evaluations, 2016*. https://www.fin.gc.ca/taxexp-depfisc/2016/taxexp1608-eng.asp#_Toc442180658.

Department of Foreign Affairs and International Trade. "January 1 marks 20th anniversary of North American Free Trade Agreement." Government of Canada, January 1, 2014. https://www.canada.ca/en/news/archive/2014/01/january-1-marks-20th-anniversary-north-american-free-trade-agreement.html.

De Pinto, Jennifer, Sarah Dutton, Anthony Salvanto, and Fred Backus. "America's unemployed: Who are the Americans who are not working?" CBS News, December 11, 2014. https://www.cbsnews.com/news/americas-unemployed-who-are-the-americans-who-arent-working.

Derbyshire, Jonathan. "The meaning of conservatism." *New Statesman*, October 8, 2009. https://www.newstatesman.com/uk-politics/2009/10/conservative-disraeli-burke.

Derviş, Kemal. "Convergence, interdependence and divergence." *Finance and*

Development (International Monetary Fund), Vol. 49, No. 3 (September 2012). http://www.imf.org/external/pubs/ft/fandd/2012/09/dervis.htm.

Desilver, Drew. "What the unemployment rate does—and doesn't—say about the economy." Pew Research Center, March 7, 2017. http://www.pewresearch. org/fact-tank/2017/03/07/employment-vs-unemployment-different-stories-from-the-jobs-numbers.

DiChristopher, Tom. "Sizing up the Trade Adjustment Assistance program." CNBC, June 26, 2015. https://www.cnbc.com/2015/06/26/is-aid-to-trade-displaced-workers-worth-the-cost.html.

Di Matteo, Livio. *A Federal Fiscal History: Canada, 1867–2017*. Fraser Institute, February 2017. https://www.fraserinstitute.org/sites/default/files/federal-fiscal-history-canada-1867-2017.pdf.

Dixon, Kim. "Romney tax plan helps rich, hurts middle class: Study." Reuters, August 1, 2012. http://www.reuters.com/article/us-usa-taxes-romney-idUSBRE8700PC20120801.

Dollar, David. "The future of U.S.–China economic ties." Brookings, October 4, 2016. https://www.brookings.edu/research/the-future-of-u-s-china-trade-ties.

Dollar, David, and Aart Kraay. "Growth is good for the poor." *Journal of Economic Growth*, Vol. 7, Issue 3 (September 2002): 195–225. https://siteresourcesqa. worldbank.org/INTRES/Resources/469232-1107449512766/Growth_is_ Good_for_Poor_Journal_Article.pdf.

———. "Trade, growth, and poverty." *The Economic Journal*, Vol. 114 (February 2004): F22–F49. https://papers.ssrn.com/sol3/papers.cfm?abstract_id=632684.

Dreher, Rod. "The death of movement conservatism." *American Conservative*, September 1, 2016. http://www.theamericanconservative.com/dreher/death-movement-conservatism.

Dugan, Andrew. "In U.S., six in ten dissatisfied with immigration levels." Gallup News, January 29, 2015. http://news.gallup.com/poll/181313/dissatisfied-immigration-levels.aspx.

Eberstadt, Nicholas. *Men without Work: America's Invisible Crisis*. West Conshohocken, PA: Templeton Press, 2016.

Editors. "The White House's welcome proposal on immigration." *National Review*, January 26, 2018. http://www.nationalreview.com/article/455837/ white-house-immigration-proposal-welcome.

Edwards, Chris. "Margaret Thatcher's privatization legacy." *Cato Journal*, Vol. 37, No. 1 (Winter 2017): 89–101. https://object.cato.org/sites/cato.org/files/ serials/files/cato-journal/2017/2/cj-v37n1-7.pdf.

Ehrenfreund, Max, and Scott Clement. "Economic and racial anxiety: Two separate forces driving support for Donald Trump." *Washington Post*, March 22, 2016. https://www.washingtonpost.com/news/wonk/wp/2016/03/22/economic-anxiety-and-racial-anxiety-two-separate-forces-driving-support-for-donald-trump/?utm_term=.b994dc5479d3.

Ehrenfreund, Max, and Jeff Guo. "A massive new study debunks a widespread theory for Donald Trump's success." *Washington Post*, August 12, 2016. https://www.washingtonpost.com/news/wonk/

wp/2016/08/12/a-massive-new-study-debunks-a-widespread-theory-for-donald-trumps-success/?utm_term=.1b277de31724.

Erbentraut, Joseph. "How these 4 major companies are tackling the autism unemployment rate." Huffington Post, May 7, 2015. http://www.huffington-post.ca/entry/autism-employment_n_7216310.

Esipova, Neli, Anita Pugliese, and Julie Ray. "Europeans most negative toward immigration." Gallup News, October 16, 2015. http://news.gallup.com/poll/186209/europeans-negative-toward-immigration.aspx.

Feulner, Ed. "Reagan's tax-cutting legacy." Heritage Commentary, July 24, 2015. http://www.heritage.org/taxes/commentary/reagans-tax-cutting-legacy.

Filner, Christine. "Two-thirds say large corporations pay too little in federal taxes (poll)." ABC News, September 26, 2017. http://abcnews.go.com/Politics/thirds-large-corporations-pay-federal-taxes-poll/story?id=50082215.

Fix, Michael, and Jeffrey S. Passel. "Immigration and immigrants." Urban Institute, May 1994. http://webarchive.urban.org/UploadedPDF/305184_immigration_immigrants.pdf.

Franck, Thomas. "McKinsey: One-third of U.S. workers could be jobless by 2030 due to automation." CNBC, November 29, 2017. https://www.cnbc.com/2017/11/29/one-third-of-us-workers-could-be-jobless-by-2030-due-to-automation.html.

Frankovic, Kathy. "Looking back at the 2008 financial crisis." YouGov, September 11, 2014. https://today.yougov.com/news/2014/09/11/2008-financial-crisis.

Friedman, Milton. "The social responsibility of business is to increase its profits." New York Times Magazine, September 13, 1970. https://www.colorado.edu/studentgroups/libertarians/issues/friedman-soc-resp-business.html.

Frum, David. "The great immigration-data debate." The Atlantic, January 19, 2016. https://www.theatlantic.com/politics/archive/2016/01/the-great-immigration-data-debate/424230.

Fukuyama, Francis. "The end of history?" National Interest, No. 16 (Summer 1989): 3–18. https://ps321.community.uaf.edu/files/2012/10/Fukuyama-End-of-history-article.pdf.

———. Trust: The Social Virtues and the Creation of Prosperity. New York: The Free Press, 1995.

Galston, William. "On immigration, the white working class is fearful." Brookings Institution, June 24, 2016. https://www.brookings.edu/blog/fixgov/2016/06/24/on-immigration-the-white-working-class-is-fearful.

Gillespie, Patrick. "Remove car imports, and U.S.–Mexico trade deficit disappears." CNN Money, January 9, 2017. http://money.cnn.com/2017/01/09/news/economy/us-mexico-trump-cars-imports-trade-deficit/index.html.

Glassman, James K. "The blessings of free trade." Cato Institute, May 1, 1998. https://www.cato.org/publications/trade-briefing-paper/blessings-free-trade.

Goodhart, David. The Road to Somewhere: The Populist Revolt and the Future of Politics. London: Oxford University Press, 2017.

Goodwin, M., H. Clarke, and P. Whiteley. "Yes, immigration really was to blame for Brexit." CapX, May 2, 2017. https://capx.co/yes-immigration-really-was-to-blame-for-brexit.

Gramlich, John. "Trump voters want to build the wall, but are more divided on other immigration questions." Pew Research Center, November 29, 2016. http://www.pewresearch.org/fact-tank/2016/11/29/trump-voters-want-to-build-the-wall-but-are-more-divided-on-other-immigration-questions.

Grant, Tavia. "Working wisdom: How workers with disabilities give companies an edge." *Globe and Mail*, February 27, 2015. https://www.theglobeandmail.com/report-on-business/working-wisdom-how-workers-with-disabilities-give-companies-an-edge/article23236023.

Hains, Tim. "Trump: My favorite book is 'The Bible!'" Real Clear Politics, August 12, 2015. https://www.realclearpolitics.com/video/2015/08/12/trump_art_of_the_deal_is_my_second_favorite_book_first_is_the_bible.html.

Hannan, Daniel. Speech, May 31, 2016. http://www.brugesgroup.com/events/10-events/1182-eu-referendum-rally-hammersmith.

Harper, Stephen J. "The political business cycle and fiscal policy in Canada." Master's thesis, University of Calgary, 1991. https://dspace.ucalgary.ca/bitstream/handle/1880/24345/1991_Harper.pdf;jsessionid=C57054E7BBF64754AF770E208D7FF590?sequence=1.

Harrington, Matt. "Survey: People's trust has declined in business, media, government and NGOs." *Harvard Business Review*, January 16, 2017. https://hbr.org/2017/01/survey-peoples-trust-has-declined-in-business-media-government-and-ngos.

Hawkins, Andrew. "Uber will teach you sign language to better communicate with deaf drivers." The Verge, September 29, 2017. https://www.theverge.com/2017/9/29/16384384/uber-sign-language-teach-deaf-driver.

Heaney, James. "Conservatism is dead; long live conservatism." The Federalist, August 6, 2016. http://thefederalist.com/2016/08/06/conservatism-is-dead-long-live-conservatism.

Heminthavong, Khamla. *Canada's Supply Management System*. Library of Parliament, Publication No. 2015-138-E17, December 17, 2015. https://lop.parl.ca/Content/LOP/ResearchPublications/2015-138-e.pdf.

Hirschman, Charles, and Elizabeth Mogford. "Immigration and the American industrial revolution from 1880 to 1920." *Social Science Research*, Vol. 38, No. 4 (December 2009): 897–920. https://www.ncbi.nlm.nih.gov/pmc/articles/PMC2760060.

Hufbauer, Gary Clyde, Cathleen Cimino-Isaacs, and Tyler Moran. "NAFTA at 20: Misleading charges and positive achievements." Peterson Institute for International Economics, May 2014. https://piie.com/publications/policy-briefs/nafta-20-misleading-charges-and-positive-achievements.

International Bank for Reconstruction and Development/World Bank Staff. *Global Economic Prospects: Trade, Regionalism, and Development*. Washington: International Bank for Reconstruction and Development/World Bank Staff, 2005. http://siteresources.worldbank.org/INTGEP2005/Resources/gep2005.pdf.

International Labour Organization and the Organisation for Economic Co-operation and Development. *The Labour Share in G20 Economies*. Report prepared for the G20 Employment Working Group, Antalya, Turkey,

February 26–27, 2015. https://www.oecd.org/g20/topics/employment-and-social-policy/The-Labour-Share-in-G20-Economies.pdf.

International Monetary Fund Staff. "Recovery from the Asian crisis and the role of the IMF." International Monetary Fund, June 2000. https://www.imf.org/external/np/exr/ib/2000/062300.htm.

Irwin, Douglas. "Ricardo and comparative advantage at 200." Vox: CEPR's Policy Portal, April 19, 2017. https://voxeu.org/article/ricardo-and-comparative-advantage-200.

Irwin, Douglas A. "Explaining America's surge in manufactured exports, 1880–1913." National Bureau of Economic Research Working Paper, July 23, 2001. https://www.dartmouth.edu/~dirwin/docs/Surge3wp.pdf.

Jackson, Chris. "Trump and the Republicans abandoned 'pocketbook populism.'" *The Hill*, December 20, 2017. http://thehill.com/opinion/campaign/365801-trump-and-the-republicans-abandoned-pocketbook-populism.

Johnson, Lyndon B. "President Lyndon B. Johnson's remarks at the signing of the immigration bill Liberty Island, New York." October 3, 1965. In *Public Papers of the Presidents of the United States: Lyndon B. Johnson, 1965*. Volume II, entry 546, 1037–1040. Washington, D. C.: Government Printing Office, 1966. http://www.lbjlibrary.org/lyndon-baines-johnson/timeline/lbj-on-immigration.

Johnson, Paul. *The Intellectuals: From Marx and Tolstoy to Sartre and Chomsky*. New York: Harper Collins, 1989.

Joint Economic Committee. "What we do together: The state of associational life in America." Social Capital Project No. 1-17, May 2017. https://www.lee.senate.gov/public/_cache/files/b5f224ce-98f7-40f6-a814-8602696714d8/what-we-do-together.pdf.

Jones, Jeffrey M. "In U.S., worry about illegal immigration steady." Gallup News, March 20, 2017. http://news.gallup.com/poll/206681/worry-illegal-immigration-steady.aspx.

Jones, Vivian C. "Trade remedies: A primer." Congressional Research Service, March 6, 2012. http://www.aiis.org/wp-content/uploads/2015/02/CRS-Trade-Remedies-Primer.pdf.

Kandel, William A. "U.S. family-based immigration policy." Congressional Research Service, February 17, 2016. https://fas.org/sgp/crs/homesec/R43145.pdf.

Katz, Lawrence F., and Robert A. Margo. "Technical change and the relative demand for skilled labor: The United States in historical perspective." In *Human Capital in History: The American Record*, edited by Leah Platt Boustan, Carola Frydman, and Robert A. Margo, 15–57. Chicago: University of Chicago Press, 2014. http://www.nber.org/chapters/c12888.pdf.

Kim, ChangHwan, Christopher R. Tamborini, and Arthur Sakamoto. "Field of study in college and lifetime earnings in the United States." *Sociology of Education*, Vol. 88, No. 4 (September 2015): 320–329. https://www.ncbi.nlm.nih.gov/pmc/articles/PMC5198720.

Kim, Seung Min. "Senate passes immigration bill." Politico, June 27, 2013. https://www.politico.com/story/2013/06/immigration-bill-2013-senate-passes-093530.

Kirchick, James. "Remember all those left-wing pundits who drooled over Venezuela?" *LA Times*, August 2, 2017. http://www.latimes.com/opinion/op-ed/la-oe-kirchick-venezuela-pundits-20170802-story.html.

Klein, Ezra. "Bernie Sanders: The Vox conversation." Vox, July 28, 2015. https://www.vox.com/2015/7/28/9014491/bernie-sanders-vox-conversation.

Kochan, Thomas. "Wages and the social contract." *Prospect Magazine*, April 22, 2007. http://prospect.org/article/wages-and-social-contract.

Kopicki, Allison. "Five years later, poll finds disapproval of bailout." *New York Times*, September 26, 2013. https://economix.blogs.nytimes.com/2013/09/26/five-years-later-poll-finds-disapproval-of-bailout.

Krause, Eleanor, and Isabel Sawhill. "What we know and don't know about declining labor force participation: A review." Brookings Institution, May 2017. https://www.brookings.edu/wp-content/uploads/2017/05/ccf_20170517_declining_labor_force_participation_sawhill1.pdf.

Krauthammer, Charles. "Alone in the universe." *National Review*, December 30, 2011. https://www.nationalreview.com/2011/12/are-we-alone-universe-charles-krauthammer.

Krogstad, Jens Manuel, Jeffrey S. Passel, and D'Vera Cohn. "5 facts about illegal immigration in the United States." Pew Research Center, April 27, 2017. http://www.pewresearch.org/fact-tank/2017/04/27/5-facts-about-illegal-immigration-in-the-u-s.

Krugman, Paul. "Notes on immigration." *New York Times*, March 27, 2006. https://krugman.blogs.nytimes.com/2006/03/27/notes-on-immigration/.

Laghi, Brian. "Working class returning to fold, Harper says." *Globe and Mail*, January 16, 2016. https://www.theglobeandmail.com/news/national/working-class-returning-to-fold-harper-says/article701725.

Lauter, David. "Trump's voters agree with him on cutting legal immigration levels." *LA Times*, October 1, 2016. http://www.latimes.com/politics/la-na-pol-immigration-poll-20161001-snap-story.html.

Lawder, David. "U.S. formally opposes China market economy status at WTO." Reuters, November 30, 2017. https://www.reuters.com/article/us-usa-china-trade-wto/u-s-formally-opposes-china-market-economy-status-at-wto-idUSKBN1DU2VH.

Levin, Yuval. "The solution: A conservative governing vision." In *Room to Grow: Conservative Reforms for a Limited Government and a Thriving Middle Class*. E-book. YG Network, 2014. http://conservativereform.com/wp-content/uploads/2014/05/Chapter-2-Introduction-The-Solution.pdf.

Littlefield, Henry. "*The Wizard of Oz*: Parable on populism." *American Quarterly*, Vol. 16, No. 1 (Spring 1964): 47–58. http://www.shsu.edu/his_rtc/2014_FALL/Wizard_of_Oz_Littlefield.pdf.

Lonsdale, Joe. "Don't just donate, innovate." Medium, October 5, 2017. https://medium.com/8vc-news/dont-just-donate-innovate-808c7cfe82e7.

Lopez, Gustavo, and Jens Manuel Krogstad. "Key facts about unauthorized immigrants enrolled in DACA." Pew Research Center, September 25, 2017. http://www.pewresearch.org/fact-tank/2017/09/25/key-facts-about-unauthorized-immigrants-enrolled-in-daca.

Marcus, Jon. "The paradox of new buildings on campus." *The Atlantic*, July 25, 2016. https://www.theatlantic.com/education/archive/2016/07/the-paradox-of-new-buildings-on-campus/492398.

Martin, Daniel. "Nation states are dead: EU chief says the belief that countries can stand alone is a 'lie and an illusion.'" *Daily Mail*, November 11, 2010. www.dailymail.co.uk/news/article-1328568/Nation-states-dead-EU-chief-says-belief-countries-stand-lie.html.

Massey, Douglas. "How a 1965 immigration reform created illegal immigration." *Washington Post*, September 25, 2015. https://www.washingtonpost.com/posteverything/wp/2015/09/25/how-a-1965-immigration-reform-created-illegal-immigration/?utm_term=.aae9fd899ae7.

McGregor, Janyce. "Supply management in Canada: Why politicians defend farm marketing boards." CBC News, July 26, 2015. http://www.cbc.ca/news/politics/supply-management-in-canada-why-politicians-defend-farm-marketing-boards-1.3166329.

McKinsey, Kitty. "Learning language key to integration, say young refugees." UNHCR, January 30, 2018. http://www.unhcr.org/news/stories/2018/1/5a6b3af64/learning-language-key-integration-say-young-refugees.html.

Merrick, Rob. "Jeremy Corbyn vows to end UK's 'failed model of capitalism' as he promises new deal for tenants and women workers." *The Independent*, September 27, 2017. https://www.independent.co.uk/news/uk/politics/jeremy-corbyn-speech-labour-leader-capitalism-conference-renting-grenfell-tower-fire-theresa-may-a7970441.html.

Migration Observatory (University of Oxford). "Migrants in the UK: An overview." February 21, 2017. http://www.migrationobservatory.ox.ac.uk/resources/briefings/migrants-in-the-uk-an-overview.

———. "Migrants in the UK labour market: An overview." December 1, 2016. http://www.migrationobservatory.ox.ac.uk/resources/briefings/migrants-in-the-uk-labour-market-an-overview.

Milionis, Petros, and Tamas Vonyo. "Reconstruction dynamics: The impact of World War II on post-war economic growth." Working Paper, August 2015.

Moss, Sasha. "Trump's 'America first' agenda requires reform at international trade agency." *The Hill*, June 29, 2017. www.rstreet.org/op-ed/trumps-america-first-agenda-requires-reform-at-international-trade-agency.

Muhlhausen, David. "Trade Adjustment Assistance: Let the ineffective and wasteful job-training program expire." Heritage Foundation, January 8, 2014. https://www.heritage.org/trade/report/trade-adjustment-assistance-let-the-ineffective-and-wasteful-job-training-program.

Murray, Alexander. *The Effect of Import Competition on Employment in Canada: Evidence from the 'China Shock.'* Centre for the Study of Living Standards, July 2017. http://www.csls.ca/reports/csls2017-03.pdf.

Naim, Moises. "Fads and fashion in economic reforms: Washington consensus or Washington confusion?" *Foreign Policy Magazine*, October 26, 1999. https://www.imf.org/external/pubs/ft/seminar/1999/reforms/Naim.HTM.

Newsome, Bruce. "Stop blaming 'populism' for everything." Berkeley Blog, December 11, 2016. http://blogs.berkeley.edu/2016/12/11/populism-cant-be-blamed-for-everything.

Nickell, Stephen, and Jumana Saleheen. "The impact of immigration on occupa-
      tional wages: Evidence from Britain." Bank of England, December 18, 2015.
      http://www.bankofengland.co.uk/research/Documents/workingpapers/
      2015/swp574.pdf.
Nowak, Peter. "Canadian cellphone rates among world's worst." CBC News,
      August 11, 2009. http://www.cbc.ca/news/technology/canadian-cellphone-
      rates-among-world-s-worst-1.800596.
———. "Internet, phone bills in Canada too high, says consumer study." CBC News,
      March 23, 2015. http://www.cbc.ca/news/business/internet-phone-bills-in-
      canada-too-high-says-consumer-study-1.3005282.
Nye, Joseph. "What are the different spheres of globalism—and how are they
      affected by globalization?" *The Globalist*, April 15, 2002. https://www.
      theglobalist.com/globalism-versus-globalization/.
Odland, Steve. "College costs out of control." *Forbes*, March 24, 2012. https://
      www.forbes.com/sites/steveodland/2012/03/24/college-costs-are-soaring/
      #631d26d61f86.
O'Donohoe, Nick. "What is the business of business?" World Economic Forum,
      February 26, 2016. https://www.weforum.org/agenda/2016/02/the-business-
      of-business-is-what.
Office of the Auditor General of Canada. "Restructuring of Chrysler and
      General Motors." *2014 Fall Report of the Auditor General of Canada*. http://
      www.oag-bvg.gc.ca/internet/English/parl_oag_201411_05_e_39963.
      html#hd5b.
Ortega, Israel, and Matt Spaulding. "Immigration reform: The need for upholding
      our national language." Heritage Foundation, June 5, 2007. https://www.
      heritage.org/immigration/report/immigration-reform-the-need-upholding-
      our-national-language.
Panetta, Alex. "Canada's immigration policy inspired Donald Trump's new plan:
      White House." Canadian Press, August 2, 2017. https://globalnews.ca/
      news/3643835/trump-immigration-canada/.
Parliamentary Budget Office. *Revenue and Distribution Analysis of Federal Tax
      Changes: 2005–2013*. May 27, 2014. http://www.pbo-dpb.gc.ca/web/default/
      files/files/files/Fiscal_Impact_and_Incidence_EN.pdf.
Patterson, Richard North. "Donald Trump and the death of principled conserva-
      tism." Huffington Post, July 11, 2017. https://www.huffingtonpost.com/
      entry/donald-trump-and-the-death-of-principled-conservatism_
      us_5964b1dce4b09be68c005531.
Payne, Adam. "Tony Blair isn't the voice of Remainers—he's partly to blame for
      Brexit." Business Insider, October 29, 2016. http://uk.businessinsider.com/
      tony-blair-brexit-immigration-eu-referendum-2016-10.
Payton, Laura. "Ottawa moves to limit foreign investment reviews." CBC News,
      May 25, 2012. http://www.cbc.ca/news/politics/ottawa-moves-to-limit-
      foreign-investment-reviews-1.1273789.
Peri, Giovanni, and Chad Sparber. "Task specialization, immigration, and wages."
      American Economic Journal, July 2009. https://www.aeaweb.org/
      articles?id=10.1257/app.1.3.135.
Pethokoukis, James. "Just how much of a socialist is Bernie Sanders?" AEI Ideas,

January 22, 2016. www.aei.org/publication/just-how-much-of-a-socialist-is-bernie-sanders/.

———. "Supply-side economics needs a 21st century update: Responding to Cato's Dan Mitchell on middle-class tax cuts." American Enterprise Institute blog, August 21, 2014. https://www.aei.org/publication/supply-side-economics-needs-a-21st-century-update-responding-to-catos-dan-mitchell-on-middle-class-tax-cuts/print.

Piccutio, Elizabeth. "Hiring people with disabilities isn't just the right thing to do—it's good for business." Daily Beast, November 27, 2014. http://www.thedailybeast.com/hiring-people-with-disabilities-isnt-just-the-right-thing-to-doits-good-for-business.

Polyakova, Alina, and Neil Fligstein. "Is European integration causing Europe to become more nationalist?: Evidence from the recent financial crisis." Paper presented to the American Sociological Association, New York City, August 9–12, 2013. http://sociology.berkeley.edu/sites/default/files/faculty/fligstein/European%20Id%203.1.pdf.

Ponnuru, Ramesh. "What reform conservatives got right about the GOP." National Review, April 21, 2016. http://www.nationalreview.com/article/434313/donald-trump-reform-conservatives-predicted-his-rise.

Putnam, Robert. Bowling Alone: The Collapse and Revival of American Community. New York: Simon & Schuster, 2000.

———. Our Kids: The American Dream in Crisis. New York: Simon & Schuster, 2015.

Pyper, Wendy. "Skilled trades employment." Perspectives on Labour and Income, Vol. 9, No. 10 (October 2008), Statistics Canada Catalogue No. 75-001-X. http://www.statcan.gc.ca/pub/75-001-x/75-001-x2008110-eng.pdf.

Reagan, Ronald W. "1988 State of the Union Address." New York Times, January 25, 1988. https://www.nytimes.com/1988/01/26/us/transcript-of-reagan-s-state-of-the-union-message-to-nation.html.

———. "The New Republican Party." Conservative Political Action Conference speech, February 6, 1977. http://reagan2020.us/speeches/The_New_Republican_Party.asp.

———. "Remarks at a White House meeting with business and trade leaders." September 23, 1985. https://reaganlibrary.archives.gov/archives/speeches/1985/92385a.htm.

Reed, Paul B., and L. Kevin Selbee. "The civic core in Canada: Disproportionality in charitable giving, volunteering, and civic participation." Nonprofit and Voluntary Sector Quarterly, Vol. 30, No. 4 (December 2001). https://www3.carleton.ca/casr/civic.pdf.

———. Patterns of Citizen Participation and the Civic Core in Canada. Paper presented at the 29th ARNOVA Annual Conference, New Orleans, November 16–18, 2000. Ottawa: Statistics Canada, no date. http://www.publications.gc.ca/Collection/Statcan/75F0048M/75F0048MIE2002003.pdf.

Reeves, Richard. "Trickle-down norms." National Affairs, Winter 2018. https://www.nationalaffairs.com/publications/detail/trickle-down-norms.

Rentoul, John. "'British jobs' blows up in PM's face." The Independent, November 4,

2007. http://www.independent.co.uk/voices/commentators/john-rentoul/john-rentoul-british-jobs-blows-up-in-the-pms-face-398892.html.

Republican Party. "Republican National Committee's Growth and Opportunity Project report." *Washington Post*, March 15, 2013. http://apps.washingtonpost.com/g/documents/politics/republican-national-committees-growth-and-opportunity-project-report/380/.

———. "We believe in America: 2012 Republican platform." The American Presidency Project, August 27, 2012. http://www.presidency.ucsb.edu/ws/?pid=101961.

Republican Party Platforms. "Republican Party platform of 1988." The American Presidency Project, August 16, 1988. http://www.presidency.ucsb.edu/ws/index.php?pid=25846.

———. "Republican Party platform of 1992." The American Presidency Project, August 17, 1992. http://www.presidency.ucsb.edu/ws/?pid=25847.

Rieger, Sarah. "The American Dream is easier to achieve in Canada." Huffington Post, January 23, 2017. https://www.huffingtonpost.ca/2017/01/23/american-dream-canada_n_14350144.html.

Roarty, Alex. "Democrats say they now know exactly why Clinton lost." McClatchy DC Bureau, May 1, 2016. http://www.mcclatchydc.com/news/politics-government/article147475484.html.

Rodrik, Dani. "Populism and the economics of globalization." *Journal of International Business Policy*, 2018. https://drodrik.scholar.harvard.edu/files/dani-rodrik/files/populism_and_the_economics_of_globalization.pdf.

———. "Put globalization to work for democracies." *New York Times*, September 17, 2016. https://www.nytimes.com/2016/09/18/opinion/sunday/put-globalization-to-work-for-democracies.html.

Rogers, Katie. "White women helped elect Donald Trump." *New York Times*, November 9, 2016. https://www.nytimes.com/2016/12/01/us/politics/white-women-helped-elect-donald-trump.html.

Rotman, David. "How technology is destroying jobs." MIT *Technology Review*, June 12, 2013. https://www.technologyreview.com/s/515926/how-technology-is-destroying-jobs.

Rubin, Jennifer. "The night Donald Trump killed conservatism." *Chicago Tribune*, December 13, 2017. http://www.chicagotribune.com/news/opinion/commentary/ct-trump-big-government-conservatism-dead-20170301-story.html.

Sala, Ilaria Maria. "Can China profit from Trump's hostility to Mexico? It's complicated." Quartz, September 4, 2017. https://qz.com/1068688/can-china-profit-from-trumps-hostility-to-mexico-its-complicated.

Savransky, Rebecca. "Majority of Americans approves of Trump's 'America First' message." *The Hill*, January 25, 2017. http://thehill.com/homenews/administration/316005-poll-majority-of-americans-approve-of-trumps-america-first-message.

Schumpeter, Joseph A. *Capitalism, Socialism and Democracy*. New York: Harper, 1975 [orig. pub. 1942].

Scott, Robert E. "Heading south: U.S.–Mexico trade and job displacement after NAFTA." Economic Policy Institute, Briefing Paper #308, May 3, 2011.

http://www.epi.org/publication/heading_south_u-s-mexico_trade_and_job_displacement_after_nafta1.

———. "Manufacturing job losses." Economic Policy Institute, Issue Brief #402, August 11, 2015. https://www.epi.org/publication/manufacturing-job-loss-trade-not-productivity-is-the-culprit.

Semuels, Alana. "Why is economic growth so lackluster?" *The Atlantic*, October 21, 2016. https://www.theatlantic.com/business/archive/2016/10/why-economic-growth-is-so-lackluster/504989.

Shambaugh, Jay, and Ryan Nunn. "Why wages aren't growing in America." *Harvard Business Review*, October 24, 2017. https://www.brookings.edu/opinions/why-wages-arent-growing-in-america.

Sharma, Mihir. "Modi disappoints at Davos." Bloomberg, January 23, 2018. https://www.bloomberg.com/view/articles/2018-01-24/modi-disappoints-at-davos.

Sharma, Ruchir. "When borders close." *New York Times*, November 12, 2016. https://www.nytimes.com/2016/11/13/opinion/sunday/when-borders-close.html?mcubz=1.

Shepard, Steven. "Poll: Voters support Trump-backed immigration bill." Politico, September 8, 2017. https://www.politico.com/story/2017/08/09/trump-immigration-polls-241422.

Shirley, Craig. "The GOP has lost its way. Here's how it can return to its roots." *Washington Post*, November 9, 2012. https://www.washingtonpost.com/opinions/the-republican-party-must-go-back-to-go-forward/2012/11/09/55947d9e-2a87-11e2-96b6-8e6a7524553f_story.html?utm_term=.3f5534d6bda4.

Shivani, Anis. "Everyone's wrong on immigration: Open borders are the only way to defeat Trump and build a better world." Salon, March 15, 2017. https://www.salon.com/2017/03/15/everyones-wrong-on-immigration-open-borders-are-the-only-way-to-defeat-trump-and-build-a-better-world.

Shleifer, Andrei, and Daniel Treisman. "Normal countries: The East 25 years after communism." Working Paper, September 12, 2014. https://scholar.harvard.edu/files/shleifer/files/normal_countries_draft_sept_12_annotated.pdf.

Siekierski, BJ. "In Canadian anti-dumping regulations, China's market-economy status will have to wait." iPolitics, May 14, 2013. https://ipolitics.ca/2013/05/14/in-canadian-anti-dumping-regulations-chinas-market-economy-status-will-have-to-wait.

Smith, Matthew. "International survey: Globalisation is still seen as a force for good in the world." YouGovUK, November 2016. https://yougov.co.uk/news/2016/11/17/international-survey.

Solon, Olivia. "More than 70% of US fears robots taking over our lives, survey finds." *The Guardian*, October 4, 2017. https://www.theguardian.com/technology/2017/oct/04/robots-artificial-intelligence-machines-us-survey.

Speer, Sean. "Canada's participation rate could be the populist 'canary in the coal mine.'" *Globe and Mail*, February 2, 2017. http://www.macdonaldlaurier.ca/why-ottawa-should-worry-over-canadas-stagnant-labour-force-participation-rate-sean-speer-in-the-globe.

————. "Christine Lagarde gives Trudeau just the spectacularly bad advice he wanted to hear." *Financial Post*, September 15, 2016. http://business. financialpost.com/opinion/christine-lagarde-gives-trudeau-just-the-spectacularly-bad-advice-he-wanted-to-hear.

————. "Natural resources are a win for rural communities." *Toronto Sun*, August 5, 2017. http://torontosun.com/2017/08/05/natural-resources-are-a-win-for-rural-communities/wcm/fd5af06b-a154-499d-afa6-eef6ac769b6a.

————. "Regulatory budgeting: Lessons from Canada." R Street Institute, March 2016. https://www.rstreet.org/wp-content/uploads/2016/03/RSTREET54.pdf.

Spiegel, David, and Anthony Volastro. "As global populism rises, so does fear among corporate elites: Survey." CNBC, December 14, 2016. http://www.cnbc.com/2016/12/14/populism-increases-fears-of-elite-global-corporations-cnbc-cfo-survey.html.

Statistics Canada. "Aboriginal people and the labour market." *The Daily*, March 16, 2017. http://www.statcan.gc.ca/daily-quotidien/170316/dq170316d-eng.htm.

————. "High-income trends among taxfilers, 1982 to 2012." *The Daily*, November 18, 2014. http://www.statcan.gc.ca/daily-quotidien/141118/dq141118b-eng.pdf.

————. "Population by sex and age group." 2016 Census, accessed on May 11, 2018. http://www.statcan.gc.ca/tables-tableaux/sum-som/l01/cst01/demo10a-eng.htm.

————. "Table 376-0051—International investment position, Canadian direct investment abroad and foreign direct investment in Canada, by country annual (dollars x 1,000,000)." Accessed on April 2, 2018. http://www5.statcan.gc.ca/cansim/a26?lang=eng&id=3760051.

————. "Table 477-0053—Registered apprenticeship training, registrations, by age groups, sex and major trade groups annual (number)." *The Daily*, October 26, 2015. http://www.statcan.gc.ca/daily-quotidien/151026/t001a-eng.htm.

Stein, Jeff. "The Bernie voters who defected to Trump, explained by a political scientist." Vox, August 24, 2017. https://www.vox.com/policy-and-politics/2017/8/24/16194086/bernie-trump-voters-study.

Steverman, Ben. "Get rid of capitalism? Millennials are ready to talk about it." Bloomberg, November 6, 2017. https://www.bloomberg.com/news/articles/2017-11-06/get-rid-of-capitalism-millennials-are-ready-to-talk-about-it.

Stokes, Bruce, Richard Wike, and Dorothy Manevich. "Post-Brexit, Europeans more favorable toward EU." Pew Research Center, June 15, 2017. www.pewglobal.org/2017/06/15/post-brexit-europeans-more-favorable-toward-eu.

Strategy One and Edelman PR Worldwide. *The Relationship among NGOs, Government, Media and Corporate Sector.* January 2001. https://cms.edelman.com/sites/default/files/2017-03/2001-Edelman-Trust-Barometer.pdf.

Swanson, Ana. "U.S.–China trade deficit hits record, fueling trade fight." *New York Times*, February 6, 2018. https://www.nytimes.com/2018/02/06/us/politics/us-china-trade-deficit.html.

Swarns, Rachel. "Failed amnesty legislation of 1986 haunts the current immigration bills in Congress." *New York Times*, May 23, 2006. http://www.nytimes.com/2006/05/23/washington/23amnesty.html.

Szabo, David. "As Germany heads to the polls, a growing split between European voters and elites." Fox News, September 22, 2017. http://www.foxnews.com/opinion/2017/09/22/as-germany-heads-to-polls-growing-split-between-european-voters-and-elites.html.

Tamney, John. "There are no 'myths' or exceptions about free trade: It's always unrelentingly good." Forbes, October 9, 2016. https://www.forbes.com/sites/johntamny/2016/10/09/there-are-no-myths-or-exceptions-to-free-trade-its-always-unrelentingly-good/#37da139a26a1.

Tanenhaus, Sam. "Can the GOP be a party of ideas?" New York Times, July 2, 2014. https://www.nytimes.com/2014/07/06/magazine/can-the-gop-be-a-party-of-ideas.html?mtrref=www.google.ca&gwh=C8E8B3EFA4B9757F4E5F9E4A3BE21A04&gwt=pay.

Tankersley, Jim, and Scott Clement. "Among American workers, poll finds unprecedented anxiety about jobs, economy." Washington Post, November 25, 2013. https://www.washingtonpost.com/business/economy/among-american-workers-poll-finds-unprecedented-anxiety-about-jobs-economy/2013/11/25/fb6a5ac8-5145-11e3-a7f0-b790929232e1_story.html?utm_term=.a042ba4a1c8d.

Tarnoff, Curt. "The Marshall Plan: 70th anniversary." CRS Insight, April 18, 2017. https://fas.org/sgp/crs/row/IN10688.pdf.

Tartar, Andre. "How the populist right is redrawing the map of Europe." Bloomberg, December 11, 2017. https://www.bloomberg.com/graphics/2017-europe-populist-right.

Tavernise, Sabrina. "Sanctuary bill in Maryland faces a surprise foe: Legal immigrants." New York Times, May 8, 2017. https://www.nytimes.com/2017/05/08/us/legal-immigrants-who-oppose-illegal-immigration.html.

Taylor, Michael. "Migration, productivity, living standards, and all that." Policy Exchange, August 7, 2016. https://policyexchange.org.uk/migration-productivity-living-standards-and-all-that.

Tett, Gillian. "Has the nation state had its day?" Financial Times, March 21, 2014. https://www.ft.com/content/3c14ccee-afc3-11e3-9cd1-00144feab7de.

Thompson, Derek. "Who are Donald Trump's supporters, really?" The Atlantic, March 1, 2016. https://www.theatlantic.com/politics/archive/2016/03/who-are-donald-trumps-supporters-really/471714.

Timiraos, Nick. "5 questions on Trade Adjustment Assistance." Wall Street Journal, June 15, 2015. https://blogs.wsj.com/briefly/2015/06/15/5-questions-on-trade-adjustment-assistance.

Trump, Donald J. "Transcript: Donald Trump's foreign policy speech." New York Times, April 27, 2016. https://www.nytimes.com/2016/04/28/us/politics/transcript-trump-foreign-policy.html.

Trump Donald J., with Tony Schwartz. The Art of the Deal. New York: Ballantine Books, republished in 2004.

Tyson, Alec. "Americans generally positive about NAFTA, but most Republicans say it benefits Mexico more than U.S." Pew Research Center, November 13, 2017. http://www.pewresearch.org/fact-tank/2017/11/13/americans-generally-positive-about-nafta-but-most-republicans-say-it-benefits-mexico-more-than-u-s.

U.S. Census Bureau. "Annual Estimates of the Resident Population for Selected Age Groups by Sex for the United States, States, Counties, and Puerto Rico Commonwealth and Municipios: April 1, 2010 to July 1, 2016, 2016 Population Estimates." Accessed on May 11, 2018. https://factfinder.census.gov/faces/tableservices/jsf/pages/productview.xhtml?src=bkmk.

———. "The foreign-born population in the United States." Date unknown. https://www.census.gov/newsroom/pdf/cspan_fb_slides.pdf.

———. "Trade in goods with Canada, 2017." Accessed on April 2, 2018. https://www.census.gov/foreign-trade/balance/c1220.html.

———. "Trade in goods with Mexico, 2017." Accessed on April 2, 2018. https://www.census.gov/foreign-trade/balance/c2010.html.

U.S. Department of State. "Visa bulletin." No. 9, Vol. IX (June 2009). https://web.archive.org/web/20090603213642/http://travel.state.gov/visa/frvi/bulletin/bulletin_4497.html.

Valverde, Miriam. "Have deportations increased under Donald Trump? Here's what the data show." Politifact, December 19, 2017. http://www.politifact.com/truth-o-meter/article/2017/dec/19/have-deportations-increased-under-donald-trump-her.

Vance, J.D. Hillbilly Elegy: A Memoir of a Family and Culture in Crisis. New York: HarperCollins, 2016.

Vandaelle, Ian. "Canadian banks need some 'protectionism': Toronto mayor urges vigilance on NAFTA." BNN, July 19, 2017. https://www.bnn.ca/canadian-banks-need-some-protectionism-toronto-mayor-urges-vigilance-on-nafta-1.808223.

Vedder, Richard. "Mitch Daniels has the right stuff for Purdue." James G. Martin Center for Academic Renewal. May 2, 2018. https://www.jamesgmartin.center/2018/05/mitch-daniels-has-the-right-stuff-for-purdue/.

Walters, Simon. "Ed Miliband hires the former Trotskyite who claimed Gordon Brown 'pandered to fascists' as his new aide." Daily Mail, January 13, 2013. http://www.dailymail.co.uk/news/article-2261520/Ed-Miliband-hires-Trotskyite-claimed-Gordon-Brown-pandered-fascists-new-aide.html.

Walther, Matthew. "Conservatism is dead." The Week, November 27, 2017. http://theweek.com/articles/739147/conservatism-dead.

Watson, William. "Who knew? Turns out the Harper government was actually terrific for wage growth." Financial Post, November 16, 2017. http://business.financialpost.com/opinion/william-watson-turns-out-the-harper-government-was-actually-terrific-for-wage-growth.

Watt, Nicholas, and Patrick Wintour. "How immigration came to haunt Labour: The inside story." The Guardian, March 24, 2015. https://www.theguardian.com/news/2015/mar/24/how-immigration-came-to-haunt-labour-inside-story.

Weiss, Bari. "Meet the renegades of the intellectual dark web." New York Times, May 8, 2018. https://www.nytimes.com/2018/05/08/opinion/intellectual-dark-web.html.

White House Office of Management and Budget. "Table 1.2—Summary of receipts, outlays, and surpluses and deficits (-) as percentages of GDP: 1930–2022." Historic Tables, accessed on January 3, 2018. https://www.whitehouse.gov/omb/budget/Historicals.

World Bank Staff. "Manufactures exports (% of merchandise exports)." World Bank, accessed on April 2, 2018. https://data.worldbank.org/indicator/TX.VAL.MANF.ZS.UN.

Wright, Daniel, and Rachel Case. "Leave voters felt ignored and left behind as post-Brexit poll reveals extent of economic division across UK." Joseph Rowntree Foundation, July 15, 2016. https://www.jrf.org.uk/press/leave-voters-felt-ignored-and-left-behind-post-brexit-poll-reveals-extent-economic-division.

Yergin, Daniel, with Joseph Stanislaw. *The Commanding Heights: The Battle for the World Economy*. New York: Touchstone, 2002.

Yip, Chi Man. "On the labor market consequences of environmental taxes." *Journal of Environmental Economics and Management*, Vol. 89 (May 2018): 136–152. https://www.sciencedirect.com/science/article/pii/S009506961730551X.

ACKNOWLEDGEMENTS

Perhaps because this book is principally a product of personal experience and personal opinion, the circle involved in it was much smaller than is typical. However, several individuals deserve note.

Significant thanks is due to my former policy adviser from the Prime Minister's Office, Sean Speer. His research, insights, and advice helped to refine the book's evidence and arguments. Sean has become an impressive thinker in his own right in the areas of modern conservatism, economics, history, and public policy. I have no doubt that he will be a key voice in these areas for many years to come.

Considerable assistance in the writing and publishing process was also rendered by my former senior staff members and now business partners at Harper & Associates, Ray Novak and Jeremy Hunt. As always, they went above and beyond, as did Anna Tomala, who keeps all of us on track.

Several other people reviewed the manuscript and offered helpful and insightful comments (but are innocent of any of the views expressed). They include John Walsh, the best national president any political party in Canada has ever had. The same superlative can be bestowed on my former policy director, Rachel Curran, who also took a look. And I must add my children, Ben and Rachel. I am fortunate that such young adults can be both so knowledgeable and critical.

Throughout the process of writing and publishing this book, I was ably assisted by the fine people at Penguin Random House Canada. Doug Pepper, publisher of Signal, was a pleasure to work with, in spite of being a tough taskmaster and critical editor. Tara Tovell, the meticulous copy editor, also warrants mention, as do

McClelland & Stewart publisher Jared Bland, managing editor Kimberlee Hesas, designer Rachel Cooper, proofreader Heather Sangster, and publicist Josh Glover.

As with my last project, agent Michael Levine again deserves accolades for managing the contracts and relationships between all the parties, including the headstrong author.

I should say something about the development of the ideas in this publication. There are countless thousands of people I could credit for furthering my interest in politics and public policy over many decades, from friends and supporters, to teachers and writers, and through to political staff, colleagues, and officials. I risk much ire by mentioning only a few by name.

I begin with my parents, who required me to be informed on current affairs by reading the newspaper—and the liberal *Toronto Star* at that—from a young age. Dr. Robert Mansell, now of the University of Calgary School of Public Policy, stands out from my college days. So, too, do the two Members of Parliament who once employed me: Jim Hawkes and Deborah Grey. And I would be very remiss if I did not mention Preston Manning. In spite of our occasional disagreements, Preston has had as lasting an influence on my political thinking as any living person.

Finally, I owe so much to the long-suffering Laureen. My wife demonstrates incredible love and patience as I go from one project and distraction to another, including this latest one. And she makes all of them possible.

That will have to do in terms of doling out credits. For any failings and deficiencies, I accept full responsibility.

INDEX

The letter n following a page number indicates a note; e.g.: 182n4 indicates note 4 on page 182.

Bush, George W.: auto-sector bailout, 89–90; G20 meeting, 19; internationalism, 49, 125; NAFTA, 40
Bush, Jeb: voter views of, 12
business leaders: advocacy by, 154; and decline in public trust, 156
business sector: decline in public trust, 155–57; profit focus, 162–63; public opinion of, 153, 155; rebuilding public trust, 157–59, 163–64; relationship-building, 159–60; relationship with government, 164–65; role in public policy, 160–62; social responsibility, 163

Cameron, David, 101, 191n33
Campbell, Gordon, 121
Canada: economy of 1970s, 21; economy of 1980s, 23, 38–39; immigration history and policies, 57, 69, 141–46; job losses, 44; nationalism in, 52; trade with U.S., 36, 38–40, 43, 108, 113, 117–18; wage and price controls, 23
Canada–U.S. Free Trade Agreement (FTA), 38–39, 108, 113
Canadian Armed Forces, 130
Canadian Reform Conservative Alliance Party, 14
capitalism, see also markets/market system: and 2016 U.S. election, 29–30; in Asian countries, 28–29; benefits of, 20, 28, 103–4; and financial sector, 92, 187n2; in former Soviet countries, 27–28; growth in 1990s, 26–28; international, 92; Marx's study of, 85; public opinion of, 20–21, 192n37
carbon taxes, 102, 162, 191n34, 199n23
celebrities: advocacy by, 154, 161
Chetty, Raj, 189n15
China: global trade, 41–42, 44, 46, 110, 114–15; growth of capitalism, 26; immigrants from, 68; oil sands investment, 116; trade with Canada, 109, 115, 193n13, 194n19;

trade with U.S., 18, 33–34, 42, 43–44, 114–15, 118–19, 194n19
citizenship: ceremonies, 137; and immigration, 62, 63–65, 150–51; and positive nationalism, 122, 130; regulations, 144–45; value of, 144
civil society: erosion of, 128–29, 131; strengths and importance, 122, 130–32
Clement, Tony, 96
Clinton, Bill: deregulation under, 30; globalization advocacy, 58; immigration policies, 64; and market economy, 26–27; trade with China, 33–34
Clinton, Hillary: Chinese imports and voter choices, 44; globalization views, 3; immigration views, 64; voter views of, 12
Cold War: effects on nationalism and foreign policy, 50, 52; and socialism, 164, 176n9; and trade, 40; won by conservatives, 2
communications: and business markets, 161; business messaging, 157–58; and business relations, 159–60; telecommunications policies, 95; traditional vs. social media, 158–59
communism: in China, 26, 41; decline by 1990s, 25–26; decline effects, 27–28; endurance in academia, 27, 86, 103–4, 120; failures, 85–86, 103, 104
Conservative Party of Canada: 2006 election, 14; and foreign investments, 115–16; government costing regulations, 189n20; immigrant support, 61, 142–43, 145; populist conservatism approach, 77; tax cuts, 94
conservatives/conservatism: belief in markets, 20; contextual/empirical nature, 80, 82, 83, 84; and market economy, 90, 97–98, 105; options today, 79–81, 87, 168–69; populist, 77–78, 84–85, 169; as right path, 171; in U.S., 82, 83–84, 186n4; values, 2, 104

fascism: Europe rescued from, 51; and radical immigrants, 68; as variant of socialist mindset, 104

Fast, Ed, 109

financial sector, *see also* economy; markets/market system: bailouts, 11–12, 19, 24, 31, 89–90; central banking, 91; central to capitalism, 187n2; driving forces, 91; policies and regulations, 91–92, 187n3; trade protections, 111–12, 119

Finley, Diane, 138

Flaherty, Jim, 94, 102

foreign investment: residential real estate, 116–17; review and approval process, 115–16

foreign policy: and global security, 49; history, 50–51; and nationalism, 126–27; of Trump administration, 49, 126–27; under Harper, 126–27; U.S., 125, 127–28

foreign students, 140–41

foreign workers *see* temporary foreign workers

Fortier, Michael, 109

France: EU membership, 181n4; immigration policies, 140; as part of ECSC, 38; populism, 167; rise of Macron, 180n2, 200n4

free trade *see* trade agreements

Friedman, Milton, 199n24

Fukuyama, Francis, 27, 176n9

G7 (Group of 7 nations): Harper's experiences, 5; Russia joins, 28, 41; tax rates, 94

G20 (Group of 20 nations): first meeting, 19; and global financial crisis, 119; Harper's experiences, 127

"Gang of Eight" bill (2013) (U.S.), 63, 65–66

Germany, *see also* West Germany: EU membership, 51–52, 181n4; immigrants from, 69; immigrants to, 73–74; populism, 167

globalism/globalists: backlash against, 130–31; balancing with

nationalism, 122, 127–28, 135; definition, 180n3; extremes of, 123, 127; and perceptions of Trump, 57; political domination of, 56; Trump's perceptions of, 58; values, 53

globalization: benefits of, 42; and deregulation, 31; history, 15–16, 36; liberal advocacy for, 57–58; and multinational production chain, 178n10; need for healthy nationalism, 55–56, 122; as political choice, 59; problems of, 2, 28–29, 43–44, 122; public opinion of, 20, 42, 48, 57; today, 16–17, 53, 54

global security *see* security, global

Gorbachev, Mikhail, 25–26

Gore, Al: immigration policies, 64

government intervention: 1970s–1980s Canada, 38–39; appropriate role, 32, 95; conservative views, 23; and environment, 101–2; and job losses/creation, 100–102; Keynesianism, 21–23, 29; in markets, 89–90, 91, 95–96, 156–57

Greece: EU membership, 181n4

Gulf War, 50

Hannan, Daniel, 58–59, 108

Harper, Stephen: 2006 election, 14; apology for Chinese "head tax," 68; apology for residential schools, 130; and bailout package, 89–90; at Davos, 47; economic policy views, 23, 94; educational policies, 99, 132; education and experience, 14, 21, 24, 33, 78; and global financial crisis, 77, 188n10; immigration policies, 61–62, 141–45; trade agreements, 34, 107–9, 112

Heritage Foundation, 144

history, national: celebrating, 129–30

Hungary: EU membership, 181n4; nationalists in power, 124

immigrants: integrating, 140–41, 143–45, 151; streams/classes, 141–42;

228 • STEPHEN J. HARPER

liberals/liberalism: abstract, non-
empirical nature, 83, 84–85, 86;
anti-nationalism, 49, 52, 57, 134;
boosters of free trade, 46; corporatism of, 20, 120; and immigration,
63; immigration policies, 63, 148–
50; "middle way" efforts, 26–27, 30;
response to populism, 81; supply
and demand views, 188n10; and
trade, 119–20
localism/localists: defined, 54; for
domestic politics, 122, 132; and perceptions of Trump, 57; political
diversity, 56; role in nationalism,
132
Lonsdale, Joe, 163
Luxembourg: as part of ECSC, 38

Maastricht Treaty (1993), 38
MacKay, Peter, 14
Macron, Emmanuel, 180n2, 200n4
Manning, Preston, 14
Mao Zedong, 41
markets/market system, *see also* capitalism; financial sector: benefits,
flaws and complexities, 20, 31–32,
90, 91, 103–4; and corporate bailouts, 89–90; as "creative destruction," 31, 177n15; and
globalization, 55; government
interventions, 95–96; growth in
1990s economies, 26–27; and job
losses/creation, 100–101; overconfidence in, 30–31; policies under
Harper, 95–96; as political choice,
59; public opinion, 20–21; and
public trust in business, 156; supply
and demand, 188n10
Marxism, 27, 85–86, 103
media, traditional, *see also* social media:
alienism in, 134; decline in public
trust, 155, 157; dying, 158; and
immigration, 65, 149; and Trump,
10, 158
Merkel, Angela, 101
Mexico: border wall, 72, 146; immigrants from, 70; NAFTA, 38–39,

118; trade with China, 194n19;
trade with U.S., 18
Michigan: Chinese imports and voter
choices, 44
Michnik, Adam, 177n12
Moore, James, 95
Moore, Roy, 93
Mulroney, Brian, 39, 40
multiculuralism policies: good vs. bad,
137–38, 150

National Citizens Coalition, 33
National Energy Program (Canada), 23
nationalism: alive and well, 121–22;
"America First," 18, 48–49, 52,
56–57, 58, 126–27; of Americans,
52; balancing with globalism, 54,
122, 127–28, 132, 135; in Canada,
52; dark side of, 48–49, 50–51, 122,
133; in EU, 123–24, 167; and foreign policy, 126–27; of Germany,
51–52; of Quebec, 124; role of
civil society, 132; since World War
II, 50–51; and social solidarity,
129–30; of U.K., 51; of Western
countries, 134
nativism: defined, 133
Netherlands: EU membership, 181n4;
as part of ECSC, 38; populism, 167
Nixon, Richard, 22, 38
North American Free Trade
Agreement (NAFTA): birth and
negotiations, 38–40; effects on
workers, 43; as example of global
supply chain, 178n10; Liberal campaign against, 108; and Trump,
117–18
North Atlantic Treaty Organization
(NATO): founded, 50; U.S. contributions, 126
North Korea: nuclear program, 125
Northrop Grumman, 160
Nye, Joseph, 180n3

Obama, Barack: auto-sector bailout,
89; "birther" theory, 1; foreign
policy, 125; and Harper, 47; as

president, 81, 89, 119, 125, 149; trade, 119; and Trump, 52, 134
Obhrai, Deepak, 196n7
oil and gas industry: foreign ownership, 116; job losses and environmental concerns, 102, 191n35; NEP, 23
Oliver, Joe, 94
Olympic Games, 121
open borders: and immigration, 72, 138, 149; and trade, 56, 59

Paradis, Christian, 95
patriotism: vs. nationalism, 50
Pennsylvania: Chinese imports and voter choices, 44
People's Party, U.S., 15, 16
people with disabilities: labour force participation, 160
Philippines: public opinions on globalization, 42
Phillips, William, 22
Poland: EU membership, 181n4; nationalists in power, 124
Ponnuru, Ramesh, 81
populism: and conservatism today, 4, 6, 77–81, 84–85, 87, 168–69; disruptive to business, 153–54; in Europe, 123–24, 167; history in U.S., 15; of the left, 102–3; and localists vs. globalists, 48, 56–57, 170–71; and trade, 44, 108; uses and meanings, 13–14
populist conservatism, 77–78, 169
poverty: and globalization, 2, 16, 42; and social erosion, 131
Prentice, Jim, 95, 101
Procter & Gamble, 160
Progressive Conservative Party of Canada: 1984 election, 39; FTA and NAFTA negotiations, 39–40; merger with Reform Alliance, 14; timid tax policies, 39
public opinion: of business sector, 153, 155; of capitalism, 20–21, 192n37; divergence from political elites, 3, 13–14; effects of recession, 20–21; in EU, 51, 181n4; of globalization,

20, 42, 57; of immigration, 63, 66, 71–72, 74, 138–39, 140, 146, 148–49
Purdue University, 190n27
Putin, Vladimir, 28

Quebec, 52, 124

racism/bigotry: and "America First," 48–49; and immigration, 63, 72, 74, 138
Reagan, Ronald: and Cold War, 2; conservatism, 83–84, 186n1; economic policies, 23, 25, 30, 92; immigration policies, 148; rapport with Mulroney, 39; trade policies, 45–46, 49, 180n25
real estate: foreign investment, 116–17
recession of 2008–2009: aftereffects, 20; and decline in trust in business, 155–56; G20 efforts, 119, 127
Reform Party of Canada: as populist party, 14, 39, 78
refugees: to Australia, 143, 196n2; benefits for, 145; to Germany, 73–74; humanitarian considerations, 140, 141; private sponsorship, 132, 145
religion/faith: as conservative value, 6, 78, 85, 87; and globalists, 53, 86; and immigrants, 137, 149; and refugee sponsorship, 132; as societal value, 7, 130–31, 137
Republican party, U.S.: 2012 tax platform, 92–93; 2016 primaries, 29–30; failures of conservatism, 81; immigration policies, 64–65; member characteristics, 57; policies convergent with Democrats, 11; policies divergent from public opinion, 13, 66; trade policies, 45–46
residential schools, 130
Ricardo, David, 35, 177n5
right see conservatives/conservatism
Rodrik, Dani, 180n3
Romney, Mitt, 52
Roosevelt, Theodore, 16
Rubio, Marco, 186n4